Staking Claims
to a Continent

Staking Claims
to a Continent

John A. Macdonald, Abraham Lincoln, Jefferson Davis, and the Making of North America

James Laxer

ANANSI

Published in Canada and the USA in 2016 by House of Anansi Press Inc.

20 19 18 17 16 1 2 3 4 5

Library and Archives Canada Cataloguing in Publication

Laxer, James, 1941–, author
Staking claims to a continent : John A. Macdonald, Abraham Lincoln, Jefferson Davis, and the making of North America / James Laxer.

Includes bibliographical references and index.
Issued in print and electronic formats.
ISBN 978-1-77089-430-3 (bound).—ISBN 978-1-77089-431-0 (html)

1. Davis, Jefferson, 1808–1889. 2. Lincoln, Abraham, 1809–1865.
3. Macdonald, John A. (John Alexander), 1815–1891. 4. United States—History—1849–1877. 5. Canada—History—1841–1867. 6. Canada—History—1867–1914. I. Title.

E415.7.L39 2016   973.7   C2015-906877-0
C2015-906878-9

Library of Congress Control Number: 2015953899

Book design: Alysia Shewchuk

We acknowledge for their financial support of our publishing program the Canada Council for the Arts, the Ontario Arts Council, and the Government of Canada through the Canada Book Fund.

Printed and bound in Canada

MIX
Paper from
responsible sources
FSC® C016245

To Sandy, Michael, Kate, Emily, Jonathan

Contents

Author's Note

In this book, I have chosen to use the words "natives" and "native peoples" when discussing indigenous peoples in both the United States and Canada. The terms "First Nations" and "aboriginal peoples," while commonly used in Canada, are not regularly used in the United States. The usual reference today in the United States is either to "Native Americans" or to specific groups, such as "Shawnees." The word "Indian" is used when it appears in quotes from the writings of the period.

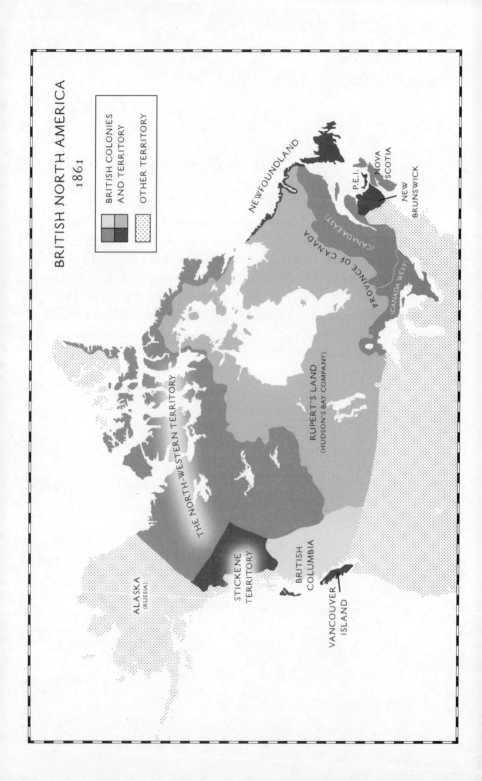

BRITISH NORTH AMERICA
1861

BRITISH COLONIES
AND TERRITORY

OTHER TERRITORY

NEWFOUNDLAND

P.E.I.

NOVA
SCOTIA

NEW
BRUNSWICK

PROVINCE OF CANADA

(CANADA EAST)

CANADA WEST

THE NORTH-WESTERN TERRITORY

RUPERT'S LAND
(HUDSON'S BAY COMPANY)

ALASKA
(RUSSIA)

STICKENE
TERRITORY

BRITISH
COLUMBIA

VANCOUVER
ISLAND

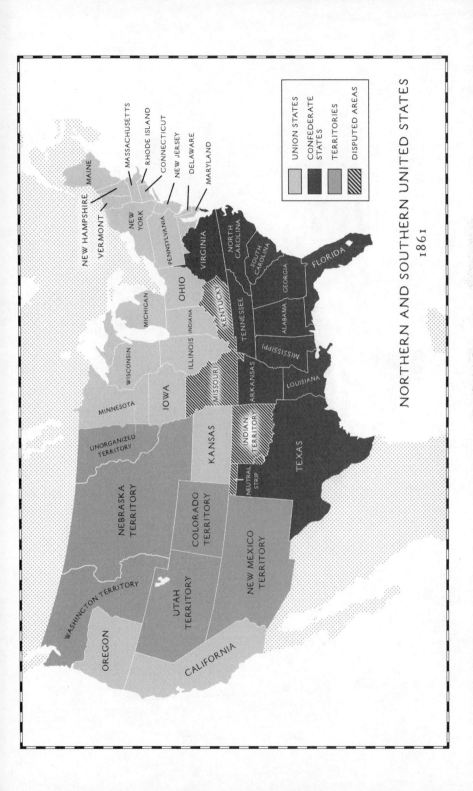

NORTHERN AND SOUTHERN UNITED STATES
1861

UNION STATES
CONFEDERATE STATES
TERRITORIES
DISPUTED AREAS

NEW HAMPSHIRE
VERMONT
MAINE
MASSACHUSETTS
RHODE ISLAND
CONNECTICUT
NEW JERSEY
DELAWARE
MARYLAND
NEW YORK
PENNSYLVANIA
OHIO
MICHIGAN
WISCONSIN
MINNESOTA
IOWA
ILLINOIS
INDIANA
MISSOURI
KENTUCKY
TENNESSEE
VIRGINIA
NORTH CAROLINA
SOUTH CAROLINA
GEORGIA
FLORIDA
ALABAMA
MISSISSIPPI
ARKANSAS
LOUISIANA
TEXAS
INDIAN TERRITORY
NEUTRAL STRIP
KANSAS
UNORGANIZED TERRITORY
NEBRASKA TERRITORY
COLORADO TERRITORY
NEW MEXICO TERRITORY
UTAH TERRITORY
WASHINGTON TERRITORY
OREGON
CALIFORNIA

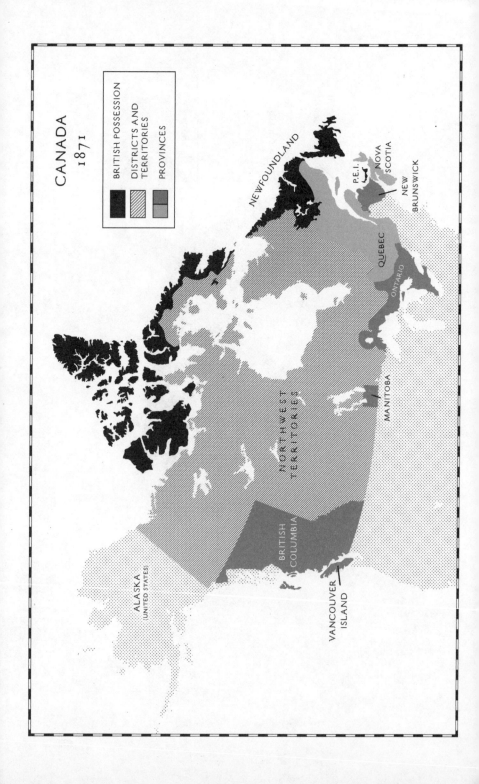

CANADA
1871

BRITISH POSSESSION

DISTRICTS AND
TERRITORIES

PROVINCES

NEWFOUNDLAND

P.E.I.

NOVA
SCOTIA

NEW
BRUNSWICK

QUEBEC

ONTARIO

MANITOBA

NORTH WEST
TERRITORIES

BRITISH
COLUMBIA

VANCOUVER
ISLAND

ALASKA
(UNITED STATES)

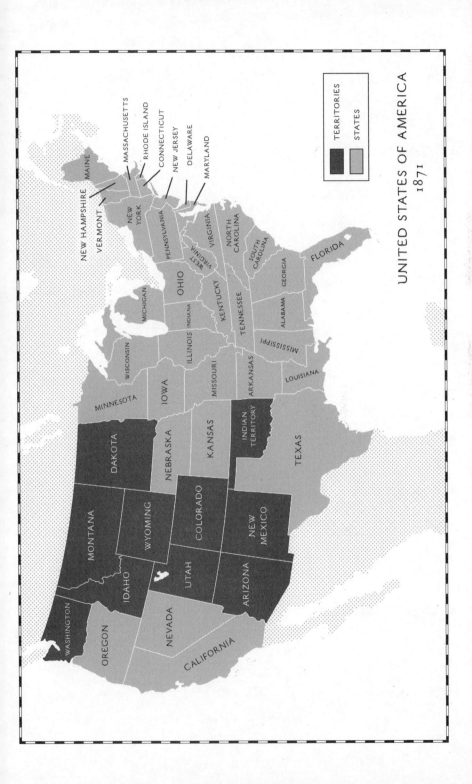

UNITED STATES OF AMERICA
1871

TERRITORIES
STATES

WASHINGTON
OREGON
NEVADA
CALIFORNIA
IDAHO
MONTANA
DAKOTA
WYOMING
UTAH
COLORADO
ARIZONA
NEW MEXICO
NEBRASKA
KANSAS
INDIAN TERRITORY
TEXAS
MINNESOTA
IOWA
MISSOURI
ARKANSAS
LOUISIANA
WISCONSIN
ILLINOIS
INDIANA
MICHIGAN
OHIO
KENTUCKY
TENNESSEE
MISSISSIPPI
ALABAMA
GEORGIA
FLORIDA
SOUTH CAROLINA
NORTH CAROLINA
VIRGINIA
WEST VIRGINIA
PENNSYLVANIA
NEW YORK
MAINE
NEW HAMPSHIRE
VERMONT
MASSACHUSETTS
RHODE ISLAND
CONNECTICUT
NEW JERSEY
DELAWARE
MARYLAND

Introduction

Three Nation State Projects and Three Unlikely Leaders

THE ELECTION OF Abraham Lincoln as president of the United States of America was the opening salvo that launched three nation state projects on the North American continent. Lincoln's November 1860 victory brought the new Republican Party — a party exclusively of the North — to power in the American Republic. For political leaders in the South, Lincoln's election amounted to a revolution that threatened the survival of their slavery-based economic and social system.

Within a few months, seven states in the Deep South seceded, thus initiating the new nation state of the Confederate States of America and triggering the bloodiest war in the history of the continent.

North of the two warring republics, the political leaders of the British North American colonies were compelled by the continental crisis to launch their own nation state project. That project sought to unite populations that spoke English and French and that had carved out their homelands on the territories of native peoples.

Inward-looking conceptions of the Civil War fall far short of capturing how the conflict fits into the broader themes of mid-nineteenth-century Western history. The mid-nineteenth century was a great age of nationalism on both sides of the Atlantic. In 1848, a wave of revolutionary uprisings erupted across Europe, triggered by a republican upheaval in Paris that led to the overthrow of the Orléans monarchy of King Louis Philippe. The Revolution in France and those across the continent combined demands for political transformation — typically centred on the goal of universal manhood suffrage — with nationalism. Initially, in most places, the middle class and the working class were broadly united in their political aspirations. But the working class, inspired by trade union and socialist movements, struggled for economic and social reforms. This put workers in conflict with the members of the middle class whose reform goals were restricted to a liberal political agenda.

The 1848 revolutionary risings were followed by a year of reaction, during which the radical gains of the previous year were mostly reversed. In Germany, Austria, and Eastern Europe, liberal nationalist assemblies and regimes were driven from power by conservatives who were intent on halting the advance of political democracy.

The promise of the 1848 European revolutions had an impact on politics and thinking across the Atlantic. Many saw the revolutions as an expression of the values of the American Revolution. However, not all political forces in the U.S. were positive about the developments across the Atlantic. Southern Democrats who spoke for the slave owners of the region were fearful about how the end of serfdom in Europe could affect their own social system.

During this distinct phase in the emergence of modern capitalism, many peoples attempted to erect their own sovereign nation states, with these attempts failing more often than they succeeded. One of those failures was the Confederate States of America.

A distinction needs to be made between "national projects" and "nation state projects." Typically, national projects emerge over a long historical period, as particular peoples develop a consciousness of those characteristics that make them distinct from other peoples. Examples of national projects abound in the contemporary world: in Scotland, Catalonia, and Quebec, key groups in the population have drawn attention to the features that mark off their national communities. Distinctive language, literature, culture, history, dress, and unique symbols can all be components of these national projects that exist within the framework of a larger state. A nation state project, on the other hand, takes matters a step further. This is when leading elements in a nation, which exists within the framework of a larger state, undertake a political campaign to achieve secession and eventual sovereignty. In Scotland, Catalonia, and Quebec, movements exist whose goal is to convert their national projects into nation state projects. In the South, leading elements in the population had long honed a sense of the unique identity of their society. When the Southern states seceded from the United States and launched the Confederate States of America, they transformed a national project into a nation state project.

The case made here is that from the time of the American Revolution and the drafting of the American Constitution in 1787 to the outbreak of the Civil War in 1861, the American Republic encompassed two nascent national projects within the framework of a single state: the Northern project, or Union; and the Southern project, or the Confederate States of America. The fact that the Northern project evolved in defence of the existing United States obscures this reality, but should not stand in the way of our comprehending it. New socioeconomic projects can develop within the institutional framework of existing states. That was the case with Lincoln's North. Northerners were effectively pouring new wine into an old bottle.

Three political leaders presided over the reshaping of the North American continent during the fiery 1860s. In an earlier era, it would have been highly unlikely for men such as Abraham Lincoln, Jefferson Davis, and John A. Macdonald to rise to such political heights. They personified an age of social and economic transformation, thrust to the top by the very forces that tore the continent apart. Lincoln, Davis, and Macdonald came to the fore at a time when nation states were being established on both sides of the Atlantic. Davis tried to create a country by ripping the South out of the United States and establishing the Confederate States of America. Lincoln's crusade to save the Union honed the industrial-military power that would one day dominate the world. Macdonald led the drive to shepherd the diverse British North

American provinces into a federal state that would secure the northern half of the continent and keep Canada out of American hands. Lucky in their careers and the bearers of misfortune in their personal lives, Lincoln, Davis, and Macdonald were products of mid-nineteenth-century capitalism. The three honed national visions that won the broad political support of their peoples and that furthered the interests of the dominant capitalists in their respective societies.

Jefferson Davis and Abraham Lincoln were both born in Kentucky, Davis in 1808 and Lincoln the following year; John A. Macdonald was born in Glasgow, Scotland, in 1815. All three were Protestants (as a youth, Davis attended a Catholic school for a time), the sons of fathers who were far from successful in life. Fortunately, each had strong mothers — Lincoln a mother and a stepmother — who instilled in them an indomitable belief in their own self-worth. Luck played a significant part in the success of the three men; so too did fortuitous connections with influential people.

If the three were lucky at key points in their careers, all suffered severe personal misfortune, even tragedy, in their lives. Davis's first wife, Sarah, died of malaria at the age of twenty-one, after only several months of marriage. Of the six children Davis had with his second wife, only three survived to adulthood. In the spring of 1864, Joseph Evan, the young son of Jefferson and Varina Davis, fell to his death from an upper-storey window of the Confederate White House in Richmond, Virginia. At the age of nine, Lincoln watched his mother die of a disease known as "milk sick," an affliction suffered from drinking the milk of cows that had eaten the poisonous white snakeroot plant. In 1862, eleven-year-old Willie, the much-loved son of Abraham and Mary Lincoln, died after a lengthy illness. Mary Lincoln never fully recovered from the loss of her son. For more than a decade, John A. Macdonald watched his wife, Isabella, suffer from illness before she died in 1857. During this time, John Jr., the young son of the Macdonalds, perished. Macdonald's second wife, Agnes, gave birth to a daughter, Mary, in 1869, who was never able to walk and never fully developed mentally.

Two of the three leaders — Lincoln and Macdonald — were remarkably flexible in their ability to adapt to changing conditions and never lost sight of their central objectives. Davis, on the other hand, while singularly devoted to his cause, was rigid in its pursuit, often losing himself in petty details of administration and missing the wider picture.

While the three projects differed in vitally important ways, they had one thing in common: all three were white settler projects. The three leaders shared the broad conviction that white Europeans, especially the Anglo-Saxon race (a term they found inoffensive), brought superior gifts to the development of energetic, prosperous societies. The three men considered the native peoples of the continent as primitive and backward. For the most part, they believed that these peoples should be ignored and left alone, except when they stood in the way of white settlement and the progress it promised.

When it came to the black race, all three shared the view that whites were naturally superior. That said, the way the three leaders and their national projects related to blacks differed enormously.

While Abraham Lincoln was a visceral opponent of slavery all of his adult life, his statements about African Americans were often tinged with racism. His Northern project was based on free labour capitalism and promoted the interests of working men and capitalists, interests he saw as compatible. Lincoln and the members of his political base regarded the slave owners of the South, the slaveocracy, as the deadly foes of ordinary people, and therefore, of liberty. In the years before the Civil War, Lincoln staunchly opposed the spread of slavery to the new territories acquired by the United States. In a speech in Chicago in July 1858, he set out his doctrine and that of his fellow Republicans as follows: "The Republican party is made up of those who, as far as they can peaceably, will oppose the extension of slavery, and who will hope for its ultimate extinction." He, and those in his party, he continued, wished to prevent "the new lands of the continent" from being grasped by slave owners who would thus keep "them from the settlement of free white laborers, who want the land to bring up their families upon."¹ It was these white labourers — free labourers who hoped to make something of themselves — who formed his core constituency.

Although slavery had existed on a small scale in eighteenth-century British North America, by 1833 it had been abolished throughout the British Empire. For John A. Macdonald, who lived in a country where slavery was illegal — a country that was the northern terminus of the Underground Railroad — blacks were unimportant in his political calculus. But race and Macdonald's national project were inextricably intertwined in his government's quest to annex the vast territory of the Hudson's Bay Company that lay beyond the Great Lakes. The Macdonald government was prepared to ignore the interests of native peoples and the Métis, the new people of mixed European and native ancestry who lived in the British North-West (the area north of the 49th parallel, west of Lake Superior, and east of the Rocky Mountains). His government relied on white immigration to push aside the existing population and prepare the territory for economic development and some form of self-government.

In May 1885, in a debate on Chinese immigration and voting rights in Canada, Macdonald made his broad sentiments on race clear in a speech to the House of Commons: "If you look around the world you will see that the Aryan races will not wholesomely amalgamate with the Africans or the Asiatics. It is not to be desired that they [the Chinese] should come; that we should have a mongrel race; that the Aryan character of the future of British America should be destroyed...the cross of those races, like the cross of the dog and the fox, is not successful; it cannot be, and never will be."²

Black slave labour was the foundation on which Jefferson Davis's project rested, the productive engine that drove the economy. When Senator Jefferson Davis of Mississippi rose in his place in the United States Senate on January 21, 1861, to bid farewell to his fellow members, on whom he had made a great impression over the years, the question of race was central to his thoughts. His own state of Mississippi had seceded from the Union a few days earlier. The Senate chamber and its galleries, which were filled to capacity, grew still on this fateful day, as the man who was soon to be sworn in as the provisional president of the Confederate States of America addressed the body.

In his brief speech, Davis pointed to Northern attacks on slavery as critical to Mississippi's decision to secede from the United States. In his thinking, the misrepresentation by Northerners of the phrase in the Declaration of Independence of 1776 that "all men are created equal" was at the heart of the quarrel between the state of Mississippi and the Union.

"It has been a conviction of pressing necessity," declared Davis, "it has been a belief that we are to be deprived in the Union of the rights which our fathers bequeathed to us, which has brought Mississippi into her present decision. She has heard proclaimed the theory that all men are created free and equal, and this made the basis of an attack upon her social institutions; and the sacred Declaration of Independence has been invoked to maintain the position of the equality of the races."

To Davis, the contentious phrase "all men are created free and equal" applied solely to "the men of the political community" and made no "reference to the slave." "Had the Declaration announced that negroes were free and equal," he continued, "how was the Prince [King George III] to be arraigned for stirring up insurrection among them? And how was this to be enumerated among the high crimes which caused the colonies to sever their connection with the mother country?"

The future president of the Confederate States of America also pointed out that the United States Constitution, drafted in 1787, made provision for slaves "as property": "They were not put upon the footing of equality with white men," he stated, "not even upon that of paupers and convicts; but, so far as representation was concerned, were discriminated against as a lower caste."[3]

Lincoln, Davis, and Macdonald were exceptionally talented at burnishing visions that not only advanced the interests of the most powerful elements of their societies but also mobilized a broad range of political support extending far beyond the circles of the elites. Each in his own way was a new kind of leader. Each had to win and to retain the backing of a popular constituency that was white and male.

The three set out to launch, or in the case of Lincoln to sustain, a sovereign nation state on the North American continent.

DURING THE CIVIL War era, a technological and economic revolution reshaped the North and the Midwest. The war against the South enhanced the pace of the transformation. The North's connection with the American past was important, but so too was the launch of an urban, industrial America that would have been unrecognizable to those who had lived only a few decades earlier.

Historians have often been blinkered in their contemplation of the nation state projects of both the South and the North. In recent decades many historians have concluded that the North's grand objective in the conflict was to safeguard the great cause of liberty that was enshrined in the American Union and to extend it through the abolition of slavery.

While it is highly misleading to see the slave-owning capitalism of the South through the post–Civil War lens of "Lost Cause" thinking, it is equally misleading to believe that the free-labour capitalism of the North was dedicated to an ethical crusade against slavery. Although the emancipation issue grew in importance over the course of the war, as did the recruitment of freedmen into the Union forces, these issues proved to be deeply divisive in the North. The slavery question should not be discounted, but neither should the primary war aim of the North, the preservation of the Union, be underplayed.

The deadly struggle between the South and the North assumed a critical role in propelling the political leaders of the British North American provinces to take urgent steps to create a nation state of their own: the Dominion of Canada.

As was the case with the Southern national project, the Canadian nation state was conceived within the framework of another state system, the British Empire. That similarity was negated, however, by a fundamental difference: while the Confederacy fought a major war to exit the American federal system, British North Americans created their new nation state within the British Empire, a venture that enjoyed the encouragement, and at times vigorous support, of Westminster.

All three nation state projects had their strengths and severe weaknesses. Each could have succeeded or failed. Analysts looking back on events now long in the past are strongly inclined to regard the outcomes as inevitable and often amass evidence to show why things turned out the way they did. But the importance of contingency is vital to sound historical analysis. And the success or failure of the projects would have consequences not only for the long-term future of the continent but for the global order to the present day.

Chapter 1

Manifest Destiny

O N T H E M O R N I N G of September 12, 1847, American artillery units commenced a barrage on the Mexican position at Chapultepec Castle, which controlled the gateway to Mexico City. While the Americans always referred to the solid stone structure as a fortress, it had been originally intended as a palace and later converted into a military college. Taking the castle would open the way for the commanding U.S. general, Winfield Scott, and his forces to occupy the Mexican capital. It would be the climactic encounter in a war that had begun in May 1846.

The Mexican forces enjoyed a formidable defensive position. After the U.S. shelling had begun to take its toll on the enemy, Robert E. Lee, a U.S. captain of engineers, set out with another officer to reconnoitre Chapultepec, which was situated on a ridge that rose to a height of about 190 feet and extended in length for 600 yards.

Having completed his reconnaissance, but still unsure what defences the Americans would face during their ascent to the castle, Lee returned to the artillery batteries, where he received an order that General Winfield Scott wished to see him at once. [1] Over the course of the march from Veracruz toward Mexico City, Scott had come to value the skill of the Virginian captain of engineers. Although he had not slept in more than thirty hours, Lee headed off to Tacubaya to report to the general at his headquarters.

Scott and his staff had to decide whether to attack at once or to wait until dawn the following day. The general concluded that the advantage of having a whole day for the assault outweighed the risk of allowing the Mexicans to repair their defences. Just after 8 a.m. on September 13, the infantry stormed the grounds and made the ascent toward the castle, deploying scaling ladders where necessary.

After making his way back to the position of the commanding general, Lee rode with Scott in the advance. And then, for the first and only time in his life, he fainted. The following day, restored to his usual self, Lee accompanied Scott as the U.S. forces took Mexico City and watched as the United States flag rose over the palace in the great square at the heart of the fallen capital. [2]

Thirteen years later, many of the men who had taken part in the war against Mexico, Robert E. Lee and Ulysses S. Grant among them, would fight again, this time against each other in the war between the South and the North.

THE VICTORY OVER Mexico opened the way for the largest single acquisition of territory in American history, and as a consequence it provoked the final struggle between the South and the North that led to the Civil War. The Mexican War was the handiwork of Democratic President James Polk, who was elected to a single term in the White House in 1844. Polk came to office during the time of Manifest Destiny, when territorial expansion, by conquest if necessary, topped the political agenda. American columnist and editor John L. O'Sullivan, who came up with the phrase "Manifest Destiny," exulted: "Yes, more, more, more! More...till our national destiny is fulfilled and...the whole boundless continent is ours." [3]

Manifest Destiny was the political outlook of the Democratic Party. The Whigs, while not averse to territorial expansion, were more disposed to using peaceful means to achieve this end and were more inclined to place their faith in the force of American ideas than in the might of American arms.

The Polk administration lusted for expansion both in the north and in the south. In the north, the battle cry among settlers in what the Americans called the Oregon Country was "Fifty-four forty or fight." The slogan referred to the latitude at the southern boundary of Russian-controlled Alaska on the Pacific coast. For decades, the west coast of North America had been the site of geopolitical struggles among competing powers. Prior to Mexico's independence from Spain in 1820, the British, Americans, Russians, and Spaniards each staked out their territorial claims. After 1820, the first three powers maintained their intense interest in the region, while the Mexicans replaced the Spanish as the possessors of California.

In his inaugural address on March 4, 1845, Polk declared that he would "assert and maintain by all constitutional means the right of the United States to that portion of our territory which lies beyond the Rocky Mountains. Our title to the country of the Oregon is 'clear and unquestionable'." [4] On April 26, 1846, two weeks before the United States declared war on Mexico, the president gave notice that the U.S. was abrogating the Convention of 1818, which set up a regime that established joint occupancy of the disputed territory by the United States and Great Britain. Behind the scenes, however, Polk let the British know that he was prepared to compromise.

Faced with the unappetizing prospect of battling on two fronts, Polk decided to make peace with the British in the north so as to pursue war against Mexico in the south.

British foreign minister Lord Aberdeen instructed Richard Pakenham, the British ambassador to Washington, to propose the 49th parallel as the boundary between the United States and the British colonies, from the Rockies to the Pacific, with Britain to retain the whole of Vancouver Island and navigation rights on the Columbia River. On June 15, 1846, the two countries signed the Oregon Treaty in Washington, D.C. By the time of the signing, the U.S. was already at war with Mexico.

The Polk administration's ambitions in the south were enormous. When Mexico refused to sell New Mexico and Upper California — California north of 31 degrees latitude — and would not concede the Rio Grande as the border between Texas and Mexico, the United States declared war.

By February 2, 1848, the United States and Mexico signed the Treaty of Guadalupe Hidalgo, which ended the war. Under the treaty, the United States annexed one million square miles of territory, including the present states of California, Nevada, Utah, and New Mexico, most of Arizona and Colorado, and sections of Oklahoma, Kansas, and Wyoming. The Rio Grande was also declared the undisputed border between Texas and Mexico. Mexico was paid a sum of $15 million for the ceded territory and was also ordered to pay $3.25 million to the U.S. to cover the debts owed by the Mexican government to American citizens.

The vast annexation of Mexican territory provoked political controversy in the United States. Some Democrats wanted to annex all of Mexico, in order to extend the cotton farmers' territory. For instance, Mississippi Senator Jefferson Davis moved an amendment in the United States Senate, which failed by a vote of 44–11, that would have added most of northeastern Mexico to the territory acquired under the treaty.

Since the American Revolution, the slave states of Louisiana, Missouri, Arkansas, Florida, and Texas had been added to the Union as a consequence of territorial acquisition. The only free state to have been admitted was Iowa.[5]

In the eighteenth and nineteenth centuries, the quest for land was the mother's milk of the politics of the Thirteen Colonies and the United States. A key trigger of the American Revolution was the desire of colonial leaders to dislodge the barrier to westward expansion, which the British had erected with the Royal Proclamation of 1763. The Royal Proclamation drew a line along the Appalachians, limiting colonial settlement to the east of the range and reserving lands to the west to native peoples. Blocking access to more land was a fetter imposed on colonists that they found unendurable.

If the drive for land made some Americans immensely wealthy and the United States more powerful, it also fostered severe tensions within the American state. Each time the American Republic acquired territory, a crisis erupted over the question of slavery in the new territory and more generally over the balance between the slave states and the free states in the Union. These crises exposed the great question confronting the American Republic from the time of its creation until the end of the Civil War: whether the United States was a single nation state or contained within its boundaries two national projects, one in the North and another in the South.

Prior to the conclusion of the war, philosopher Ralph Waldo Emerson made a fateful prediction: "The United States will conquer Mexico, but it will be as the man swallows the arsenic, which brings him down. Mexico will poison us."[6]

Many Whig politicians, notably Abraham Lincoln, had opposed the Mexican War. One of the first bitter squabbles erupted during the early months of battle, in August 1846, when David Wilmot, a first-term Democratic congressman from Pennsylvania, rose in the House of Representatives during a debate to move an amendment on appropriations, should the U.S. win territory at the end of the war: "That, as an express and fundamental condition of the acquisition of any territory from the Republic of Mexico, neither slavery nor involuntary servitude shall ever exist in any part of said territory."[7]

The amendment ignited a firestorm. The so-called Wilmot Proviso won the support of Northern Whigs as well as Northern Democrats and passed in the House. It failed in the Senate, however, where the South was more heavily represented. The measure was again introduced in February 1847, once more passing in the House and losing in the Senate. An attempt to include it in the Treaty of Guadalupe Hidalgo also failed.

By the time the furious debate erupted over the Wilmot Proviso, the South and the North had been following ever more distinct and divergent socio-economic paths. Two national entities were taking shape within the framework of the American Republic. There were very tangible, material reasons for this. The South's interests lay in the surging production of cotton and the shift in the locus of the economy from Virginia to the cotton belt of Georgia, Mississippi, and Alabama. Meanwhile, the North was the centre of an industrial revolution that was transforming this populous region, to which immigrants were drawn, into an ever more urban economic powerhouse.

So much romance has been associated with the "Lost Cause" of the South — the pro-Southern narrative honed in the years following the Civil War — over the past century and a half that it is hard to comprehend that the Confederate States of America was a modern mid-nineteenth-century nation state. Cotton, its growth and harvesting, was at the core of the Southern project. The enormous profits gleaned from cotton drove the rise of the New South in the decades leading up to the Civil War and was the most consequential among its long-term causes. As historian Sven Beckert states in his book *Empire of Cotton: A Global History*: "Cotton, the nineteenth century's chief global commodity, brought seeming opposites together, turning them almost by alchemy into wealth: slavery and free labour, states and markets, colonialism and free trade, industrialization and deindustrialization." [8]

Although cotton had been harvested and rendered into cloth for thousands of years in many parts of the world, Europe was late in entering the production of cotton textiles because the plant could be grown in only a few southern extremities of the continent. The rise of cotton manufacturing around Manchester in the late eighteenth century was protected by the British Empire against imports from India. It also took off as a consequence of the development of mechanized methods of production.

In 1784, an industrialist named Samuel Greg opened a small factory on the banks of the River Bollin near Manchester, where he set up water-frames, new spinning machines for the manufacture of cotton yarn. This was the first time in history that machines powered by energy from a non-animate source were used to produce yarn. [9]

Greg also put orphaned children and labourers from surrounding villages to work in the factory. Children as young as six years of age had to crawl under the dangerous machines to retrieve bits of cotton that were blown away in the process of production.

Soon tens of thousands of workers were employed in the factories. Despite the frequent efforts of weavers to block the use of the new machines, which were depriving them of work, productivity in the cotton industry advanced dramatically. By 1797, there were about nine hundred factories in the immediate area surrounding Manchester. Three decades later, one in six labourers in Britain was employed in the cotton industry. [10]

During the 1780s, British and French plantation owners in the West Indies deployed slave labour to produce cotton; exports from the islands to Britain quickly rose. As it happened, the Caribbean was serving as a proving ground for the use of slave labour to produce cotton in the Southern states. Greg's raw cotton was imported from the Caribbean. By 1780, none of the raw cotton being used in mills in Lancashire was imported from North America. [11] That was about to change, and so too was the economy of the states of the American South.

Later in the nineteenth century, the production of cotton fabrics became the world's leading mechanized industry. This made the new South the indispensable source of raw material for mills in the English Midlands, in Lyons, France, and in the U.S. Northeast.

Prior to the American Revolution, cotton had been grown in the American colonies in small amounts. By the 1780s, some owners were utilizing slave labour to grow and harvest a special variety of cotton on the sea islands off the coast of Georgia and along the coasts of Georgia and South Carolina. Production further inland was only possible with other strains of cotton, but removing seeds from the fibre of these new strains was highly labour-intensive. This difficulty was eradicated by Eli Whitney's famous 1793 invention: the cotton gin.

Whitney's invention allowed the efficient removal of cotton seeds, and it opened the door to a tragic chapter in the history of human labour: the use of slaves on an enormous scale across a vast territory to produce cotton for export. As historian Sven Beckert puts it: "The United States more than any other country had elastic supplies of the three crucial ingredients that went into the production of raw cotton: labour, land and credit."[12] By 1802, the United States had become the largest supplier of cotton to the English mills.[13]

The farming methods used by the plantation owners were exceptionally wasteful. Soil was quickly degraded and was seldom refurbished through the planting of other restorative crops. Instead, the plantation owners sought fresh, fertile land to which they could move their slaves. The very operations of the cotton plantations of the New South necessitated territorial expansion to acquire fertile new land for the slave owners. The Louisiana Purchase of 1803, the acquisition of Florida in 1819, the annexation of Texas in 1845, and the enormous conquest of territory from Mexico in the 1846–48 war added immense stretches of land to the American Republic on which the cotton growers of the South could expand their operations. In 1860, 85 percent of cotton in the South was produced by owners whose assets included more than one hundred acres. Labouring on these large farms were 91.2 percent of all the slaves working on the cotton fields.[14] When necessary, which it often was, native peoples were driven out of their traditional territories, one way or another, to open new expanses for the growth of cotton.

As a result, slave labour became more central and indispensable to the Southern economy. It was the cheapest, most profitable way to grow and harvest cotton. The members of the slaveocracy — the major slave owners who were the dominant economic and political actors of the South — were intent on territorial expansion to bring new and potentially profitable lands into their domain.

Much of the land that was newly acquired by the United States was too far north or was otherwise unsuited for cotton, which is why political leaders such as Jefferson Davis, to whom the interests of cotton growers were always a major concern, favoured the acquisition of Cuba, other Caribbean islands, and land in Central America in addition to expanding the territorial reach of the American Republic on the continental mainland. Cuba headed the list of territories in the Caribbean that plantation owners were eager to acquire. Indeed, in the years prior to the Civil War, Cuba's Spanish rulers bloodily repulsed operations undertaken by American freebooters to seize the island. Pro-slavery freebooters also made failed attempts to secure Guatemala and Nicaragua.

So great was the demand for slaves on the eve of the war, that in the South some political leaders advocated the reopening of the transatlantic slave trade. "If it is right to buy slaves in Virginia and carry them to New Orleans," queried Senator William Lowndes Yancey of Alabama, "why is it not right to buy them in Africa and carry them there?"[15] In March 1858, South Carolina Senator James Hammond expressed the expansive confidence of the planters when he told the United States Senate: "The slaveholding South is now the controlling power of the world. Cotton, rice, tobacco and naval stores command the world...No power on earth dares...to make war on cotton. Cotton is King."[16]

On the new plantations, slaves were put to work clearing the land and then growing and harvesting cotton. The shift in the locus of slavery in the U.S. was dramatic, from Virginia in the Upper South to South Carolina and Georgia, and then to Alabama, Louisiana, Mississippi, Arkansas, and Texas. So swift was the move to the new, unspoiled terrain that by the end of the 1830s, Mississippi, the home state of Jefferson Davis, produced more cotton than any other state.

The use of ever more slaves, often purchased from Virginia, can be seen by the increase in the proportion of slaves to the total population over the decades. In 1790, slaves made up 18.4 percent of the population of four upcountry counties in South Carolina. In 1820, the proportion had surged to 39.5 percent, and by 1860, it had reached 61.1 percent.[17] By 1830, one million people in the United States, the overwhelming majority of them slaves, sowed and harvested cotton. By 1860, three-quarters of American cotton was grown west of South Carolina and Georgia.[18]

The most advanced industrial capitalism of the mid-nineteenth century, centred in Lancashire, fitted like a hand in a glove with slavery as the principal source of labour in the New South. During the quarter century before the ending of the importation of slaves in 1808, slave traders transported approximately 170,000 slaves across the seas from West Africa to the United States. In 1853, an article in the *American Cotton Planter* contended that "slave labour must also continue, for it is idle to talk of producing Cotton for the world's supply with free labour. It has never yet been successfully grown by voluntary labour." [19] The same year, Karl Marx wrote that "bourgeois civilization" and "barbarity" were joined together. [20] By 1860, about one million slaves had been moved from states in the Upper South, principally Virginia, to the Deep South. [21] That slavery was immensely profitable is shown by the steep rise in the price of slaves over the decades. In 1800, a young adult male slave drew about $500 at auction in New Orleans. On the eve of the Civil War, the price for this man had climbed to about $1,800. [22]

In the process, families were ruthlessly torn apart. And whenever the price of cotton rose, thus increasing demand, slaves felt it with the sting of the lash. In 1854, a fugitive slave recalled the savagery: "When the price [of cotton] rises in the English market, the poor slaves immediately feel the effects, for they are harder driven, and the whip is kept more constantly going." [23]

The slave owners and the politicians who served them were acutely aware of the need for an active state that supported their aspirations. Likewise they were deeply alarmed at any prospect that the U.S. federal government could fall into hostile hands.

As late as 1830, the widespread assumption in the North and even in much of the South was that slavery was an institution that was on its way to extinction. Many Southerners joined Northerners in the conviction that slavery was morally reprehensible as well as being an economic fetter standing in the way of the emergence of a dynamic and productive society. Between 1830 and 1860, however, the very industrialism that promoted the rise of the North and the Midwest breathed new life into slave labour as a source of vast wealth for those who owned plantations in the cotton belt. Far from being a vestigial remnant of earlier times, Southern slavery was linked to centres of capital that were among the most advanced in the world.

During the decades prior to the Civil War, challenges to slavery were treated as threats to a very wealthy and politically powerful ruling class. Publicists and thinkers who expressed the outlook of the Southern gentry had stopped defending slavery as a necessary evil. Instead, they promulgated the view that slavery was a positive good, benefitting both the slaves, who lived in a supposedly benign condition of cradle-to-grave welfare, and the white owners, who were suited to their paternal position as a natural consequence of their racial superiority. By the middle of the nineteenth century, the very rationale for slavery was shifting from traditional and biblical justifications to the new and savage biological theories of racial differences.

As producers of cotton and other primary products, Southern businesses lived off the profits of exports. They had an interest in keeping the price of imported industrial goods low and were just as happy to buy manufactured products from England or France as from the North. As a consequence, they naturally favoured low tariffs. The political economy of the South clashed with that of the North not only on the question of slavery but also on the issue of the tariff. As a primary producing region with a vital connection to European markets, the South desired state policies that were at odds with the policies favoured in the North.

The collision between the South and the North as a result of diverging socio-economic systems can be readily grasped. Over the course of the 1850s, as the North industrialized, the South focused even more on the production of a few staple products, destined for export to Europe and the North. While cotton prices had been low in the 1840s, during the following decade the average price increased by more than 50 percent to 11.5 cents a pound. Toward the end of the 1850s, the annual cotton crop doubled to four million bales. The prices and production of sugar and tobacco, two other important Southern staples, also increased sharply during these years, while the output per capita of food production actually declined over the course of the decade. The

South was becoming a highly specialized region, more able to profit from exports than to feed itself. [24]

THOUGH THE RULERS of the South regarded themselves as the helmsmen of a rising power, the North and the Midwest were ascending in economic and demographic might even more rapidly. Over the course of the 1840s, 1.7 million immigrants entered the United States. During the decade, the population of the country increased by over six million people, with most of the growth in the North and Midwest. With labourers flooding into the new industries of the North, the population balance between the free states and the slave states was shifting ever more in favour of the former and against the latter.

The perilous decade of the 1850s opened with a last, Herculean attempt to achieve a viable accommodation between the slave states and the free states: the Compromise of 1850. The five bills, passed in September 1850 and signed into law by President Millard Fillmore, were cobbled together by Whig Senator Henry Clay of Kentucky and Democratic Senator Stephen Douglas of Illinois.

For more than four decades, Henry Clay had played a major role in American politics. An economic nationalist and the founder of the Whig Party, Clay believed in American expansion. During the War of 1812, he was committed to driving Britain from the continent through the invasion and annexation of Canada. Among his admirers was a young Abraham Lincoln.

Senator Stephen Douglas, dubbed the "little giant," was a politician who made up in intellect and oratorical prowess for his short stature. A former state court judge and a rising star in the Democratic Party, Douglas had his heart set on winning the White House. Regarded by many as the finest orator in the country, Douglas used his political standing to steer the elements of Clay's Compromise through Congress.

The 1850 Compromise was fiercely opposed both by Southerners, who thought it did not sufficiently protect slavery and the South, and by Northerners, who felt it didn't serve the interests of the free states. As such, it could not be passed as a single package. Douglas divided the package up into five separate bills, largely the work of Clay, which were passed individually by narrow congressional majorities. The five bills were as follows:

- The admission of California as a free state. What made this bill controversial was that the state extended well south of the parallel 36 degrees 30 minutes north, the line that was agreed upon in the 1820 Missouri Compromise as the northernmost limit at which slavery was to be allowed in the territories in the West that had not yet been admitted as states.

- The slave trade — the sale of slaves — was abolished in Washington, D.C., but the institution of slavery was still permitted in the national capital.

- The territories of New Mexico (which included present-day Arizona) and Utah were to administer themselves under the rule of "popular sovereignty," allowing citizens to determine whether to allow slavery or to ban it. To Northern opponents of slavery, it was anathema that Utah, which lay entirely north of 36/30, could choose whether to permit slavery.

- A Fugitive Slave Act, which permitted Southern slave owners to pursue their runaway slaves into free states and to call on the authorities to seize and return them to bondage. This element of the Compromise generated explosive hostility in the North because it was seen as an unwarranted extension of the power of the slave owners into states that did not allow slavery.

- Texas gave up western lands it had previously claimed. In exchange, the state received $10 million in compensation, and the money was earmarked to pay off the debt that had been accumulated during its time as an independent republic.

Initially, the Compromise proved highly popular in both the North and the South, because it appeared to stave off the nation's descent into armed conflict. Its viability and political legitimacy did not endure long, however.

In the short term, it staunched what historians have called "the first secession crisis."[25] From 1846 to 1850, a number of political leaders and thinkers in the South had concluded that their section of the country was increasingly under siege. For instance, in December 1849, Congressman Alexander Stephens, who later became vice president of the Confederacy, wrote in a letter to his brother: "I find the feeling among the Southern members for a dissolution of the Union — if the antislavery [measures] should be pressed to extremity — is becoming more general than at first."

The drive for secession was strongest in Mississippi, Alabama, Georgia, and South Carolina. Southern-rights political groups formed and held conventions to consider available political options. In June 1850, at the Nashville Convention in Tennessee, pro-secession Southerners pushed their agenda, but they were outnumbered by moderates who still favoured the retention of the Union provided the South's rights were respected.

In Georgia, Governor George Towns, acting on the instructions of the state legislature, called a special election to select delegates to a state convention to decide how to respond to the Compromise. In December 1850, following five days of deliberations in Milledgeville, Georgia, the 264 delegates issued the Georgia Platform, a qualified endorsement of the Compromise that was conditional on the further diminution of the rights of slave owners.

Meanwhile, in the North, political leaders who were to play a major role in the sectional debate were making their voices heard. One of those was Senator William Henry Seward from New York State, who was destined to play a central role in the great debate about the terms of the Compromise of 1850. By then, the New York politician had come a long way in his evolution as a rousing orator. Earlier in life, Seward had suffered from stage fright, and while his intelligence and reasoning powers were evident, he was a far from gifted speaker.

William Henry Seward was born in Florida, New York, in 1801, one of five children of Samuel Sweezy Seward, a doctor and successful businessman. The 1820 census counted seven slaves as belonging to the Seward household. As a child, William Seward spent a great deal of time with the slaves' children. Seward's father was unique in the village in permitting these children to attend the local school. According to Seward, his parents "never uttered an expression that could tend to make me think that the negro was inferior to the white person." Two years before Seward's birth, the New York state legislature had passed a law to phase out slavery. The law did not apply to slaves who had been born before 1799. [26]

In the early 1820s, Seward moved to Auburn, New York, in the heart of the Finger Lakes, a town bustling with entrepreneurial energy. New sawmills, cloth factories, flour mills, newspapers, and other businesses were being opened during these years. The town was located about fifteen miles south of the Erie Canal, the vital commercial corridor that linked New York City with Lake Erie, making it the most effective way, at the time, to ship goods from the Great Lakes to the Atlantic Coast.

In Auburn, Seward joined the law firm of Elijah Miller, a retired judge and one of the most influential men in the region. It was not long before the young lawyer married the judge's daughter Frances. The marriage came with an odd request from Seward's father-in-law: that the young couple should reside in Miller's house, which was located on four acres of beautiful land. There, they lived not only with widower Elijah Miller but also with his aging mother and his sister, Clara. [27]

Vitally important to William Seward was his close friendship with Thurlow Weed, a political operative and rainmaker in the Whig Party in New York State. Seward and Weed formed a highly productive political partnership, with Seward as the elegant idea man and Weed as the backroom deal maker who knew how to twist arms when necessary. Seward served as a member of the New York State Senate from 1831 to 1834, and in 1834 he ran unsuccessfully as the Whig candidate for state governor, losing to the incumbent Democrat, William L. Marcy. In 1838, Seward again challenged Marcy, and this time he was elected governor, a position he held on to in the subsequent election of 1840. In March 1849, when a U.S. Senate seat for New York needed to be filled, Seward put himself forward, and his friend Weed worked to great effect behind the scenes to get him the votes to win. This was in a day when United States senators were still elected by the members of state legislatures. With Weed's ability to make deals, Seward won the vote in the New York state legislature by the wide margin of 121 to 32.[28]

The United States Senate was the ideal forum for Seward to propound his views on slavery. When he arrived in the Upper Chamber, he did not wait long to make those views known. In one early speech, he said he had grown tired of hearing slave owners and their political backers make the case that slavery would come to an end "in time." Impatiently, Seward told his fellow senators: "Slavery has existed here under the sanction of Congress…undisturbed…the right time, then has not passed…it must therefore be a future time. Will gentlemen oblige me, and the country, by telling us how far down in the future the right time lies?"[29]

At the conclusion of another address, Seward directed his caustic remarks to Southern senators: "I simply ask whether the safety and interests of the twenty-five million free, non-slave-owning white men ought to be sacrificed or put in jeopardy for the convenience or safety of 350,000 slaveholders?"[30]

On March 11, 1850, he rose in the Senate to oppose the terms of the Compromise. While he supported the admission of California as a free state and the banning of the slave trade in Washington, D.C., Seward refused to support the terms of the Compromise that could extend the territorial scope of slavery. He also opposed the Fugitive Slave Act, which would turn Northern free states into hunting grounds for the pursuit and capture of runaway slaves. But most importantly, he changed the terms of the slavery debate in the United States so that the question could never again be approached as it had been in the past.

First, he addressed the issue of the territories and asked his fellow senators to consider this matter not merely from the viewpoint of those who lived in the territories at present, but from the viewpoint of those who would live there hundreds of years in the future. He said those voices in the future were crying out to say: "The soil you hold in trust for us, give it to us free — free from the calamities and sorrows of human bondage."

But what he said later reverberated across the country. Traditionally, both advocates and opponents of slavery had conducted debates about the institution from the premise that slavery was legal under the U.S. Constitution. Seward rejected that premise, declaring that the Constitution was devoted "to union, to justice, to defense, to welfare, and to liberty. But there is a higher law than the Constitution, which regulates our authority over the domain, and devotes it to the same noble purposes. The territory is a part — no inconsiderable part — of the common heritage of mankind, bestowed upon them by the Creator of the universe. We are his stewards, and must so discharge our trust as to secure, in the highest attainable degree, their happiness." [31]

Seward's Higher Law speech was an immediate sensation in both the North and the South. The speech was printed by Seward's office, and by many others, and was distributed in pamphlet form to hundreds of thousands of people. [32]

In the North, abolitionists took to calling themselves the "higher law people." [33] In the South, Seward was condemned as the deadliest foe of the region.

Southern newspapers were vituperative: the New Orleans *Picayune* described him as "an unscrupulous Demagogue," while a writer for the *Richmond Enquirer* said that Seward was "a wretch whom it would be a degradation to name."

Even the venerable Henry Clay wrote that "Mr. Seward's latest abolitionist speech...had eradicated the respect of almost all men for him." [34]

Clay's comment was a sign of the times. Clay, Daniel Webster of Massachusetts, and South Carolina pro-slavery theorist John Calhoun, who had long dominated the United States Congress and had often put their differences aside to achieve results, were going to their graves. Indeed, Calhoun died on March 31, 1850, while the debate about the Compromise was underway. In his later years, Calhoun became ever more embittered as opposition to slavery grew in the North. He theorized about the positive benefits of slavery, both for master and for slave, and made the case that states had a right to secede from the Union. Webster died in January 1852, a few months before Clay's passing.

Among those who would take the place of the power brokers of the past was Jefferson Davis, the senator from Mississippi.

Chapter 2

Irrepressible Conflict

B Y 1854, two issues had plunged the United States into a renewed state of political crisis. The first was territorial: Were new territories permitted to resolve the issue of slavery on their own? The territorial issue boiled to the surface with the creation of the territories of Nebraska and Kansas, which lay north of the 36/30 parallel.

Anxious to hold on to his political supporters in both the North and the South, Senator Stephen Douglas advanced a formula he hoped would keep the Kansas issue local: the concept of popular sovereignty. Popular sovereignty would allow citizens of Kansas and Nebraska to decide for themselves whether to allow or to ban slavery, thus confining the issue to each territory and avoiding a great national debate. Douglas insisted that popular sovereignty was in keeping with the republican principles upon which the American constitutional system was based.

Southerners in Congress were determined to gain one further concession before they would support Douglas's Kansas-Nebraska Act. Kentucky Senator Archibald Dixon introduced an amendment to the act that would explicitly repeal the section of the Missouri Compromise that prohibited slavery in territories north of 36/30. In part, Dixon was motivated by the desire to demonstrate to Southerners that the Whigs were strong defenders of slavery. Southern Democrats had been effectively demolishing the Whigs in the South on the slavery issue. Douglas was well aware that this concession would "raise a hell of a storm" in the North.[1]

Despite his reservations, he decided he had to go along with Dixon's amendment. The searing debate over Kansas-Nebraska went on for four months in the Senate and the House. On March 4, 1854, the Senate passed the bill. Free state senators voted 14–12 in support of it, while slave state senators overwhelmingly backed it by a vote of 23–2.

First delayed, then filibustered, and finally intensely debated in the House of Representatives, the Kansas-Nebraska Act was passed by a vote of 113–100. In the North, Democrats supported the bill by a narrow margin of 44–42. All forty-five Northern Whigs voted against the bill. In the South, Whigs backed the measure, 12–7, while Democrats overwhelmingly supported it, 57–2. On May 30, 1854, President Franklin Pierce signed the Kansas-Nebraska Act into law.

If Kansas-Nebraska stoked the flames of sectional conflict, so too did the 1857 Dred Scott case, which deeply strained the relations between the supporters and the foes of slavery. In 1830, Dred Scott had been purchased in Missouri by an army surgeon, Dr. John Emerson. Scott went with Emerson in 1833 to free territory — Fort Armstrong at Rock Island, Illinois. After three years there, he accompanied Emerson to Fort Snelling, near present-day Saint Paul, Minnesota, which was then in the Louisiana Territory. Scott returned with the doctor to Missouri in 1838. When the doctor died in 1843, Dred Scott tried to buy his freedom from Emerson's widow. She refused, and Scott petitioned for his freedom at the Missouri Circuit Court in St. Louis. He made the argument that since he had lived for three years in the free state of Illinois, he should thereby have gained his freedom.

Although Scott lost this case on a technicality, he won at a second trial in 1850. This time a Missouri court came down on his side of the argument, ruling that a slave who was taken out of Missouri should be considered free.[2]

Mrs. Emerson appealed the court's ruling to the Missouri Supreme

Court, which in turn reversed the decision made by the lower court. The Missouri Supreme Court ruling was upheld by a federal court. Scott appealed his case to the Supreme Court of the United States.[3] In 1856, the case went to trial. Presiding was Chief Justice Roger B. Taney, who had been appointed the fifth chief justice in 1836. Prior to his accession to that position, Taney, who had been born into a wealthy slave-owning family in Maryland in 1777, had held the positions of attorney general and secretary of the treasury in the administration of President Andrew Jackson.

In December 1856, Montgomery Blair, an attorney and former resident of St. Louis, presented the case for Scott, contending that when Dr. Emerson took his client to the free state of Illinois and to the Louisiana Territory, which prohibited slavery, he thereby liberated the slave. He argued that five states had recognized African Americans as citizens, and that the state of Missouri had done so in the past.[4]

During the oral arguments the following February, Senator Henry Geyer of Missouri contended that "blacks are not citizens" even if they accompany their masters to free territory. A former attorney general of the United States, Reverdy Johnson, made the case for slavery before the court: "Slavery promises to exist through all time," he argued, "so far as human vision can discover."[5]

The incoming president of the United States, James Buchanan, took a considerable interest in the Dred Scott case, convinced that its outcome could settle the issue of slavery in the territories once and for all. In fact, a few days before his inauguration, Buchanan was told by Chief Justice Taney how the verdict would go. Armed with this prior knowledge, Buchanan used his inaugural address to contend that the Dred Scott case would soon "be speedily and finally settled," and that when the decision was handed down, "in common with all good citizens, I shall cheerfully submit."[6]

Throughout his presidency, Buchanan, a Pennsylvania Democrat, took the side of the slave owners, obstinately believing that the rising tide of opinion against the institution in the North was the consequence of agitation by fanatical abolitionists. His utter failure to face the reality of the critical debate about the extension of slavery to the territories was an important reason that 1860 became the year of Lincoln's election and the year when the secession of Southern states commenced.

Taney's opinion, issued two days after Buchanan's inauguration, dismissed Dred Scott's appeal, and did so not on narrow grounds, but on such broad grounds that it ended up stoking anti-slavery feeling in the North. Central to the chief justice's opinion, which coincided with the majority — the verdict against Scott was 7–2 — was the inflammatory assertion that slaves were not human, and that therefore they had no legal standing to file a suit in court. In his decision, Taney declared that blacks were "unfit to associate with the white race... and so far inferior that they had no rights which the white man was bound to respect."[7]

The second finding of the Supreme Court was that the U.S. Congress did not have the constitutional authority to exclude slavery from federal territories. This decision had the effect of rendering unconstitutional the Missouri Compromise of 1820, which had barred slavery from the territories of the Louisiana Purchase that lay north of the latitude 36/30, with the exception of Missouri. Taney had to engage in constitutional legerdemain to reach this conclusion. He conceded that the first Congress of the United States had enacted the Northwest Ordinance of 1787, but ruled that subsequent Congresses lacked the constitutional right to bar slavery from territories acquired by the United States thereafter. The third finding in Taney's ruling was that Dred Scott was a slave, and would permanently be one, under Missouri law.[8]

The Supreme Court's ruling, so much more political than judicial in character, had, in fact, been influenced by the incoming president. Prior to the issuing of the ruling, Southern congressmen and the president-elect were concerned that if the split on the Supreme Court pitted the five Southern justices (a majority of the nine-member court) against the Northerners, the legitimacy of the verdict would be undermined. In February 1858, Justice John Catron of Tennessee wrote to

Buchanan, advising him to exert influence on Supreme Court Justice Robert Grier of Pennsylvania to come down on the side of Taney and the other Southerners in the Dred Scott case. The president-elect secretly wrote to Justice Grier, who was a fellow Pennsylvanian, to urge him to find against Scott. By doing so, Buchanan violated the prohibition against any interference by the executive branch in the proceedings of the judiciary. Grier did end up voting with Taney and the majority in the Court, and sent a letter to Buchanan revealing that he was well aware of the impropriety: "We will not let any others of our brethren know," he wrote, "about the cause of our anxiety to produce the result." In his letter, he acknowledged that what was happening was "contrary to our usual practice." [9]

If President Buchanan, Taney, and the other justices who voted on the majority side of the verdict thought the decision in the Dred Scott case would calm the mood of American politics, they were dead wrong. Leading Republicans and prominent newspaper editors denounced the decision. The *New-York Tribune's* Horace Greeley wrote that the court's ruling was "atrocious," "wicked," and "abominable." [10]

The Dred Scott case and its judicial outcome dramatically increased the tension between the South and the North. But even more important in stoking the discord between the sections was one of the measures adopted as a main feature of the Compromise of 1850: the Fugitive Slave Act.

THE SECOND ISSUE that strained North-South relations was intended as a measure that would damp down the resentment of Southern slave owners against the rising hostility of Northerners toward slavery. The Fugitive Slave Act led to numerous cases in which runaway slaves were hunted down on Northern territory, sometimes making good their escapes and sometimes being returned by law enforcement officials to their masters.

John Price was in his twenties when he fled on horseback with two other slaves on a cold night in January 1856. The three headed north from the Kentucky farm where they lived, and when they reached the Ohio River, they safely crossed it into Brown County, Ohio. There, they met a Quaker who was a member of the Underground Railroad and [11] whose mission was to provide safe houses and support for runaway slaves as they made the treacherous journey to a reasonably safe location in the North or to Canada. By 1860, about thirty thousand former slaves had escaped to freedom in Canada.

The Quaker helped Price and his two companions journey to Oberlin, a very special northern Ohio town in which runaway slaves were welcomed and often provided with work and a dwelling. The racially integrated town had been founded as a "utopian" community where religious Protestants could live together in a society free from racism, and where communitarian values could prevail. Its residents, who numbered just over 2,200, detested the Fugitive Slave Act and were inclined to act on behalf of captives, caring little whether they were runaways or not. Oberlin College, established in 1833, included many African Americans among its students. [12]

John Price, who chose to remain in Oberlin rather than to go on to Canada, eked out an existence with support from the townspeople. He did odd jobs and harvested crops. On September 13, 1858, while he was harvesting potatoes for a local farmer, two slave hunters from Kentucky, accompanied by a deputy marshal from Oberlin, seized Price and pulled him into their carriage.

Just as runaway slaves were drawn to Oberlin, so too were those who sought them out. They would bring a document from a Southern court, or sometimes a warrant, which allowed them to bring their captive before a federal commissioner. During a hearing, the alleged runaway slave was not permitted to testify. In the event that the commissioner issued a "certificate of removal," which allowed the slave hunters to take the unfortunate captive with them, the commissioner was paid a fee of $10. Should the commissioner find on behalf of the captive and determine that he should be released, he received a sum of only $5. [13]

The men who seized John Price took him to a hotel in the nearby town of Wellington, where they proceeded to eat lunch in his presence. Assuming they were safe, the captors were unaware that two Oberlin students had spotted them during their journey. The students alerted others as to Price's whereabouts, and a large posse of determined rescuers — both whites and blacks — congregated in Oberlin and travelled the ten miles to Wellington, where they surrounded the hotel. A large crowd of Wellington residents joined them. Under siege, the captors took John Price to an upstairs room and barred the door. [14]

The slave hunters tried to negotiate with the crowd, holding up the papers they claimed gave them a right to return John Price to Kentucky. They even brought their captive out onto the balcony where the visibly shaken man told the people below that since the men had the papers for him, he supposed he would have to return with them to Kentucky.

This incensed the crowd even more. The standoff ended when two groups of men from Oberlin, led by African Americans, burst into the hotel. They ascended the two flights of stairs, broke down the door, and carried Price down to the crowd below. He was swiftly taken by carriage back to Oberlin and was spirited across the border to Canada.

The rescue of John Price was a public and highly publicized challenge to the Fugitive Slave Act. Members of President James Buchanan's administration saw the rescue as a brazen assault on the administration's stance on slavery. Buchanan agreed with Attorney General Jeremiah Black that they had to make an example of the rescuers. Initially, they even considered charging them with espionage, in which case convictions would have carried the death penalty. They decided instead to charge thirty-seven of the rescuers with violating the Fugitive Slave Act. [15]

In Cleveland, Judge Hiram V. Willson impanelled a grand jury to weigh the evidence against the accused. The judge revealed his bias against the rescuers from the moment he instructed the jurors on their duties. He told them their task was to determine whether Price's rescuers had breached the law, not to rule on whether slavery was right or wrong. [16] Not only was the judge biased against the rescuers; the members of the grand jury were a one-sided lot as well. All of them were Democrats, whereas those whose cases they were considering were abolitionists and Republicans.

The trials of the rescuers, under the glare of nationwide publicity, commenced on March 8, 1859. The prosecution tried the accused one by one. Prosecutor George Belden focused on the town of Oberlin and abolitionists in general in trying the first case. He airily dismissed what he called "the saints of Oberlin." In concluding his argument, he declared: "When the Oberlin men went down to Wellington they proclaimed that they did so under the Higher Law, for they knew they were outraging the law of the land."

Albert Riddle, the defence attorney, did not back away from the ethical argument. "And now, as to the matter referred to, the so-called dogma of the Higher Law...I am perfectly frank to declare, that I am a votary of that Higher Law." [17]

Defendant Charles Langston, an African American who was a leader of the black abolitionist movement in Ohio, was found guilty by the jury. He was then permitted to address the court.

Everyone, Langston declared defiantly to the judge, "had a right to his liberty under the laws of God...If ever a man is seized near me, and is about to be carried Southward as a slave, then we are thrown back upon those last defences of our rights, which cannot be taken from us, and which God gave us that we need not be slaves."

Surprisingly, Langston's speech, which drew sustained applause from the observers in the courtroom, evoked sympathetic remarks from Judge Willson and a comparatively light sentence for the convicted man.

"We appreciate fully your condition," said the judge, "and while it excites the cordial sympathies of our better natures, still the law must be vindicated. On reflection, I am constrained to say that the penalty in your case should be comparatively light."

Willson proceeded to sentence Langston to twenty days in jail and a fine of $100, which was virtually the lightest possible sentence. [18] The prosecution and members of the Buchanan administration regarded the sentence as a blow to their hopes for a sharp rebuke to the abolitionists.

In addition to those committed to rescuing runaway slaves or helping them flee to Canada, there were those who were determined to attack the entire system of slavery and to abolish it.

IN OCTOBER 1859, a man named John Brown and a small force of men, including both whites and African Americans, set out on a mission that was to bring him martyrdom and that was to unleash a wave of fear across the white South. Brown's plan was to seize the armoury at Harper's Ferry, Virginia, on the south bank of the Potomac River. Once he and his men had made off with an ample supply of weapons, they would head south along the Appalachian Mountains, fomenting the slave rebellion as they went. Many who had been invited to join Brown's expedition, including the renowned African-American writer and militant Frederick Douglass, had turned him down. Douglass was convinced that Brown was setting out on a suicide mission.

Born in Connecticut in 1800, John Brown could trace his forebears back to the seventeenth-century English Puritans. His family moved to Ohio when he was five years old. At the age of sixteen, Brown left home, aspiring to become a Congregationalist minister. When he ran out of money and suffered health problems, he was forced to give up his religious studies in Litchfield, Connecticut. He returned to Ohio, where he married.

Moving his family to Franklin Mills, Ohio, in 1836, Brown established a tannery, raised cattle, and made additional money surveying. He borrowed heavily to underwrite his various ventures and then fell into debt during the 1839 economic downturn. His struggles to get out of debt led him into new ventures and even to the occupation of a farm he had owned, against the claims of the new owner. For this, he was jailed for a time.

By the late 1830s, Brown had become a militant opponent of slavery, taking an oath before witnesses that he would consecrate his life to the destruction of the institution. In 1846 he moved to Springfield, Massachusetts, where he came in contact with abolitionists and became involved in the Underground Railroad. He helped make the town an important stop on the route to freedom for runaway slaves.

Increasingly, Brown came to believe that the problem with most of the abolitionists was that they were all talk and no action. He reached the conclusion that only the mobilization of slaves in armed struggle would secure their freedom.

In mid-1855, he set out for Kansas to determine whether the territory would enter the Union as a slave or a free state. The father of twenty children, John Brown moved to a piece of land that had been settled by six of his sons and a son-in-law. Brown's sons had already joined a military company that was on the side of the free-soil advocates and was engaged in the undeclared war against the pro-slavery side.

On an expedition to defend the town of Lawrence, Kansas, against pro-slavery fighters from Missouri, Brown and his companions learned that the town had been pillaged. Infuriated, Brown shouted in front of witnesses: "Something must be done to show these barbarians that we, too, have rights." [19] He decided that the time had come for brutal retaliation. Reckoning that the pro-slavery marauders had killed at least five free-soil men since the troubles in Kansas had commenced, Brown set out with four of his sons and three other companions to hunt down supporters of slavery. Near Pottawatomie Creek, Brown and his men broke into the cabins of pro-slavery settlers, seized five men, and murdered them with broadswords. It made no difference to him that these men were not themselves implicated in any murders.

Although two of Brown's sons had not been involved in the murders, they were later arrested by federal officials, and pro-slavery units burned down their homesteads. John Brown and his companions were never captured and did not face charges arising from the shocking affair at Pottawatomie. [20]

In 1858, Brown visited Canada and met with other active opponents of slavery, including Harriet Tubman, the extraordinary woman who had led so many people to freedom. Brown referred to her as the "general." [21] Brown organized a gathering in Chatham, Canada West (formerly Upper Canada), [22] to plan an operation that would fail utterly to motivate slaves to throw off their chains but would succeed in inflaming public opinion in both the South and the North beyond its author's wildest expectations, in a foretaste of the great war to come.

On the evening of October 16, 1859, Brown led eighteen men into Harper's Ferry, which lay in a bowl far below the crest of a ridge, a mousetrap if there ever was one. They quickly captured the armoury. Brown then dispatched a few men to spread the word among the slaves that the revolt had begun. Only a few slaves were brought back by Brown's patrol. The next morning, local residents began sniping at Brown's small force. Virginia and Maryland militia closed in on the town, as did a company of U.S. Marines, commanded by Colonel Robert E. Lee and Lieutenant J. E. B. Stuart. Over the course of the afternoon of October 17, eight of Brown's men, among them two of his sons, were killed, along with three residents of the town.

Seven members of the expedition managed to escape, two of whom were later captured. Lee finished off Brown's revolt when he sent in the Marines, who killed two of the raiders while losing one of their own. The wounded Brown was captured. [23]

On October 27, John Brown went on trial in nearby Charles Town, Virginia. He was charged with murdering four whites and one African American, with conspiring with slaves to set off a rebellion, and with treason against the state of Virginia. On November 2, the jury found Brown guilty on all three counts.

Before his sentence was pronounced, Brown proclaimed to the court: "I deny everything but what I have all along admitted of a design on my part to free slaves... Had I interfered in the manner which I admit... in behalf of the rich, the powerful, the intelligent, the so-called great... every man in this Court would have deemed it an act worthy of reward rather than punishment...

"Now, if it is deemed necessary that I should forfeit my life for the furtherance of the ends of justice, and mingle my blood further with the blood of my children and with the blood of millions in this slave country whose rights are disregarded by wicked, cruel and unjust enactments, I say, let it be done." [24]

Brown was sentenced to be hanged at a public execution on December 2.

The response across both the North and the South revealed how perilous was the state of the American Union. Ralph Waldo Emerson predicted that John Brown would "make the gallows as glorious as the cross."

On the day of his execution, church bells tolled in many Northern towns, ministers preached sermons on the lessons of Brown's sacrifice, and thousands of people bowed their heads to commemorate the man they viewed as a martyr to liberty. Henry David Thoreau wrote that Brown was "a crucified hero."

Across the white South, the reaction to Brown's failed rebellion, and to the sympathy expressed for him in much of the North, was of shock and foreboding. All slave-owning societies, dating back at least as far as ancient Sparta, have lived in terror of slave uprisings. Even in times of peace, the fear of the slave is never far from consciousness. In the U.S. South, the period from the late 1840s to the hanging of John Brown was one of an ever ascending sense of encirclement by a hostile North.

Benjamin Perry, a South Carolina politician who had been a strong defender of the Union and of poorer citizens in opposition to the slave-owning elite, expressed the fears of Southern whites when he wrote that the stance of the North was designed to make the slave "the equal of his master... [and]... to go with him to the polls and vote, to serve on juries... to meet the white man as an equal and visit his family, intermarry with his children and form one society and one family."

In his diary, John C. Rutherfoord, a well-known Virginia politician who had served in the early 1840s as acting governor of the state, noted: "The Harper's Ferry affair has had the fortunate effect of revealing to the people of the white South, as if by one vivid flash of light, the true character of [the] danger." [25]

The trials of Brown and his followers provoked wrath against the Fugitive Slave Act and the slave owners of the South. Far from calming the tension between South and North, as it was intended to do, the act brought anger between the sections to a fever pitch and pushed the United States toward civil war.

A CONSEQUENCE OF the Fugitive Slave Act — one that became dramatically apparent in the case of John Price — was that slaves who managed to escape to free states, such as Ohio, were by no means safe. This had major implications for Canada, which quickly became an important destination for fugitives from slavery.

Prior to its final elimination north of the U.S. border in the 1834, the institution of slavery had existed in the British North American colonies on a small scale. By the late seventeenth century, a few African slaves were held in Canada under the French regime. Later, following the conclusion of the American Revolutionary War, Loyalists brought about five hundred slaves with them to the Maritimes. Loyalists also took slaves to Upper Canada, where they met with the staunch opposition of John Graves Simcoe, who was appointed as the province's first governor in 1791. Simcoe oversaw the passage of a law in 1793 that banned the further introduction of slaves into the province. The law also established that from then on all children born to slaves would be free. [26] In 1807, Britain declared the Atlantic slave trade illegal and from then on used the Royal Navy to intercept ships carrying human cargo.

In the decade prior to the outbreak of the Civil War, Canada was inexorably drawn into the conflict that was tearing the American Republic apart. The fact that the Underground Railroad terminated in Canada meant that Canada was bound to become involved in the slavery question. In 1851, the year he was elected to the legislative assembly, George Brown played a role in founding the Anti-Slavery Society of Canada. [27]

That same year, a young black woman who was a determined fighter for the abolition of slavery in the United States paid a visit to Toronto. Mary Ann Camberton Shadd was nearly twenty-eight years old when she came to get a first-hand view of the opportunities in Canada for men, women, and children who were fleeing slavery. Shadd had been born into a free black family in the slave state of Delaware, where the prospects for an education for a free black child were very poor. By the time Mary was ten years old, her family had moved to West Chester, Pennsylvania, not far from Philadelphia. According to the story passed down from her family, Mary was educated by Quakers. [28]

During her decades-long struggle to educate blacks and to free them from slavery, she showed herself to be the most remarkable member of an exceptional family. Her father, Abraham Shadd, a shoemaker, fought actively for the cause of abolition. Dangerous though this was, he made his house a way station on the Underground Railroad. For a time, he was the president of the National Convention for the Improvement of Free People of Color in the United States. Later, he was the first black person to be elected to public office in Canada West.*

After she finished school, Mary Shadd returned to Wilmington, Delaware, to open a school for black children. She also taught school for a time in Trenton, New Jersey, and in New York City.

It was her continuing work for the liberation of her people that brought her to Canada West in 1851. At a meeting in Toronto, she heard prominent abolitionists, as well as Henry Bibb, the founder of *Voice of the Fugitive*, a newspaper published in the little community of Sandwich, near Windsor. Mary Shadd liked what she saw in Canada, and she wanted to play a direct role. After a visit to Buffalo, she travelled by steamer to the Detroit-Windsor area. In Windsor, then a tiny hamlet with a population of about two hundred, she got a first-hand view of the wretched conditions endured by runaway slaves at this terminus of the Underground Railroad.

---

* After slavery was abolished, during the brief period of Reconstruction before the political rights of blacks were once again stamped out, Mary Shadd's brother Isaac served in the Mississippi legislature between 1871 and 1877, part of that time as Speaker of the House. Her brother Abraham was a lawyer in Mississippi and Arkansas. [29]

The blacks who arrived in the Windsor area faced not only rising prejudice against them but also poverty, poor housing, and disease. It was an uphill struggle for the freed slaves to adapt to the climate and laws of Canada West. For Shadd, the most appropriate way to help this struggling community was to establish herself as a teacher. Unwilling to teach in a racially segregated school, she managed to set up a private school. Initially, she charged four shillings a month, but later she was forced to drop this to three shillings. She carried on, raising money where she could, despite having become embroiled in a bitter factional dispute with Henry Bibb and his wife, who also ran her own school.

A year after her arrival in Canada, Mary Shadd wrote and published a forty-four-page pamphlet, *Notes of Canada West*, on the possibilities for blacks north of the border. Of the alternatives, she wrote that tropical Africa was "teeming... with the breath of pestilence, a burning sun and fearful maladies." In the slave-owning South, she commented, blacks confronted "the probability of worse than inquisitorial inhumanity." In Canada, while blacks would confront prejudice, she wrote, they would find conditions that were superior to the alternatives:

"Coloured persons have been refused entertainment in taverns (invariably of an inferior class), and on some boats distinction is made; but in all cases, it is that of distinction that is made between poor foreigners and other passengers... it is an easy matter to make out a case of prejudice in any country. We naturally look for it, and the conduct of many is calculated to cause unpleasant treatment, and to make it difficult for well-mannered persons to get comfortable accommodations. There is a medium between servility and presumption, that recommends itself to all persons of common sense, of whatever rank or complexion; and if coloured people would avoid the two extremes, there would be but few cases of prejudice to complain of in Canada. In cases in which tavern keepers and other public characters persist in refusing to entertain them, they can, in common with the travelling public, generally, get redress at law." [30]

At this time, not only were slave hunters removing slaves from

Northern states, often to a terrible fate; in many cases free blacks were seized and carried south as well. On some occasions, the slave hunters ignored the border and tried to capture blacks on Canadian soil. On one occasion, hunters tracked a black youth into Chatham, where they seized him. Shadd burst upon the hunters and tore the boy away from them. She then ran to the courthouse and rang its bell. The townspeople crowded into the street to find out what was going on, and the hunters, without their prey, made their escape.

Shadd also made herself the driving force behind the *Provincial Freeman*, an abolitionist paper published in Canada. Although for a time, while she was actually editing and raising funds for the newspaper, the nominal editor of the newspaper was a male, she eventually became the editor in name as well as in practice. On a tour in the United States to raise money for the newspaper and to promote the cause of black immigration to Canada, she was feted in Philadelphia as the first black woman in North America to edit a newspaper. [31]*

The flight of slaves to Canada drew the ire of the governors of Southern states as early as the 1820s. Even Northern governors could get into scrapes with Canada on the issue. In 1829, in reply to a query from the state of Illinois about an escaped slave, a Canadian government official wrote to Illinois Governor Ninian Edwards: "The state of slavery is not recognized in the law of Canada nor does the law admit that any Man can be the proprietor of another." [33]

In December 1859, Otho R. Singleton, a Democratic Mississippi congressman, expressed the wrath of Southern politicians and slave owners at the ability of runaway slaves to escape to Canada: "Men cannot afford to own slaves when, by crossing an imaginary line, they fall into the hands of our enemies, and friends who aid them in their

---

* To complete Mary Shadd's extraordinary story: she managed to play her own distinct part in the Civil War. Beginning in early 1864, she helped recruit blacks in Canada to enlist in the Union army. After the war, she returned to the United States. She taught in Detroit and then in Washington, D.C. In her later years, she was deeply involved in the women's rights movement, giving an address to the national convention of the National Woman Suffrage Association in 1878. She died in Washington, D.C., in 1893. [32]

flight... Do you think, gentlemen, that we will remain quiet while this is being done? The south will never submit to that state of things. It matters not what evils come upon us; it matters not how deep we may have to wade through blood; we are bound to keep our slaves and their present condition."[34]

The Underground Railroad was one of the flashpoints driving the sectional division between the South and the North toward an explosion. The Compromise of 1850, including the Fugitive Slave Act, was intended to ease tensions. Instead, it exacerbated them.

Chapter 3

A House Divided

THE PASSAGE OF the Kansas-Nebraska Act opened the way in Kansas for an often bloody struggle between pro- and anti-slavery forces to draft a constitution. That constitution would then be subjected to a referendum. Once passed, it would be sent to Washington to open the way for the admission of Kansas as a state. In 1855, free state advocates assembled in Topeka and drafted what came to be called the Topeka Constitution, which would have banned slavery in Kansas. Two years later, pro-slavery forces met in Lecompton, the designated capital, where they drafted a constitution under which Kansas would be admitted as a slave state. The Lecompton Constitution proved highly consequential in subsequent national political developments.

With an eye to shoring up his administration's standing with the staunchly pro-slavery Southern wing of the Democratic Party, President James Buchanan endorsed the Lecompton Constitution and called on Congress to admit Kansas as a slave state. While this won the support of the Southern Democrats, Senator Stephen Douglas of Illinois opposed Lecompton. As Douglas later explained, following a stormy meeting with Buchanan: "My objection to the Lecompton Constitution did not consist in the fact that it made Kansas a slave state." His problem was that Lecompton "was not the act and deed of the people of Kansas, and did not embody their will."[1]

Douglas took the politically risky step of breaking with the president and Southern Democrats on this critical issue to safeguard his own political future. He faced a Senate re-election campaign the following year. Had he not opposed the Lecompton Constitution, his doctrine of popular sovereignty would have been regarded as a sham.

A large number of Northern Democrats backed Douglas, including members of the newly founded Republican Party. In 1858, the House of Representatives soundly defeated the Lecompton Constitution.[*]

The most important result of the political struggle over Kansas-Nebraska was the creation of the Republican Party. The existence of a powerful new party established only in the North was of exceptional importance in driving the American Republic toward war. Disaffected Northerners, including Whigs, Free Soilers, and many Democrats, held meetings in a wide range of states, including Michigan, Wisconsin, Vermont, Maine, Ohio, Indiana, and Iowa, to form a common front and, if possible, a new political party to block the advance of slavery. The Whig Party, which had been the major national alternative to the Democratic Party, was disintegrating, and as a result other political forces were emerging. Among them were the Liberty Party, the Free Soil Party, and the anti-immigrant, anti-Catholic Know Nothings. The Republican movement was known by different names at first, but it is likely that the label "Republican" was first used at a meeting in Ripon, Wisconsin, in February 1854.

The leaders of this coalescing political force gave voice to a common stock of political ideas that bound them together. They favoured protective tariffs to foster industry and government outlays to finance internal improvements, chiefly railroads, canals, and roads. And they supported the opening of public lands in the West to encourage settlement.

What distinguished Republicans from the earlier Whigs was that the members of the new party were outraged by the very idea that slavery could be allowed in new territories such as Kansas and Nebraska,

---

[*] Kansas was admitted as a free state in 1861, when the Civil War was underway.

as well as in the territories acquired from Mexico in the recent war. Most Republicans were not abolitionists who favoured the immediate abolition of slavery. Many, if not most, held the view that slavery must be limited to the states where it currently existed, so that it would eventually die out.

Republicans believed that the slave power would not rest until slavery was established in every state in the Union. The wealthy and powerful slave owners of the South, they argued, were determined to spread the institution not only to new American territories but also to the Caribbean and Central America.

The Republican Party proved to be much more potent politically than the Whig Party. Since the new party existed only in the North, its adherents did not spend much time or political capital trying to sell its ideas or adapting its political line to a Southern audience. The new party quickly brought politicians who had been active Whigs to the fore.

One member who played exceptionally important role was William Seward.

HAVING TURNED DOWN numerous speaking engagements in the summer and fall of 1858, Senator William Seward accepted an invitation to address an audience in Rochester on behalf of his friend Edwin Morgan, the Republican candidate for governor of New York. The speech lit a fire in both the North and the South that would be remembered long after the gubernatorial race, indeed long after the Civil War. "Two radically different political systems," Seward declared, existed in the United States, "the one resting on the basis of servile or slave labour, the other on the basis of voluntary labour or freemen.

"These antagonistic systems are continually coming into closer contact and collision results.

"Shall I tell you what this collision means," he asked rhetorically. "They who think it is accidental, unnecessary, the work of interested, or fanatical agitators, and therefore ephemeral, mistake the case

altogether. It is an irrepressible conflict between opposing and enduring forces, and it means that the United States must and will, sooner
or later, become entirely either a slave-holding nation, or entirely a
free labour nation."[2]

Once the words "irrepressible conflict" were out of Seward's
mouth, they struck those who read them in newspapers or pamphlets
in both North and South with a palpable shock. A major Northern figure, thought by many as the man most likely to win the presidency in
1860, had declared that no long-term modus vivendi could be reached
between slavery and free labour.

Even though Seward had made essentially the same case in
speeches many times in preceding years, this speech had an altogether different impact, for two reasons. First, by the autumn of 1858,
the sinews of the Union had been stretched almost to the breaking
point. Second, the phrase "irrepressible conflict" captured the prevailing mood in deadly fashion. Its undeniable implication was that
a showdown was soon to come, and that it would settle the question
one way or the other.

For Seward, the speech was also decisive. Having once spoken
those fateful words, even if it at times for tactical political reasons he
wanted to qualify them, he could not. The speech may well have cost
William Seward the Republican presidential nomination. Seward had
painted himself onto the abolitionist side of the Republican spectrum,
and that left the way open for an alternative candidate to secure the
nomination.

That alternative candidate was Abraham Lincoln.

A FEW MONTHS before Seward delivered his speech in Rochester, the
much less well-known Abraham Lincoln, a former Whig who was
now a Republican, made a speech addressing the coming crisis over
the question of slavery in Illinois when he accepted the Republican
nomination for the U.S. Senate. On June 16, 1858, Lincoln drew on a
famous line from the Bible (Mark 3:25) in his "House Divided" speech:

We are now into the *fifth* year, since a policy was initiated [the Kansas-Nebraska Act], with the *avowed* object and *confident* promise, of putting an end to slavery agitation.

Under the operation of that policy, agitation has not only, *not ceased,* but has *constantly augmented.*

In my opinion, it will not cease, until a crisis shall have been reached, and passed.

A House divided against itself cannot stand.

I believe this government cannot endure, permanently half *slave* and half *free.*

I do not expect the Union to be *dissolved* — I do not expect the house to *fall* — but I *do* expect it will cease to be divided.

It will become *all* one thing, or *all* the other.

Either the *opponents* of slavery, will arrest the further spread of it, and place it where the public mind shall rest in the belief that it is in course of ultimate extinction; or its *advocates* will push it forward, till it shall become alike lawful in *all* the States, *old* as well as *new* — *North* as well as *South.* [3]

The evening before he delivered the historic address, Lincoln had read a draft of it to a dozen friends, seeking their advice. The response of most was that it was too radical, too far in advance of public thinking, and that it could have the effect of driving many voters away from the Republicans, voters who had recently come over from the Democrats.

Lincoln listened but decided to go ahead with the address as drafted, telling his advisors: "The time has come when these sentiments should be uttered." [4]

Abraham Lincoln was an unlikely prospect to rise to the supreme leadership of his country. Born into a family in Kentucky that was far from wealthy or well-established, Lincoln had to toil physically to support himself for much of his early life.

In 1859, Lincoln answered the query of an Illinois newspaper for the story of his life and origins with a brief and characteristically unvarnished reply: "My parents were both born in Virginia, of undistinguished families."[5]

When Lincoln won the Republican presidential nomination in May 1860, to the surprise of almost everyone, newspaper editors rushed to satisfy the public appetite for information about the man and his past. John Locke Scripps, a senior editor of the *Chicago Press and Tribune*, convinced Lincoln, who was reticent about indulging in musings about his life, to write an autobiographical sketch from which a campaign biography could be written. Lincoln produced three thousand words, the longest work he ever wrote about himself. He wrote it in the third person, often calling himself "A" for Abraham.

On his education, he wrote: "A. now thinks that the aggregate of all his schooling did not amount to one year. He was never in a college or Academy as a student; and never inside of a college or academy till since he had a law-license. What he has in the way of education, he has picked up."[6]

Although he was habitually plain-spoken, Lincoln was always calculating. In his mid-nineteenth-century frontier surroundings, he was well aware of the advantages of appearing self-made. Lincoln was actually more interested in his ancestry than he let on in public. He tried to trace his lineage but could not get much farther than his paternal grandfather.

In fact, his earliest New World forebears arrived in New England in the early decades of English settlement.[7] In 1637, his first American ancestor, Samuel Lincoln, set out on the two-month voyage to Salem, Massachusetts. He was one of the migrants who left England during the troubled era on the eve of the English Civil War. These settlers sought a better life for themselves that would include freedom from religious persecution.

An apprentice linen weaver by trade, Samuel Lincoln made his home in Hingham, fifteen miles south of Boston. There, he found a surfeit of weavers, and so he chose for a time to try his hand at farming. Later, he was successful in business ventures, enabling him to build a substantial house.[8] Future generations of Lincolns migrated south and west to New Jersey and Pennsylvania, some of them successful in business and in the acquisition of land.

Abraham Lincoln's grandfather, also named Abraham, was born in Pennsylvania in 1744. With his wife and sons, he set out for the near west of the day, Kentucky, whose attractions for settlers had been much hyped by the famed frontiersman and publicist Daniel Boone. White settlers in Kentucky made their homes on traditional Shawnee hunting grounds, leading to a decades-long conflict. In 1786, on farmland just east of today's Louisville, near the log cabin Abraham Lincoln had built, a native warrior, likely Shawnee, shot and killed him.

Thomas Lincoln, the father of the future president, was only six years old when he watched his own father die on a farm field. Although he did receive some support from relatives, Thomas had to work for three shillings a day at a mill that served neighbouring farms. For a time, he laboured on an uncle's farm in Tennessee. When he returned to Kentucky, he served as an apprentice carpenter and cabinetmaker in Elizabethtown.[9]

Despite his initially hard lot in life and his almost complete lack of formal education, Thomas Lincoln did manage to acquire a large farm by the time he was twenty-five, as well as other property that ranked him as owning the fifteenth-most valuable property out of a total of ninety-eight in Hardin County, Kentucky, in 1814.[10] While he was far from rich, he accumulated more than is usually thought by those who portray Abraham Lincoln as a self-made man who rose from nothing to attain the White House.

Having sold his first farm in December 1808, Thomas Lincoln acquired a second one, twelve miles southeast of Elizabethtown. On the Sinking Spring Farm, named for its freshwater spring, he built a one-room log cabin with a stone fireplace, a dirt floor, and possibly a window without glass, covered over with greased paper. It was in this rude dwelling that the future president, named for his assassinated grandfather, was born on February 12, 1809.[11]

In 1816, the family moved once more, this time to forty acres of land in heavily forested Indiana, north of the Ohio River. On the free soil of Indiana, in contrast to Kentucky, where slavery was legal, young Abraham Lincoln learned to use an ax and assisted his father in building a new cabin and establishing the farm. [12] It was in Indiana that Lincoln grew to early manhood, six feet and four inches in height, weighing over two hundred pounds, powerful and physically adept, qualities prized by local farmers on the lookout for wage labourers.

His childhood was marked by tragedy when he watched his mother die in September 1818 of the "milk sick." It was a terrifying and mysterious disease; its source — milk tainted by white snakeroot — was not yet known.

Just over a year after his wife's death, Thomas Lincoln returned to Kentucky. In Elizabethtown, he called unannounced at the home of Sarah Bush Johnston, a widow he had known previously. He was on a mission to propose marriage, a practical idea for himself and his children, as well as for the widow, who had three children of her own. Thomas pledged to pay off Sarah's debts, and the two were married in Elizabethtown in December 1819. He was forty-one and she was thirty-two.

The Lincolns, made up of two wounded families, set out for their property in Indiana. Sarah brought order, cleanliness, and loving concern for the children to the home, which she insisted had to be outfitted with a floor, a door, and decent furniture. Before they could resume farming, the family, under Sarah's direction, carried out home renovations. In the brief autobiography prepared for his presidential campaign, Lincoln wrote of Sarah: "She proved a good and kind mother to A." [13]

Abraham Lincoln's father was often rough with him, on occasion knocking him down. Sarah, though, supported him lovingly and took pains to encourage his education. In his brief sketches about his parents, the future president was much cooler in tone toward his father than his birth mother and his stepmother: "Owing to my father being left an orphan at the age of six years, in poverty and in a new country," he wrote in reply to a question from a Massachusetts relative about family history, "he became a wholly uneducated man; which I supposed is why I know so little of our family history." [14] Of his mother, although it was not clear whether he was referring to Sarah or his birth mother, he told William Herndon, his law partner: "God bless my mother; all that I am or ever hope to be I owe to her." [15]

While Abe was strong and could do physical labour, his real passion was for learning. He was ten years old when he and his sister first attended school in a log cabin in Spencer County, Indiana. In those days, children whose parents paid a subscription for enrollment attended such a school for only several months a year. Their teachers were an odd assortment of people who mostly had had little education themselves. Lincoln later wrote sardonically that in this region of the country, if someone knew a little Latin, he or she was regarded as a wizard. [16]

As a youth, Lincoln had few books to read, and he made much use of the Bible, *Pilgrim's Progress*, and *Aesop's Fables*. He drew moral lessons from these works, including the crucial conviction that individuals could make a difference to the world around them.

By the age of thirteen or fourteen, Lincoln's size and strength allowed him to work for farmers as a rail splitter. Within a couple of years, when he attained his adult stature, his skill with an ax made him eminently employable. Farmers needed fences to mark off their properties from those of their neighbours and to keep animals in or out. Fence rails, made from ash, hickory, oak, poplar, or walnut trees, were normally ten feet long and four inches wide. [17] A skilled rail splitter could make up to four hundred rails in a day — Abraham often worked from dawn to dusk to earn twenty-five cents.

In the autumn of 1828, Lincoln, along with the son of a local businessman, navigated a flatboat containing a cargo of goods down the Ohio River and then the Mississippi to New Orleans. This was the young man's first encounter with a major city, a city alive with the pulses of French, Creole, Spanish, English, and African cultures. New Orleans was also home to a busy slave market, where men, women, and children were traded daily as commodities. [18]

In the winter of 1830, the wanderlust struck Lincoln's father once more, and he decided to move, this time to the prairies of Illinois. Selling off all but their most essential possessions, the family set out on the 225-mile trek westward, with Abraham Lincoln driving one of the wagons. A few miles out of Decatur, Thomas and Abraham constructed a log cabin, a smokehouse, and a barn. Abraham split the rails for the fence to mark off the perimeters of their land.

At the age of twenty-two, Abraham Lincoln left his family home and walked to New Salem, Illinois, a distance of nearly 180 miles, to begin life on his own. There, he initially worked for a local store owner. In 1832, the twenty-three-year-old Lincoln made his initial foray into politics, declaring himself a candidate for a seat in the state legislature. Although this first bid for office failed, he succeeded in winning the votes of those in his own local community.

That same year, when the Black Hawk War provoked fear among Illinois settlers, Lincoln joined the militia. His popularity with his fellow recruits moved them to elect him to the temporary position of captain of his unit.

In 1834, Lincoln tried a second time for a seat in the state legislature and this time he prevailed. His politics — and he was to remain committed to a broad set of principles throughout his career — turned on strong support for internal improvements such as the building of canals and railroads and a high national tariff to protect local industry. He aligned himself with the Whigs but succeeded in avoiding an image of narrow partisanship and often won support for his proposals from Democrats.

From the beginning, Lincoln was a spokesman for a frontier version of Northern capitalism. Across the North and Midwest, capitalist enterprises were burgeoning, driven by the demand that accompanied the construction of canals and railroads, which knitted markets together and opened the way for an ever larger scale of production. To Lincoln, a young man who had risen from the ranks of wage labourers, there was no apparent or serious contradiction between the interests of the wage earner and those of the proprietor or capitalist. Hard work and an open door to upward mobility went together, in his experience.

In 1836, Lincoln won a second term in the Illinois legislature. Even though he was only twenty-seven years old, House Whigs elected him as their floor leader. In December 1836, at a time of widespread public support for improvements, Lincoln led the campaign for a statewide system of canals, railroads, and roads that would promote development and economic expansion.[19] Meetings were organized throughout the state, attracting farmers and businessmen who threw their weight behind these projects. Lincoln argued that the legislature should appropriate $10 million to be financed by state bonds. To those such as Illinois Governor Joseph Duncan who advised caution and wanted only one-third of the proposed capital to be provided by the state, Lincoln insisted that any failure to act would place the state at a competitive disadvantage in relation to other states that were pursuing such projects.[20]

Lincoln and his allies succeeded in pushing the legislation through. Celebrations soon gave way to anxiety and regret when the major financial panic of 1837 struck both sides of the Atlantic. Illinois was saddled with a $15 million debt. Four years after the $10 million appropriation, state bonds had sunk in value to fifteen cents on the dollar.[21]

In the winter of 1835, during his first term in the legislature, Abraham Lincoln became interested in studying law and earning a license to practise as a lawyer. At a time when there were only seven law schools in the United States — none in Illinois — those who desired a law career usually clerked in the office of an experienced attorney while they studied.

John Todd Stuart, an established lawyer, saw potential in the young man and offered to become his mentor. Stuart placed the resources of his office, located twenty miles from New Salem, at Lincoln's disposal. The lawyer's ample law library was especially useful. Henry Dummer, Stuart's law partner, described Lincoln during his first encounters with him as "the most uncouth looking young man I ever saw." But Lincoln impressed him over time. Dummer recalled that the young man "seemed to feel timid, with a tinge of sadness visible in the countenance, but when he did talk all this disappeared for the time and he demonstrated that he was both strong and acute...He surprised us more and more at every visit." [22]

Determined to devote himself to the study of law, Lincoln purchased at an auction Sir William Blackstone's *Commentaries on the Laws of England*, written in the late 1760s. [23] Still the standard legal treatise of the day, the book demonstrated an ordered approach to the law that fitted with Lincoln's evolving outlook on life, one that prized rationality as essential to personal success and to the betterment of the community.

In March 1836, Lincoln put his name on the record of the Sangamon Circuit Court as a person of good moral character, the first formal step he needed to take toward becoming a lawyer. [24] Then he moved from New Salem to Springfield, which had been named the new capital of Illinois — a designation in which Lincoln had played a leading role. There, he was to spend many years as a legislator and a lawyer.

He received his law licence in the spring of 1837 and was fortunate to be invited by John Todd Stuart to become his partner in what became the firm of Stuart and Lincoln. Theirs was a general law practice, handling cases of libel, trespass, damage claims, and criminal matters.

When Stuart was elected to Congress and left Springfield for Washington, D.C., in November 1839, Lincoln took over the entire caseload. Twice a year, he travelled on horseback around the fifteen counties of Illinois's Eighth Judicial Circuit. On these tours, he met with other lawyers, townspeople, and farmers, contacts that would be invaluable to him in the years to come. [25]

In the winter of 1837, the volatile and divisive issue of slavery came to the fore in Illinois politics. State Governor Joseph Duncan presented a resolution to the legislature that was intended to tread a careful line on the issue. While the resolution acknowledged "the unfortunate condition of our fellow men, whose lots are cast in thralldom in a land of liberty and peace," it concluded that "the arm of the General Government has no powers to strike the fetters from them." [26] On the matter of slavery in the District of Columbia, the resolution asserted that the federal government had no right to abolish slavery there without the consent of its citizens.

Lincoln was one of six legislators to vote in opposition to the resolution, while seventy-seven voted for it. It was the first time he took a position on slavery. [27]

Together with Dan Stone — a fellow Whig, fellow lawyer, and fellow legislator opposed to slavery — Lincoln introduced what he called a "protest" in the legislature to restore balance on the slavery question. The protest affirmed Lincoln and Stone's belief "that the institution of slavery is founded on both injustice and bad policy; but that the promulgation of abolition doctrines tends rather to increase than abate its evils."

On slavery in the states, the protest conceded: "They [Lincoln and Stone] believe that the Congress of the United States has no power, under the constitution, to interfere with the institution of slavery in the different States."

However, on the matter of slavery in the District of Columbia, the protest reversed the emphasis in the resolution that had been passed. It stated: "They [Lincoln and Stone] believe that the Congress of the United States has the power under the constitution, to abolish slavery in the District of Columbia; but that that power ought not to be exercised unless at the request of the people of said District." [28]

While this was far from a stalwart anti-slavery gesture, in the politics of Illinois in the late 1830s, it was noteworthy. When Illinois achieved statehood in 1818, its constitution forbade slavery. Over the following two decades, however, most of the migrants to the state hailed from the South. In southern Illinois — Illinois stretches 390 miles from north to south — pro-slavery sentiment was pronounced. This was offset to some extent by the migration of settlers to northern Illinois from the Northeast and New England, and these newcomers tended to be anti-slavery.

By the late 1830s, the young man whose beginnings had been so lacking in promise had come a long way as a legislator and lawyer, with a growing public reputation. After serving twelve years in the Illinois state legislature, Lincoln was elected to the U.S. House of Representatives in 1846. As he had at the state level, he promoted a

Whig agenda, focused on economic development. He supported railroad projects and tariffs to protect American industry.

During his one term in the House, Lincoln vocally opposed the war with Mexico. He went as far as to challenge President James Polk's assertion that Mexican soldiers fired the first shots in the war. In the House, he skewered the president's motives and speculated about his conscience: "I more than suspect already, that he is deeply conscious of being in the wrong — that he feels the blood of this war, like the blood of Abel, is crying to Heaven against him." [29]

Lincoln's position did not endear him to the people of his district. When his congressional term was up, he did not seek re-election. He returned to Illinois to practise law, but his deep interest in politics, and the meaning of the great issues roiling the country, continued to evolve.

In 1854, Lincoln's opposition to the Kansas-Nebraska Act drew him back into active politics. Later that year, he ran for a U.S. Senate seat from Illinois as a Whig candidate. While he led in the initial rounds of voting in the legislature, when support for him began to decline, he convinced his backers to throw their weight behind an alternative candidate.

Having always been a Whig, Lincoln watched his party disintegrate over the slavery question. Retaining his established political values, he played a role in launching the Republican Party. At the new party's national convention in 1856, Lincoln placed second in the race to become the Republican candidate for vice president. What had drawn Lincoln back into politics and into the Republican Party was his determination to oppose the expansion of slavery into the nation's new territories.

Much of Lincoln's career both before and after he became president turned on his interpretation of the meaning of the Declaration of Independence. In his analysis of the Dred Scott verdict, he challenged the meaning of the Declaration advanced by Chief Justice Roger Taney and by his political opponent Stephen Douglas.

On June 26, 1857, Lincoln presented his analysis of the Dred Scott decision in the Illinois statehouse. For two weeks, he had worked on his response in the Illinois Supreme Court's law library in Springfield. Having carefully perused the opinions of the justices on both sides of the case, and having read commentaries in the newspapers, he prepared what amounted to his own legal brief on the subject. In his carefully reasoned statement, he began by observing that he did not concur with people who favoured resisting the Supreme Court ruling. "But we think the Dred Scott decision is erroneous," he made clear. "We know the court that made it has often over-ruled its own decisions, and we shall do what we can to have it to over-rule this. We offer no *resistance* to it."[30]

Several weeks before Lincoln made his statement about the Scott case, Senator Stephen Douglas delivered his own at the invitation of the U.S. District Court in Springfield, with Lincoln in the audience. In his address, Douglas made it clear that he believed the assertion in the Declaration of Independence that "all men are created equal" to be racially limited. "No one can vindicate the character, motive, and conduct of the signers of the Declaration of Independence," Douglas declared, "except upon the hypothesis that they referred to the white race alone, and not to the African, when they declared men to have been created free and equal."[31]

Lincoln's reply to Douglas contains an important insight into his interpretation of the Declaration, which was significantly broader than that of Douglas: "I think the authors of that notable instrument intended to include *all* men, but they did not intend to declare all men equal in *all* respects. They did not mean to say all were equal in colour, size, intellect, moral developments, or social capacity." Lincoln went on, however, to assert to what extent the founders did mean to include all men: "They defined with tolerable distinctness, in what respect they did consider all men created equal — equal in 'certain inalienable rights, among which are life, liberty, and the pursuit of happiness.' This they said, and this they meant."[32]

Looking to the future, in a way that pointed toward the Gettysburg Address in November 1863, Lincoln was already thinking of how the promise of the Declaration of Independence could be broadened. The authors, he said, "meant to set up a standard maxim for free society, which should be familiar to all, and revered by all; constantly looked to, constantly labored for, and though never perfectly attained, constantly approximated, and thereby constantly spreading and deepening its influence, and augmenting the happiness and value of life to all people of all colors everywhere."[33]

Far from believing that the condition of blacks was improving, Lincoln contended, despite the views of others, that it was becoming worse: "The Chief Justice does not directly assert, but plainly assumes, as a fact, that the public estimate of the black man is more favourable now than it was in the days of the Revolution. This assumption is a mistake.

"All the powers of earth seem rapidly combining against him," Lincoln said of the slave. "Mammon is after him; ambition follows, and philosophy follows, and the Theology of the day is fast joining the cry."

Lincoln took aim at Douglas and the defenders of the South who claimed that slaves were better off in the mid-nineteenth century than they had been at the birth of the United States in 1776. "They have him in his prison house," declared Lincoln on the condition of the slave. "They have searched his person, and left no prying instrument with him. One after another they have closed the heavy iron doors upon him, and now they have him, as it were, bolted in with a lock of a hundred keys; which can never be unlocked without the concurrence of every key."

Whether he believed this slur himself or gave voice to it because he saw it as the accepted wisdom of the day, Lincoln made it clear that he was not expressing support for racial equality when he said that there was "a natural disgust in the minds of nearly all white people, to the idea of an indiscriminate amalgamation of the white and black races."

But Lincoln parted company with Douglas on the issue of race. He attacked Douglas's remark that Republicans contended that the Declaration of Independence included blacks only because "they want to vote, and eat, and sleep, and marry with negroes! ... Now I protest against that counterfeit logic which concludes that, because I do not want a black woman for a *slave* I must necessarily want her for a *wife*. I need not have her for either, I can just leave her alone. In some respects she certainly is not my equal; but in her natural right to eat the bread she earns with her own hands without asking leave of anyone else, she is my equal, and the equal of all others." [34]

DURING THE YEARS when William Seward and Abraham Lincoln were staking out positions as opponents of the expansion of slavery, Jefferson Davis was becoming a leading spokesman on behalf of states' rights and the rights of slave owners. He took his place in the U.S. Senate in December 1847, when the sectional struggle over slavery, particularly whether slavery should be permitted or banned in the territories newly acquired from Mexico, was taking centre stage.

Born in a small farmhouse in Christian County in southwestern Kentucky on June 3, 1808, Jefferson Davis was the youngest of the ten children of Samuel and Jane Davis (née Cook) and was born twenty-four years after the first of his siblings, his brother Joseph, who was to have a major influence on his career and his ideas. Jefferson's father, Samuel, was fifty-three years old when this last child was born. He had spent decades in an elusive search for material well-being. A year before he died in 1824, he wrote a letter to Jefferson, who was then a student at Transylvania University in Lexington, Kentucky, offering a few life lessons to his son. "Remember the short lessons of instruction offered you before our parting," Samuel Davis advised. "Use every possible means to acquire useful knowledge, as knowledge is power, the want of which has brought mischief and misery on your father in old age." [35]

The more distant forebears of the future president of the Confederacy emigrated from Wales to occupy lands set aside by William Penn for settlers from South Wales. Thirty thousand acres of land, known as the "Welsh Tract," located in Pennsylvania and neighbouring Maryland, were conveyed to David Evans and William

Davis, who were to divide it among the newcomers. Among the farmers, carpenters, and artisans who migrated to New Castle Country, Pennsylvania, were John Davis, whose name in Wales was Shion Dafydd, and his brother David. Both were described in the land deeds as "turners," craftsmen who worked with lathes. John Davis was the direct ancestor of Jefferson Davis. His brother David, who married Martha Thomas and changed the spelling of his name to Davies, was the father of Samuel Davies, a well-known evangelist and Presbyterian minister who became the fourth president of the College of New Jersey, now Princeton University.

As for Jefferson Davis's direct lineage, his great-grandfather John Davis had two sons. The second one, Evan, went south from Pennsylvania to South Carolina, where he married a widow by the name of Mary Williams. Their son, Samuel, named for the famous Samuel Davies, was born in 1756.

When he was about twenty years old, having received a rudimentary education from his mother, Samuel Davis left home to join the Continental Army during the American Revolutionary War. He succeeded in raising a company of infantry in Georgia, and as its captain, took the unit to South Carolina, where his services were sufficiently noteworthy that the state granted him a thousand acres of land. [36]

He did not remain in South Carolina but returned to Georgia and then migrated to southwestern Kentucky in 1796. There, he tried his hand at tobacco planting and raising horses, and it was during his years in Kentucky that Jefferson was born. A year after Jefferson's birth, the peripatetic Samuel set out for Bayou Teche Parish in Louisiana. Finding the climate unsuitable to his family's health, he moved once more, to Wilkinson County, Mississippi, where he died in 1824.

Despite Samuel Davis's life journey of successes and failures, marked by a quest to "make it" that was never fulfilled, late in his own life Jefferson Davis looked back on his father with some reverence, although not much affection. By then the Confederacy had been crushed and Jefferson Davis's period of imprisonment in a federal fortress was over. He was passing his final days trying to make sense of it all.

He wrote that his father was "naturally a grave and stoical character, and of such sound judgment that his opinions were a law to his children, and quoted by them long after he had gone to his final rest."[37] He recorded that his mother, Jane Cook, met his father during his military service in South Carolina and that they were married after the war. She was, as he wrote, of "Scotch-Irish descent, and was noted for her beauty and sprightliness of mind."[38]

As a consequence of the family's frequent moves, Jefferson Davis did not develop a strong sense of rootedness in any single locale. Until the age of seven, he went to school in a log cabin close to home in Wilkinson County. Then, taken in hand by friends of his father, he travelled on horseback from Mississippi to Kentucky, where he was boarded at St. Thomas, a Dominican school noteworthy for its wealth through the Dominican Order's ownership of farmlands, flour mills, flocks of sheep, and herds of cattle. The order deployed slave labour to work its productive properties.[39]

After returning home, he was sent briefly to Jefferson College in Adams County, Mississippi, and then to the Academy of Wilkinson County. In 1821, Davis was enrolled in Transylvania University. In his final year there, his father died.

Where his father left off as a rather uncertain guide, Jefferson Davis's brother Joseph, old enough to be his father, took over and served as a mentor during the crucial next steps in Jefferson's evolution. Joseph Davis was making himself into a wealthy and successful businessman in the new Lower South, where cotton had become king.[40] Through the good offices of Mississippi Congressman Christopher Rankin, Joseph managed to obtain for Jefferson a place as a cadet at West Point, the officer training school of the United States Army. The actual appointment came from John Calhoun, who was then serving as secretary of war in the cabinet of President James Monroe.[41]

At West Point, Jefferson Davis did moderately well but far from brilliantly, placing twenty-third in a class of thirty-three. Upon graduation, he went into the army as a lieutenant and was noted for his dashing looks, spotless uniforms, and fine horsemanship. He was also

lucky, a quality much prized by Napoleon when choosing commanders and a quality that was highly useful to a young American who
could not count on the backing of a leading family or great wealth.

Davis was posted to frontier Iowa under the command of Colonel
Zachary Taylor, the future American hero of the Mexican War and
president of the United States. "Old Rough and Ready" saw potential
in the young officer and watched over his advancement. [42] In 1832, the
Black Hawk War broke out on the northwest frontier. Black Hawk, a
Sauk leader, was determined to resettle his people on land in Illinois
that had been claimed by the United States on the basis of a disputed
treaty signed in 1804.

The United States mobilized a force that included both Jefferson
Davis and Abraham Lincoln in its ranks. At the conclusion of the brief
war, Zachary Taylor received information about Black Hawk's hid-
ing place on an island in the middle of the Mississippi River. Taylor
dispatched Davis to capture the native leader, which the young man
did without a shot being fired. Jefferson Davis was newly minted as
a military hero. [43]

Despite some good luck that brought him to the attention of men
of power, the road ahead for Davis was by no means an easy one. A
rather thin-skinned man, he found himself continually at odds with
others in the military. A dispute with a superior even led to Davis
being court-martialled.

When Jefferson Davis fell in love with Sarah Knox Taylor, the second and favourite daughter of Zachary Taylor, "Old Rough and Ready"
was opposed to the young man as a prospective husband for her. While
he did not find Davis personally objectionable, he believed that marriage to a military officer would not promote Sarah's happiness.

Finally, Taylor relented, and Lieutenant Davis and Sarah Knox
Taylor were married in 1835. To celebrate the marriage and to establish
Jefferson Davis in business, Joseph bestowed on the couple two thousand acres of land on the eastern bank of the Mississippi, thirty miles
south of Vicksburg. The gift included ten slaves and a cabin adjacent
to his own dwelling. Jefferson named the plantation Brierfield. Sadly,

the couple spent only one summer there. Both were afflicted with severe cases of malaria, and while Davis survived, his wife did not.[44]

Following Sarah's death, Davis spent many months recuperating from the ravages of malaria. During this time, he travelled to Havana, then returned to his plantation and took up the life of the planter next door to his brother Joseph. Jefferson spent innumerable hours in Joseph's well-stocked library, reading history and the works of the English essayists. Joseph became a mentor to Jefferson, and the two discussed politics and government at great length.

When he acquired Brierfield, Davis made it into the ranks of the cotton-growing slaveocracy of the Lower South — the class whose interests he would faithfully represent throughout his political career. For the time being, however, he devoted himself to improving farming methods and overseeing the slaves.[45]

In 1845, following a period in which he was active in the Democratic Party in Mississippi and was gaining a reputation as an effective public speaker, Davis was elected to the U.S. House of Representatives. That same year, he married again at the age of thirty-seven. His bride, who was eighteen years old, was Varina Howell of Natchez, Mississippi.[46]

With the United States facing possible conflicts with Britain over the Oregon question and with Mexico over the Rio Grande boundary, Davis was much more willing to support the use of armed force on the southern than on the northern border. In the House of Representatives, he voted to back the war with Mexico and was in favour of raising a volunteer force.[47] A regiment from Mississippi was organized at Vicksburg, and the men, as was the system, elected their field officers, choosing Davis to serve as colonel. Despite important business before Congress, Davis chose to accept the post. At the urging of President James Polk, he did not resign his seat in the House when he left Washington to join the regiment. Davis travelled with his men to the Rio Grande front, where he served under his former father-in-law, General Zachary Taylor.[48] In February 1847, Davis led his regiment in what came to be seen as a heroic stand in the Battle of Buena Vista. Wounded in the foot, Davis stayed on the field until the fight was over. Mentioned favourably in a dispatch written by General Taylor for his coolness and bravery in battle, the future president of the Confederacy was later celebrated in New Orleans and Mississippi as a hero.

Mississippi Governor Albert Brown appointed Jefferson Davis, on his return, to take the United States Senate seat of the late Senator Jesse Speight, which he did in December 1847. [49] The following January, the Mississippi legislature unanimously elected Davis to complete the remaining two years of the Senate term. In December 1849, benefitting from his military reputation, Davis won the position of chairman of the Committee on Military Affairs. Later that month, the Mississippi legislature elected him to a full six-year term in the Senate.

By 1851, Jefferson Davis was already pointing to the secession of the slave states as a possible outcome of the struggle over slavery. In a letter, he set out his views: "The bitter waters [of North-South division] have spread far and wide and as the torrent rolls on, it will acquire volume and velocity, from inexhaustible source of supply. When it becomes palpable to every man's sense, that from the free states we have nothing to expect but eternal war upon the institution of slavery, I believe the southern people will awake and unite, not to preserve the Constitution, or the union, but to organize a government for themselves." [50]

Despite these views, Davis still managed to play a significant role in national affairs. In 1853, President Franklin Pierce appointed him to the position of secretary of war. When Pierce's term in office ended, Davis ran again to be the United States senator from Mississippi, won the election in the state legislature, and returned to the Senate on March 4, 1857.

Over the course of the 1850s, Davis learned the lesson that any gestures of amity he expressed toward Northerners would undercut his political base in the South. In 1858, this lesson was driven home when he visited Maine to convalesce from the onset of a recurring ailment. Davis suffered from herpes, which he almost certainly contracted following sexual relations with a woman who suffered from the ailment. From time to time, Davis's condition caused the onset of a neuralgia that affected his left eye, led to facial swelling, and left him weak and unable to function for weeks on end. [51]

Invited to stay for a time at the vacation home of a friend, Davis journeyed by ship with his wife and two children to Portland, Maine. He welcomed the opportunity to rest, but he was leery of any public exposure there. He thought of New England as the heart of abolitionism, where newspapers such as the *Liberator* were published. Much to his surprise, he and his family were serenaded by friendly locals when they stepped off a ship in Portland on July 9, 1858. [52]

In off-the-cuff remarks, Jefferson Davis proclaimed to well-wishers that "in proportion as a citizen loves his own State, will he strive to honour by preserving her name and her fame free from the tarnish of having failed to observe her obligations, and to fulfill her duties to her sister States." The sections of the country should sing each other's praises, he insisted: "Shall the North not rejoice that the progress of agriculture in the South has given to her great staple [cotton] the controlling influence of the commerce of the world, and put manufacturing nations under bond to keep the peace with the United States? Shall the South not exult in the fact, that the industry and persevering intelligence of the North, has placed her mechanical skill in the front ranks of the civilized world — that our mother country…was brought some four years ago to recognize our pre-eminence by sending a commission to examine our work shops, and our machinery, to perfect their own manufacture of the arms requisite for their defence?" [53]

Davis's well-received speech convinced Maine's Democrats, who were then meeting in convention, that they should invite him to deliver an address. He made a speech that stressed the need for unity at a time of crisis: "Shall narrow interests, shall local jealousies, shall disregard of the high purposes for which our Union was ordained, continue to distract our people and impede the progress of our government towards the high consummation which prophetic statesmen have so often indicated as her destiny?"

To this, people jumped up to shout "No! No! No!" [54]

Jefferson Davis had made himself a star in Maine and was the recipient of an honorary degree at prestigious Bowdoin College. He was asked to speak almost everywhere he travelled. In his speeches, he emphasized the common heritage shared by all Americans, whether from the North or the South. He told crowds slavery was a local matter, and that local matters should be left to be determined at the local level. At the end of his two-month stay in Maine, he journeyed home with his family, stopping at Boston and New York. In both cities, he spoke to receptive audiences on the issue of slavery, telling them that it was time to cool the ferocious debate on the subject: "There is nothing of truth or justice with which to sustain this agitation, or grounds for it," he told listeners in both cities. "I plead with you now to arrest fanaticism which has been evil in the beginning, and must be evil in the end…The danger lies at your door, and it is time to arrest it. Too long have we allowed this influence to progress." [55]

What came as a shock to Davis was that while Northern newspaper editors applauded his speeches for being patriotic and imbued with common sense, in the South he was castigated for having been so open and amenable to the Yankees. Among those who attacked him was Robert Rhett, the editor of the Charleston *Mercury*: "Of all the signal examples of startling Southern defection that the venality of the times has afforded," Rhett wrote, "there is none that can compare at all with this…the Jefferson Davis we knew is no more." [56]

Upon his return to his plantation, Davis thought about what had happened to him. The time had come, he concluded, when open and generous dialogue between South and North was no longer possible. Instead, the narrative had to be clear. Political leaders needed to stake out their positions so that no one, friend or foe, could misunderstand them.

This he proceeded to do in two speeches in Jackson and Vicksburg in November 1858. In Jackson, he told a large crowd that the remarks he had made in New England were of a personal nature and that while he was grateful for the kindness shown toward him and his family at a time when he was ill, he remained a fierce defender of slavery and held to the view that Northerners needed to stop their political agitation against the South.

At Vicksburg, he issued a warning for the future of the country. If the Republicans won control of both Houses of Congress and the presidency in 1860, that would constitute a "revolution," which would destroy the United States government, leaving the South no alternative but to secede. The South could not tolerate an anti-slavery president, he made clear. In his menacing conclusion, Davis called Northerners "hostile" and painted them as "enemies." In the event that the Republicans took control of the United States government, he said that he would be in "favour of holding the city of Washington...and the glorious star-spangled banner, declaring the government at an end and maintaining our rights and honour, even though blood should flow in torrents throughout the land." In the event of the Republicans winning power, he "would rather appeal to the God of Battles at once than to attempt to live longer in such a union." On the prospect of an abolitionist being elected president, he threw down the gauntlet: "Let the star of Mississippi be snatched from the constellation to shine by its inherent light, if it must be so, through all the storms and clouds of war." [57]

With these two speeches, the senator from Mississippi wiped away any stain that had been left on his reputation following his rapturous welcome in the North. In Oxford, Mississippi, the editor of the local paper wrote that Jefferson Davis's message "effectually clears away all doubts about his fidelity to the South and shows that he is still as true to her as the needle to the pole." [58]

Chapter 4

Political Deadlock in Canada

T HE SAME IMPULSES that had driven American colonists to embrace self-government and independence erupted in the British colonies in the 1830s. In 1837–38, armed rebellions broke out in both English-speaking Upper Canada and the more populous, largely francophone province of Lower Canada. In both cases, those who took up arms fought for responsible government — a reform that would vest essential power in the hands of the elected representatives of the people by allowing the leaders of the party or parties that enjoyed the support of a majority of members of the legislature to choose the members of the cabinet. They demanded an end to rule by governors appointed in England and advised by business elites, known in Upper Canada as the Family Compact and in Lower Canada as the Château Clique. Led by William Lyon Mackenzie, a Scottish immigrant who had served as the first mayor of Toronto, the Upper Canadian rebellion was a relatively small-scale affair that was quickly put down by the governor and the militia. A hot-tempered firebrand, Mackenzie on occasion hurled his red wig at people who annoyed him during debates. Before entering politics, he published the *Colonial Advocate*, a newspaper that ceaselessly attacked the Upper Canadian business elite and the colonial government. On one occasion, angry Tories broke into his office, seized his printing press, and threw it into Lake Ontario.

In Lower Canada, the rebellion, led by Louis-Joseph Papineau, the leader of the Parti Patriote in the legislative assembly, enjoyed considerable support among French Canadians. Papineau, whose party had little power in the province even though it had won a majority of seats in the assembly, was a member of the French-Canadian elite. He was a seigneur, a title left over from the Old Regime in New France before the British conquest, which meant that he enjoyed rights over small farmers on a large stretch of land along the Ottawa River west of Montreal. In his personal library, Papineau had books from the French Enlightenment philosophers, as well as works expressing the ideas of the French and American revolutions.

The Lower Canadian rebellion was much more threatening than the affair in Upper Canada and involved a number of hard-fought battles. In the autumn of 1837, Patriote forces defeated the British in a battle at Saint-Denis, only to be defeated by their foes in battles at Saint-Charles and Saint-Eustache. In French Canada, the rebellion was a struggle not only for democratic rights but also for the national autonomy of a recently conquered people. Despite the differences between the struggles in Upper and Lower Canada, the rebels in the two provinces viewed each other as allies.

To determine what was to be done with the unruly colonies in the wake of the rebellions, the British government dispatched Lord Durham, an official equipped with the power to remake the Canadian state. His Lordship, whose nickname was Radical Jack, sailed from England to Quebec, arriving on May 27, 1838; his party numbered twenty-two persons.

In his famed *Report on the Affairs of British North America*, authored after his return to England, Durham wrote that when he had arrived in Canada, he had expected to encounter a state of discontent based on a liberally motivated unhappiness with the nature of the government, as well as rebelliousness due to the current economic malaise. Instead, he concluded that the root of the problem was the existence of "two nations warring within the bosom of a single state." By this, he meant that rivalry between the English and French populations in the Canadas was the real source of the difficulties.

A graduate of Eton, Durham inherited a vast fortune upon his father's death in 1797. His wealth flowed from mining properties in England. Something of a dandy in his fastidious dress and remoteness from non-elite subjects of the Crown, he was asked in 1821 what would constitute a satisfactory income for an English gentleman. He replied "that a man might jog along comfortably on forty thousand pounds a year."* Durham, with his close ties to the Whig Party establishment, sat in the House of Commons from 1812 to 1828, when he was elevated to the peerage as Baron Durham. He served as an officer in the British army, with the rank of cornet, from 1809 to 1811. When his father-in-law, Lord Grey, held the office of prime minister, Durham was appointed Lord Privy Seal and participated in the drafting of the Great Reform Act of 1832. That historic act ended the control of the House of Commons by a small and unrepresentative electorate — in many cases, parliamentary seats described as "rotten boroughs" had been controlled by a tiny number of men. The Great Reform Act moved Britain toward a system of government that represented a much wider swath of the population. Those who brought it into being, including Lord Durham, proudly called themselves "Reformers."**

Lord Durham's Report advocated a political union between Upper and Lower Canada, a central purpose of which was to achieve the assimilation of the French Canadians. Despite his reputation as a Reformer in Britain, Lord Durham had nothing but disdain for the French Canadians. He sweepingly dismissed them as hopelessly mired in the past, as not having progressed in their approach to the economy and society for two hundred years.

"I repeat that the alteration of the character of the province ought to be immediately entered upon," he wrote, "and firmly, though

---

* That sum would have been approximately the same in value as £1.7 million in the early twenty-first century.

** To this day, a very posh Reform Club exists in London. A condition of membership is that one has to declare support for the Great Reform Act of 1832, however antiquated that may seem.

cautiously, followed up; that in any plan which may be adopted for the future management of Lower Canada, the first object ought to be that of making it an English province; and that, with this end in view, the ascendancy should never again be placed in any hands but those of an English population."[1] According to this British lord, the French Canadians lacked anything "that elevates a people."*

Upon his arrival in Quebec City, Lord Durham wielded the most extensive powers ever bestowed on any representative of the Crown in the history of Canada. In five provinces — Upper Canada, Lower Canada, New Brunswick, Nova Scotia and Prince Edward Island — he was governor-in-chief. He was also high commissioner, with the power to recommend changes to the form of government in the two Canadas, the provinces that had been the scene of the violent rebellions. Tying together his powers, he was given the title "High Commissioner and Governor General of all Her Majesty's provinces on the continent of North America, and of the islands of Prince Edward and Newfoundland."[3]

Durham had two main objectives for the governance of Canada. The first was responsible government. The second, which starkly contradicted the first, was to diminish the power of French Canadians in the governing of Canada. Not surprisingly, given his outlook, in Lower Canada Durham was enthusiastically received by members of the English speaking commercial elite, while he was met with indifference bordering on hostility by the political leadership in French Canada.

---

* This was not the first time that British governors had concluded that francophones needed to be assimilated. The most brutal expression of this view came in 1755, when the British government of Nova Scotia forcibly expelled French-speaking Acadians from their communities along the Bay of Fundy, sending thousands of people by ship to the Thirteen Colonies. The Acadian communities were burned to the ground, their fields laid waste at harvest time. As for the Acadians themselves, British rulers, such as Nova Scotia Governor Charles Lawrence, believed that expulsion would lead to their assimilation and the loss of their Acadian identity. Despite the terrible ordeal they suffered, which cost many hundreds of Acadian lives, many Acadians returned to their homeland, establishing new settlements in what is now New Brunswick, where they fiercely sustained their identity.[2]

During his stay in Canada, Durham considered the possibility of establishing a British North American federal union, an idea that had already met with considerable support in Whitehall. This was an era during which the British were reforming their own system of government and were increasingly regarding their settler colonies as more of a nuisance than an asset. With free trade the new dogma in British ruling circles, the feeling was that settler colonies would drop off the tree of the old empire when they had ripened into mature fruit. Confident that Britain led the world as an industrial power, those at the helm of government, finance, and industry were sure that a policy of selling goods in all markets and buying primary products where they were cheapest was best for the country. They were no longer interested in traditional mercantilist policies that bestowed imperial preference on Canada and other colonies. They were just as happy to buy wheat and forest products from Americans or Scandinavians.

Durham's preferred plan for Canada, entirely aimed at neutering the power of the French Canadians, was to create three provinces out of the existing provinces of Upper and Lower Canada. The central and western regions of Upper Canada were to constitute a province; the eastern portion of Upper Canada, along with Montreal and the Eastern Townships of Lower Canada, were to make up a second province; and the third province was to be erected on the territory of the remainder of Lower Canada. [4] These provinces were to be embedded in a broader British North American federation.

Not surprisingly, Durham's idea of splitting Lower Canada was staunchly resisted in French Canada. The federal scheme did not meet with a favourable response in the Maritimes, especially in New Brunswick. As a consequence, the union of Upper and Lower Canada into one province with a single legislature was the ground to which Durham shifted. [5]

Once back in England, Lord Durham turned his attention to writing his report. The idea of uniting Upper and Lower Canada into a single province was accepted. The province extended a thousand miles from the Gaspé, where the St. Lawrence emptied into the Atlantic, to the region of forest, rock, and lakes that lay north of Lake Superior. In 1841, well over a million people lived within its boundaries, 670,000 of them in the eastern half, which had been Lower Canada. Of those, about 510,000 were francophone. In the former Upper Canada, the population, almost entirely anglophone, was 480,000.

But the British government did not establish a legislative union treating the province's population as a single entity. Instead, the Act of Union, which was adopted by the British parliament in 1840, retained the old divisions of Upper and Lower Canada for purposes of electing representatives to the new provincial legislature. The initial effect of this fateful decision was to overrepresent English-speaking Upper Canada (Canada West after 1841) in the legislature by granting this section of the province an equal number of seats with Lower Canada (Canada East after 1841), despite the latter's much larger population.* The second deviation from Lord Durham's wishes was to continue to deny responsible government to the new province.

THE BRITISH MAY have believed that the arrangements they made for the Canadian state in 1841 would be enduring, but that proved not to be the case. Economic, technological, and demographic changes soon exposed the Province of Canada as, at best, a halfway house to a more durable edifice.

For the colonists who lived north of the United States, the mid-nineteenth century was a period of rapid development. Canals were constructed, followed by railways and the onset of the telegraph. While new industries in the U.S. Northeast drove the construction of railways, in Canada it tended to be the reverse: the rapid extension of railways drove industrialization.

The British Empire was also undergoing a critical economic and political transformation. In mid-century Britain, the "Little

---

* The terms "Canada West" and "Canada East" never replaced "Upper Canada" and "Lower Canada" in popular usage. Indeed, the latter terms often continued to be used in official documents.

Englanders" played a key role in shaping government policy by promoting the cause of free trade instead of classic economic empire. Men such as Richard Cobden, who was a manufacturer and reformer, and John Bright, the political reformer, opposed traditional notions of the economic role of colonies and mother country. During the long mercantilist age that preceded the mid-nineteenth century, the prevailing approach was for colonies to provide raw materials and primary products to help drive England's economic engine. However, as manufacturing rose during the industrial revolution, England became the "workshop" of the world. As British industry, centred on the production of cotton fabrics, became globally dominant, the balance of political and economic forces shifted.

British reformers embraced new economic doctrines, chief among them free trade. Why provide monetary preferences to producers of raw materials within the empire, when the British could often purchase them more cheaply in the United States, Scandinavia, or South America? British manufactured goods should be made available to the markets of the world, and the British should be able to buy cotton, grain, or timber from the cheapest possible sources. The Reformers were essentially advocating a shift from mercantilism to classical economics, the ideas Adam Smith had pioneered decades earlier. Instead of traditional concepts of economic empire, the Little Englanders argued, Britain should foster free trade. This, they believed, would make Britain wealthier. To them, colonies were costly and unnecessary.

The effect of this thinking on Canada and other colonies was enormous. Prior to the mid-1840s, Canadian merchants and financiers had benefited from imperial preference. Under the old system, Canadian grain and timber entered the British market with a preferential advantage over American produce. Indeed, the system operated so that when American producers shipped their products to Canada to be exported from there to Britain, those products were treated as imperial products. Imperial preference was vital to Canadian commercial interests and helped underwrite the costs of building canals to create a shipping route that would compete with New York State's Erie Canal.

In Britain, the aristocratic land-owning interests, which had dominated society and politics since the Glorious Revolution of 1688, were losing power to the financial interests of the City of London and the rising influence of manufacturers based in Manchester and other industrial centres in the Midlands. With the transformation of the British power structure, political support for mercantilism disintegrated.

As the shift to classical economics and free trade accelerated, British political leaders saw less point in maintaining close political control over the internal affairs of the settler colonies. In 1846, the British parliament repealed the Corn Laws, which ended imperial preference for Canadian wheat in the British market. Three years later, Britain repealed the Navigation Acts, which required that goods traded between Britain and the colonies be transported in British or colonial ships.

In 1848, the British government instructed Lord Elgin, the governor general of Canada, to institute responsible government. But Westminster did not simply bestow responsible government on Canadians. A remarkable new alliance of both French-speaking and English-speaking Reformers came together to provide the necessary leadership to convince the British government that relations with the colony would improve once the change was made.* Louis-Hippolyte LaFontaine, Robert Baldwin, and Francis Hincks — all three in their late thirties or early forties during these years — were the successors to the failed rebels, Louis-Joseph Papineau and William Lyon Mackenzie.

The immediate consequence of responsible government was the election of a ministry made up of Reformers from both Canada West and Canada East. It was a government whose achievements put Canada firmly on the path to self-rule. The two leaders of the ministry were LaFontaine of Canada East, who became first minister of Canada in

---

* The term "Reformer" or "Reform Party" was used to describe the political forces in Canada that later established the Liberal Party. Reformers were sometimes also called Grits or Clear Grits. The Reformers of the mid-nineteenth century had nothing to do with the Reform Party that was one of the forebears of the present-day Conservative Party of Canada.

1848 — he had served briefly in that position in the early 1840s — and
Robert Baldwin of Canada West. LaFontaine and Baldwin were determined to make the province a genuine democracy. Among their goals
was the restoration of the French language to an equal position with
English as a language of government. In 1848, the Reformers succeeded
in having French re-established as a language of record in the provincial government. LaFontaine and Baldwin brought co-operation
between French and English Canadians to a level that would not be
equalled again until the critical decade of the 1860s.

The Reformers were also pledged to bring justice to those who had
suffered most during the 1837–38 rebellions. In 1849, the government
passed the Rebellion Losses Bill, which provided compensation to residents in Canada East whose properties had been damaged. The bill
would also compensate those who had supported the rebellion, provided they had not been tried and convicted of high treason. A similar
bill had previously passed in Canada West. Tories were furious because
the bill would compensate French Canadians whose properties were
located in areas where support for the rebellions had been strongest. [6]

An English-speaking pro-Tory mob took to the streets of Montreal,
which was then the capital of Canada. Some of the mob attacked the
Parliament building, torched it, and left it gutted by fire. On one occasion during the week of rioting, LaFontaine and Baldwin stood in the
courtyard of the Château Ramezay, protected by police and militiamen whose numbers were far outnumbered by the mob's. [7]

As a consequence of the riots, the capital of the province was
moved out of Montreal. In future, it would alternate between Toronto
and Quebec City.

The establishment of responsible government struck a blow at the
power of the banker-merchant elite. So too did the end of imperial
preference. The empire no longer promised a secure economic haven
for the Canadian commercial class. Gone were the days when the
members of the merchant elite could be assured of cozy positions
doled out by the governor.

In 1849, leading members of the Canadian business elite drafted and signed the Annexation Manifesto, which called for the annexation of Canada by the United States. In part to assuage the choler of the commercial elite, the British government negotiated a reciprocal trade agreement with Washington to embed the British North American provinces in a free trade arrangement with the United States. Reciprocity came into effect in 1854.

Economic and political change was accompanied by demographic transformation, which rendered the Province of Canada politically dysfunctional. During the 1840s and 1850s, the Canadian population grew very rapidly. While the birth rate among French Canadians was high, the main driver of the population increase was immigration from the British Isles. By 1851, the first decennial census revealed a population of just over 1.8 million people. By that date, Canada West had overtaken Canada East with a population of 952,000 compared to 890,000. In Canada East, there were 669,000 French Canadians and 220,000 English Canadians. A decade later, the 1861 census found a total population of 2.5 million, with Canada West at 1.4 million and Canada East at just over 1.1 million.

Not only was the proportion of French Canadians dropping in Canada as a whole; the proportion of people of American origin was also declining sharply in relation to those of recent British origin. In 1861, there were 64,000 people of American origin, 127,000 from England and Wales, 90,000 from Scotland, and 241,000 from Ireland. Native-born English Canadians numbered just over 1 million, and French Canadians in Canada East 880,000.[8] While the Loyalists who arrived from the United States in the decades between the end of the American Revolution and the outbreak of the War of 1812 remained an important group, they were swamped in numbers by newcomers from across the Atlantic.

The British Isles, the source of so many migrants to Canada in the 1840s and 1850s, had itself evolved enormously both socially and economically over the previous five or six decades. The Britain of the mid-nineteenth century was a very different society from the earlier Britain from which the American colonies drew their founding

populations prior to the American Revolution. The Britain that peopled the Thirteen Colonies was pre-industrial. The early American
political culture, centred on the Declaration of Independence and the
1787 U.S. Constitution, was the product of pre-industrial commercial
capitalism. By contrast, the immigrants to Canada in the decades
prior to the 1860s population boom came from an industrial Britain
in which manufacturing and finance had grown to dominance over
commercial agriculture. From this Britain came working-class culture and ideology and the belief in free trade capitalism.

Highly significant was the immense migration of both Protestant
and Roman Catholic Irish to Canada in the terrible years following
the Irish famine in the late 1840s. Immigration to Canada was dispro-
portionately skewed — the proportion of Irish and Scottish to English
was much higher among migrants to Canada than it was in the British
Isles themselves.

John A. Macdonald was one of those immigrants, and when the
transition to a more British Canada was completed, he would be ideally
suited to offer leadership to a population with which he was very much
in tune.

Chapter 5

John A. Macdonald
Takes the Stage

JOHN A. MACDONALD was twenty-three years old and living in Kingston when the rebellions against British rule erupted in both Upper and Lower Canada in 1837. In the Loyalist town where he lived, there was virtually no sympathy for the William Lyon Mackenzie's rebels. When the news reached Kingston that rebellion was likely and then that rebels had marched southward toward Toronto, where they were met and repelled by the local militia, the members of the Kingston militia were mustered, Macdonald among them. [1]

The rebellions in the Canadas stirred up anti-British feeling in the United States. For months after the rebellions had been quelled, there were alarums along the border, with warnings that invasions of Canadian soil could be imminent. As a lawyer as well as a militiaman, Macdonald was not only mustered into the ranks on occasion but was also called upon to play a role as a lawyer in an important case when one real military incursion did occur close to Kingston. [2]

Despite the fact that Macdonald was a conservative and staunchly loyal to the British Crown, the rebellions and their aftermath were crucial in opening the way for his later political career. Even by the time of the rebellions, he was becoming a new kind of Canadian Tory — one who would find himself quite at home in the much more democratic era that was coming.

BORN IN GLASGOW, Scotland, on January 11, 1815, John A. Macdonald's early prospects were as dim as those of Jefferson Davis and Abraham Lincoln. The future architect of Canadian Confederation and prime minister of Canada was the third of five children of Hugh Macdonald and Helen Shaw, who married in 1811. Hugh Macdonald was a failed businessman whose ventures left him in debt. By contrast, his wife Helen was a forceful and determined woman who proved to be the anchor of the family. Hugh and Helen migrated from Britain with his family in 1820 and settled in Kingston, Upper Canada.

After the long voyage to Quebec City, followed by the gruelling and lengthy journey in a bateau and then in a Durham boat to Montreal and finally to Kingston, Macdonald arrived with his family in a town of about four thousand people, which at the time made it the largest municipality in Upper Canada.[3] Compared to other settlements in Upper Canada, Kingston had a lengthy and storied history. Originally founded by the French as Fort Frontenac in the seventeenth century, it had fallen under British rule following the conquest of Canada at the Battle of the Plains of Abraham in 1759. In 1784, it became a true town with the arrival of the United Empire Loyalists.

Kingston was the most important British military base in Upper Canada, home to a large contingent of British regulars and Canadian militia, and the principal base of the British fleet on Lake Ontario. During the War of 1812, American forces never succeeded in occupying Kingston, unlike York (Toronto after 1834), the provincial capital, which fell twice to American attackers in 1813.

When the Macdonalds arrived in 1820, the town remained an important military base, with Fort Henry located on its eastern edge. The Macdonalds had been drawn to Kingston in large measure because they had relatives there. The pattern was a common one, then as now, in Canada. Migrants were drawn to locations where more or less distant relatives could assist and guide them during their transition to a new homeland.

Colonel Donald Macpherson was by far Hugh Macdonald's most important connection in Kingston. Married to Hugh's wife's step-sister, the colonel had fought twice on the British side, first during the American Revolutionary War and then in the War of 1812. Retired in Kingston, Colonel Macpherson dwelt in a large stone house and was content to take in the Macdonald family while Hugh made plans for the future. [4] In those years, stone houses were a signature feature in Kingston, which was located in limestone country. Well-to-do Kingstonians built limestone houses in the heart of the town, houses that can still be seen today, especially in the city's old Sydenham Ward.

The Macdonalds may have changed continents to seek a brighter future, but Hugh Macdonald's losing ways in business did not change. After living in the colonel's home for three months, Hugh opened a general store in the centre of town. He sold a wide range of goods, his stock purchased from merchants in Montreal. [5] The six members of the family lived in the rooms above the store, which quickly failed. [6]

In 1824, Hugh Macdonald tried yet another store. He was nothing if not determined, a quality he may have passed to the future prime minister, whose nickname came to be "Old Tomorrow." This time the store was located in Hay Bay, on Lake Ontario west of Kingston. [7] John, who was then nine years old, walked to the school he attended with his sisters, Margaret and Louisa, in the village of Adolphustown, three miles from home.

His brother, James, should have been with them. Tragically, he had been killed two years earlier, at the age of five and a half, by a family servant by the name of Kennedy. Hugh and Helen left the boys in the care of this servant one day. While there are varying accounts of the tragedy that unfolded, what is certain is that Kennedy struck James with a stick, causing him to slip and strike his head. He expired from the blow. The terrible scene was witnessed by John A. Whether Kennedy was angered because James cried for his parents or he lunged at the boy while in a drunken state is not known. Kennedy was never charged for his part in the affair. [8]

With his wiry hair and his large nose, which in adulthood would give him an uncanny resemblance to Benjamin Disraeli, whose broad philosophical outlook he came to share, John A. made many friends at school, despite being taunted by some of the girls with the epithet "Ugly John Macdonald." [9] After a couple of years of schooling at Adolphustown, John A.'s parents sent him to the Midland Grammar School in Kingston, where the annual tuition fee was seventy pounds. This was a very considerable outlay for a family that was always in a state of financial difficulty.

John A. spent his summers on the Bay of Quinte, at Glenora, where his father had moved the family so that he could operate a grist mill, which soon failed. At fourteen, John A. was transferred to another school that was run by an Oxford graduate, Reverend John Cruickshank, and offered a general classical education. A coeducational institution, which was unusual for the time, the school encouraged Macdonald's natural and growing appetite for reading in a range of fields, including history and politics. [10]

At the age of fifteen, John A. Macdonald ended his school days and after an all too brief period of youth set out in quest of a legal career. As was the case for Abraham Lincoln in Illinois, there was no law school in Upper Canada and no formal law degree. To gain the position of law clerk, Macdonald journeyed by steamboat to Toronto, where the offices of the Law Society of Upper Canada were located. There, for a fee of fifteen pounds, he sat an exam before a panel of benchers that tested him on Latin and mathematics.

Just as Abraham Lincoln had been highly fortunate to be mentored by a leading attorney, Macdonald clerked for Kingston lawyer George Mackenzie — already, at age thirty-five, one of the town's most successful attorneys. [11] Crucially, Colonel Macpherson, who had done so much for the Macdonald family, introduced Macdonald to Mackenzie.

Two years after going to work for Mackenzie, John A. gained the chance, with Mackenzie's blessing, to temporarily take over the law office of Lowther Macpherson, a relative of Donald Macpherson who was sidelined with an illness. In the office in Prince Edward County, young Macdonald learned how to manage an operation on his own. [12]

George Mackenzie handled the legal work of businessmen, merchants, and farmers in the surrounding area. He offered John A. a room in his house in Kingston, which gave the young man the benefits of a well-stocked library and invaluable lessons in how to deal with clients — lessons that were at least as important as knowledge of the fine points of the law.

Mackenzie was a special kind of corporate lawyer; his progressive social and political views supported a capitalism open to many more than just the members of the established elites. He was one of the leaders of a campaign to break the monopoly of the Bank of Upper Canada through the establishment of a Kingston-based bank. A bill to charter the new bank died in the provincial legislature's appointed upper house, the Legislative Council, among whose members were many directors or stockholders of the Bank of Upper Canada. [13] It took several attempts to charter a new bank. When the Commercial Bank of the Midland District did come into being, its first lawyer was Mackenzie. [14]

Mackenzie was neither a Tory nor a Reformer. At a time when provincial politics was increasingly polarized, he preached moderate reform that was not disloyal to the Crown. His political outlook displayed features of the political philosophy of John A. Macdonald in the 1850s, when he styled himself a Liberal-Conservative. Mackenzie allowed his name to be placed in nomination to fill the seat for Frontenac County in the Upper Canada Legislature. His career ended suddenly, however, when he died of cholera in August 1834. [15]

Macdonald's own law career was advanced rather sadly by three deaths: that of Mackenzie; that of Lowther Macpherson, who died on board a ship returning from Britain, where he had undergone medical treatment; and then in 1839, with the sudden passing of Henry Cassady, another prominent attorney. The latter's death opened the way for Macdonald to acquire much of his business, including the key position of solicitor of the Commercial Bank of the Midland District.

In 1835, Macdonald opened his own law office in Kingston. In the Kingston *Chronicle*, he posted the notice: "John A. Macdonald, attorney, has opened his office…where he will attend to all the duties of the profession." [16] His claim to be an attorney in the advertisement was somewhat premature. In fact, it was not until a year later, after ·

he passed the requisite exam in Toronto, that he was actually called to the bar, at age twenty-one.

Significantly younger than Lincoln had been when he became a lawyer, Macdonald proceeded to take on two law clerks, each of whom was extraordinary in his own right: Alexander Campbell, who later served as a cabinet minister under Macdonald, and later still as lieutenant-governor of Ontario, and Oliver Mowat, [17] who would become a Liberal premier of Ontario — and, from that post, a persistent and able adversary to Macdonald.

Having launched a successful law practice, which allowed him to move with his family into a substantial house, and then into another one on a more fashionable street, Macdonald made himself the effective head of his family in place of his father Hugh, the persistent failure. [18]

From 1837 to 1839, he shifted his law practice to criminal cases. Whether or not this was his objective, high-profile criminal cases brought him to the attention of a much wider public. Two clients, charged in separate cases with murder, experienced different fates — the first client was found guilty and hanged, while the second was acquitted.

The armed rebellions of 1837–38 brought a very high-profile case his way. Following the collapse of the rebellion in Upper Canada, William Lyon Mackenzie fled to New York State. The rebellions in the two Canadian provinces provoked considerable sympathy south of the border, where many saw them as political upheavals broadly similar to the American Revolution. In 1838, so-called Hunters' Lodges, secret bodies similar to Masonic lodges, formed in the United States to launch armed attacks against the British regime in Canada.

In one such attack in November 1838, about 180 members of a contingent crossed the St. Lawrence on a steamship and a couple of schooners to Windmill Point, near Prescott, Upper Canada. The invaders were led by Nils Gustaf von Schoultz, a romantic revolutionary of Swedish origin who had fought at the side of Poles defending Warsaw against the forces of the Russian czar. After ending up in the United States, Schoultz was drawn to the cause of liberating Canadians from British rule. He and the members of the contingent had been told that reinforcements would soon arrive from the U.S. to buttress their attack. The reinforcements never came.

In short order, members of the local militia and British regulars surrounded the attackers, then brought up cannon and forced them to surrender.

John A. Macdonald offered to defend Schoultz and Daniel George, who had raised funds to outfit members of the expedition. [19] As invaders of Canadian soil, the two were to be tried before a court martial. Macdonald was in no position to defend the accused as he could have in a normal criminal trial. Acting in the belief that all manner of accused deserved a defence, he did what he could. Both men were sentenced to death. Macdonald was able to assist Schoultz in drafting his will, while refusing any payment to himself as a clause in the will. Schoultz went bravely to his death, walking calmly to the scaffold and placing the noose around his neck and his hands in his pockets to await his execution. [20]

In 1839, Macdonald handled his final criminal case when he represented a Mohawk native who had been charged with the murder of another Mohawk man. Macdonald's defence turned on the fact that the house where the crime had been committed had been dark, and that it was therefore uncertain who had plunged the knife into the victim. While Macdonald did not get his client acquitted, the accused was convicted of manslaughter and was sentenced to only six months in prison. As in other cases, Macdonald's imaginative and energetic defence drew admiration. [21]

From then on Macdonald practised corporate law. A good deal of work flowed from his position as the solicitor of the Commercial Bank of the Midland District. He extended his practice to commercial issues in nearby towns such as Belleville and eventually Montreal, which was then the financial and business hub of Canada. Real estate drew ever more of his attention. While at first he profited from buying and selling lots and parcels of land in Kingston, a sharp contraction of the real estate market wiped out his previous gains.

His law practice placed him ever more at the centre of business. He

became a director of Kingston-based firms that specialized in canals
and railways, among other things.

A journey to Britain in 1842, the year after the death of his father,
allowed him to develop contacts that ultimately paid off when, for
instance, he became the solicitor for the Trust and Loan Company of
Upper Canada, whose headquarters were in London.[22] The trip also
deeply reinforced his love for England and for Canada's connection
to the British Empire.

Britain was at the peak of its imperial dominance. The Napoleonic
Wars were behind it, and it had not yet entered the era that would
come a few decades later, when new industrial powers, principally
Germany and the United States, became serious economic competi-
tors. In the 1840s, Britain was the workplace of the world. The Royal
Navy was the master of the oceans. And the Bank of England, the Old
Lady of Threadneedle Street, regulated global commerce and played
a dominant role in determining where infrastructure projects such
as canals, harbours, and eventually railways would be undertaken in
many parts of the world.

In the days following the failed rebellions, it was no surprise that
a young man, conscious of his Scottish origins and connections, who
had absorbed the staunchly British attitudes of Upper Canadians
should find London the embodiment of wealth, style, and power, and
the home of a political system he could admire. With its population
of two million people and its vast influence on events everywhere,
London captivated Macdonald the way, a century later, many young
people were captivated by New York. He had also fallen in love with
his first cousin Isabella Clark, who was to become his wife.[23]

Home from England, Macdonald decided to try his hand at politics — a natural decision for a lawyer with considerable experience in
business who had shown a notable flair when arguing cases before
judges and juries. In 1843, he ran and won an aldermanic seat in
Kingston. In the spring of 1844, leading Kingstonians — only men
with property enjoyed the right to vote — asked Macdonald to stand
for a seat in the legislature in the upcoming election.

Agreeing to be a Conservative candidate, Macdonald declared that he took a practical view of politics: "In a young country like Canada, I am of the opinion that it is of more consequence to endeavour to develop its resources and improve its physical advantages than to waste the time of the legislature and the money of the people on abstract and theoretical questions of government." [24]

Practicality and support for improvement though the construction of railways, canals, and roads were to be key tenets of Macdonald's approach throughout his long political career. Close to the business community and anxious to promote its success, Macdonald, like Lincoln, did not see a separation between the interests of business and the role of the state. Macdonald believed in an active state precisely because he was pro-business. As a lawyer, he had shifted from criminal cases to commercial law, representing important financial interests and going into business himself. He bought and sold large parcels of land in various parts of the province. He sat as a director on the boards of a number of Canadian and British companies. His interest in playing a role in the politics of the province grew along with his role as a lawyer tied to business.

In the autumn of 1844, just prior to the provincial election, Macdonald included the following assertion in his election manifesto published in the Kingston *Chronicle*: "I...need to state my firm belief that the prosperity of Canada depends upon its permanent connection with the Mother Country and that I shall resist to the utmost any attempt which may tend to weaken that union." [25]

On October 14 and 15, voters came to cast their votes by shouting out their choices (this election predated the secret ballot). Macdonald prevailed easily, winning 275 votes against his opponent's 42. The greatest career in nineteenth-century Canadian politics was well and truly launched.

Beginning in 1847, Macdonald served for the first time in a cabinet, spending seven months as receiver general and three months as commissioner of Crown lands, in governments headed by William Henry Draper and Henry Sherwood. In 1848, Macdonald resigned with the rest of the Conservative government when the Reformers won office under the leadership of Robert Baldwin and Louis-Hippolyte LaFontaine. He returned to the cabinet in September 1854 in the important position of attorney general for Canada West in the government jointly led by Sir Allan MacNab and Augustin-Norbert Morin. Taking advantage of financial scandals that had wracked the reputation of Reformer Francis Hincks earlier that year,[26] Conservatives had broadened their political base by forging an alliance with the more centrist elements among the Reformers in Canada West as well as a tighter alliance with conservative politicians in French Canada.

In this newly reconfigured Conservative Party, the Liberal-Conservative coalition, Sir Allan MacNab was too much a relic of the past to stay on for long as leader. Indeed, it had been Macdonald, not MacNab, who had played the central role in staking out the new ground for the remade Liberal-Conservatives. In 1856, in a virtual coup d'état, MacNab was forced to resign as leader of the government and leader of the Conservative Party. His departure opened the way for Macdonald to become co-leader of the government with Étienne Taché, who served as premier. He also became leader of the Conservative Party, a position he was to hold until his death in 1891.

Chapter 6

Leaders of Canada's Two Solitudes: George-Étienne Cartier and George Brown

T HE ESTABLISHMENT OF a single Canadian province through the merger of Upper and Lower Canada was Lord Durham's problematic legacy. The result was a unitary state in which an ongoing struggle for power between English and French Canadians was a constant reality. The two leaders who most personified that struggle were George-Étienne Cartier and George Brown.

From 1841 to 1867, four parties dominated the politics of the Province of Canada: the Conservative and Reform parties in Canada West, and the Bleu (conservative) and Rouge (reform) parties in Canada East. As time passed, it became increasingly difficult for political leaders to form coalition ministries — typically with one party from each section — to provide stable governments. Instead, governments came and went with increasing frequency. Long-term planning for the future development of the province shuddered to a halt.

If the English and French could work out a system of government that was not mired in deadlock, and if Canadian capitalists could act successfully as middlemen in this portion of the British Empire, much might be achieved. But as always, the rising power of the American Republic to the south could choke off Canada's potential to serve as the core of a great state.

While political gridlock in Canada became an ever more acute problem, it did not halt important economic and demographic changes from taking place.

Reciprocity quickly opened the way for closer north-south trade ties between Canada and the United States. Especially important was the export to the United States of highly desirable white pine from the Bruce Peninsula region of Canada West, on the shores of Georgian Bay. In the other direction, U.S. manufacturers found markets for their products north of the border.

Making use of their time off from farming, thousands of Canadian men spent their winters in the logging camps. With spring breakup, enormous squared rafts of timber were steered down the rivers, and the timber was transported on the new rail lines to markets.

By the late 1850s, most of the best arable land in the Province of Canada had already been occupied. Farther north, colonization drives were directing farmers in both Canada West and Canada East to much more marginal land. Those who moved there ended up as poor farmers, and their farms, which have mostly been abandoned, lie in ruins, mute testimony to a policy gone wrong. Thousands of people in Canada West sought land across the border in Michigan and Wisconsin, and thousands of French Canadians migrated south to take jobs in the mill towns of New England.

The high birth rate, especially in French Canada, and the huge wave of immigration from Britain kept the Canadian population growing briskly despite the steady flow of both French and English Canadians to the United States.

The French Canadians, who had initially been underrepresented in the provincial legislature in 1841, now found themselves overrepresented by the 1850s. Their leaders were determined to hang on to the share of seats that had been granted to Canada East in the Act of Union.

ONCE THE POPULATION of Canada West soared past that of the eastern half of the province, anglophones of Canada West began a campaign for reform. Politicians took up the cry for Representation by Population. Rep by Pop opened the door to George Brown, who emerged as a towering figure in the politics of Canada in the 1850s. And while Brown demanded change, political leaders in French Canada were forced to defend the existing constitutional order, the most prominent of these being George-Étienne Cartier.

Cartier was born in 1814 in Saint-Antoine-sur-Richelieu, Lower Canada, into a well-to-do family that earned its living in the business of milling and exporting grain. In honour of King George III, his name was given the English spelling, George, rather than the French spelling, Georges. He graduated from the Sulpician Collège de Montréal and was called to the bar in 1835.

Two years later, he was inspired by the cause of Louis-Joseph Papineau and joined the nationalist Société des Fils de la Liberté (Society of the Sons of Liberty). He took up arms and fought valiantly alongside Wolfred Nelson, one of the leading rebels, at the Battle of Saint-Denis on November 23, 1837, the one major battle that was won by the rebels against the British regulars, who were led by Colonel Charles Gore.

Following the defeat of the rebellion, Cartier managed to escape into exile in Vermont. In 1838, his petition for a right to return was successful, and he took up residence in Montreal, where he resumed the practice of law. In his legal career, Cartier grew in importance, taking on railways, banks, and orders of the Catholic Church as clients. In 1841, he became active in politics as Louis-Hippolyte LaFontaine's campaign manager. In 1848, he ran and won a seat in the legislature and soon became a cabinet minister.

In 1855, following the transformation of John A. Macdonald's party the previous year, Cartier entered the Liberal-Conservative cabinet. It was far from immediately evident to Macdonald that this solid, squat, and rather square-faced man was to become his most important French-Canadian partner during the critical years to come. [1] What would certainly become clear over time was Cartier's uniqueness among French-Canadian politicians. A former rebel, then a Rouge and later a Bleu, Cartier remained a moderate French-Canadian nationalist who was prepared to stand up as a staunch defender of French Canada's position in the province. His ties to Montreal business and to the Church rendered him a highly valuable ally, especially in an era when major decisions had to be made. Over time, Macdonald would come to see past Cartier's hot-tempered, intimidating manner in debate[2] to perceive an ally with whom he could form a close and enduring political relationship.

By 1857, when Macdonald's position had become paramount in the government, he left it largely to Cartier to make decisions for Canada East, including the selection of cabinet ministers from that part of the province.[3]

In 1858, following a brief shakeup in the government, with the Reformers in power for only a few days, the Liberal-Conservatives once again took office, this time with Cartier as first minister and Macdonald as the key minister from English Canada.[4] Later that year, faced with the growing difficulties in governing the province, with demands for Rep by Pop a constant reality, both Macdonald and Cartier were won over in principle to the concept of a federal union that would include all of the British North American provinces.[5]

It was one thing to perceive the potential for such an approach as a way out of the political log-jam, but quite another to translate this into practical politics. Tentative steps taken by the Canadian government to garner initial support for the idea of a federation received a cold shoulder from the British Colonial Office, whose officials saw the proposal as a narrowly partisan move on the part of the Canadian government that had little actual backing from the other British North American provinces.[6] This initial gesture on the part of Macdonald and Cartier in favour of federalism went nowhere.

In 1861, when the new Canadian decennial census was published, it revealed that the population of Canada West had come to exceed that of Canada East by approximately 285,000 people. The number shocked politicians in Canada West into renewed demands for electoral reform. With Macdonald's support, Cartier addressed the House on the subject for nearly five hours, during which he announced that the government did not plan to introduce a bill that would alter the system of equal electoral representation for the two sections of the province.[7] Cartier made it clear that he would not countenance any change to the political place of French Canada in the province as long as it remained a unitary state.[8]

Two weeks later, Macdonald addressed the House to support the position Cartier had staked out. Macdonald remained at Cartier's side in the debate even when it was not politically convenient to do so. As he had once written about French Canada: "Treat them as a nation and they will act as a free people generally do — generously."[9]

Significantly, Macdonald's speech came exactly one week after the Confederates assaulted Fort Sumter on April 12, 1861, in the opening shots of the Civil War.[10] That conflict would prove decisive in shifting the parameters of the Canadian debate.

Meanwhile, it fell to Cartier to safeguard the interests of French Canada. In that struggle, his most formidable opponent was George Brown, the owner and editor of the *Globe* newspaper in Toronto and the leader of the Canada West Reformers. Where Brown insisted on change, Cartier defended the existing order.

LIKE JOHN A. Macdonald, George Brown was an immigrant from Scotland. Unlike Macdonald, Brown was tall, large, red-headed, and far from physically agile. His physique announced his personality and even his manner of thinking. Stolid, fervently attached to a set of ideas, and anything but subtle, Brown embodied the political outlook of Canada West.

Born in 1818 in the small port of Alloa, west of Edinburgh on the River Forth, George Brown began his education in a small parish school. When he was eight years old, his family moved to Edinburgh. There, he attended the city's high school, where famous men such as Adam Smith and the radical MP Joseph Hume had been educated.[11] Young Brown soon convinced his family that he should transfer to the Southern Academy of Edinburgh, where the renowned educator

Dr. William Gunn taught him. George Brown excelled at the academy, becoming Dr. Gunn's star pupil. When Brown graduated, Dr. Gunn heaped praise on him: "This young gentleman is not only endowed with high enthusiasm but possesses the faculty of creating enthusiasm in others." [12]

George Brown's father, Peter, passed on to his son his love of learning, his appetite for an active life, and his commitments to political reform and economic progress under the banner of liberalism. He imbued George with a strong dislike of aristocratic privilege and of Tory doctrines. Young George was raised in the Presbyterian faith of his family, [13] an influence that was bound to make him view John A. Macdonald with skepticism and distrust.

In April 1837, when George Brown was eighteen, he set out with his father from Liverpool on an American brig bound for New York. There, Brown's father established a print shop, and the young man served as his sole assistant. The following year, Brown's mother and his other siblings made the voyage to America. In 1842, Peter Brown founded the *British Chronicle*, a newspaper that catered to British migrants in the city. George worked with his father on the paper and made a tour of Canada on behalf of the publication. The following year, the Browns once again pulled up stakes, closing down their New York newspaper and moving to Toronto. [14]

There, Peter and George Brown were naturally drawn to the moderate liberalism of Robert Baldwin's Reform Party. The Browns, who were never attracted to the populist, democratic thrust of American liberalism, had always preferred British-style liberalism, a doctrine that promulgated gradual reform. They rented a shop on Toronto's King Street and established a new newspaper, the *Banner*, a publication that soon aligned itself with the Reformers and that favoured a moderate liberalism anchored in loyalty to the British Crown.

In 1844, Reform supporters encouraged George Brown to found a new newspaper that would be less concerned with ecclesiastical issues in the Presbyterian Church and that would be a more forceful political voice. With their backing, Brown launched the *Globe*, first as a weekly that shared facilities and even some of its columns with the *Banner*, which continued to be edited by Peter Brown.

Soon the leading newspaper in Canada West, the *Globe* became the most important voice of Reformers (later Liberals) in the province and made Brown a power to be reckoned with. The paper expressed the sentiments not only of Reformers but of commercial interests in the city of Toronto, the urban centre that was already beginning to challenge the dominance of Montreal as Canada's most important metropolis. Before long, Brown began to speak as a Reform politician for much of Canada West, in particular Toronto and rural regions west of the city.

IN 1851, BROWN won a seat in the province's legislative assembly. Over the course of the 1850s, he became the leading spokesman of Canada West's Reformers. As the champion of the western section of the province, Brown made the case that English-speaking Canada West was effectively under the thumb of French Canadians and the Roman Catholic Church. He thundered that, given its large population, Canada West should be represented by the majority of members in the assembly.

For more than a decade, Brown unleashed fire and brimstone not only on French Canadians but on his Conservative rivals, branding them as thoroughly corrupt. His personal quarrel with John A. Macdonald became so intense that the two men would not speak to each other.

In response to George Brown's demand for Rep by Pop, French-Canadian Rouge politicians, the heirs to Louis-Joseph Papineau's Patriote rebels of 1837, who were the natural allies of Brown's Reformers, advanced what they called a Double Majority. Ideologically, the Reformers and the Rouges stood on the liberal side against Macdonald's Conservatives (the Liberal-Conservatives) and George-Étienne Cartier's Bleus. In practice, the Reformers and the Rouges were deeply divided around Rep by Pop. The Rouges' proposition of a Double Majority held that for legislation to pass it should require a majority of legislators from both halves of the province, Canada East and Canada West, thus recognizing the existence of two peoples in Canada. For his part, Brown pushed the much different idea that each vote should be equal, a position which, taken to its logical conclusion, would undermine the political position of the French Canadians.

If Brown's fight for Rep by Pop situated him in a battle with those to his east, his politics also faced west. Using the *Globe* as his vehicle for propagating the idea, Brown became a proponent of the expansion of Canada into the British territories that lay to the west. To give the idea broad appeal, he needed to show that acquiring the West would benefit more than Toronto commercial interests — that it also held the promise of plentiful prairie land for the sons of the farmers of Canada West.

The prospect of ready farmland was an attractive one for Canadian farmers. But there was debate between those who insisted that the prairies were desolate northern lands and those who maintained that the summers were warm enough and long enough in the region to support the large-scale growth of wheat.

In addition, Canadian business was increasingly feeling the tug of the North-West, where riches were to be gleaned from mineral deposits reported to exist north of Lakes Huron and Superior. If Canadian railways could hook up with a line of steamships plying the Upper Lakes, Canadian business could venture into this distant region, reestablishing a commercial tie with the old fur trade country to which Canada had once been linked.

There was sporadic discussion among political leaders and businessmen and in the newspapers about the possibility of annexing the North-West, including the immense lands controlled by the Hudson's Bay Company in the interior of the continent. Others saw Canada forming a transcontinental union on British territory that would extend as far Vancouver Island and would encompass the vast interior of what is now British Columbia. In the early 1850s, there was even some talk of the building of a transcontinental railway linking Canada to the west coast, passing along the southern tier of the Hudson's Bay Company lands.

Well before the rise of tensions between Britain and the United States during the Civil War, Canadian ideas of western expansion inevitably involved a strong defensive element — the need to protect the northern half of the continent against American aggression. Westward expansion always took into account the northward American population migration, which could lead to calls for U.S. annexation of territory.

By the end of 1856, Reformers and opinion leaders in Canada West were calling for the annexation of the Hudson's Bay Company territory. In January 1857, several hundred Reformers attended a meeting at Temperance Hall in Toronto, where they drafted a platform for the coming legislative session as well as for the anticipated provincial election. The eighth plank in the platform, alongside Rep by Pop, called for Canada's annexation of the company lands. [15]

Decisive events south of the border were soon to compel British North Americans to cope with the issues that had come to divide them.

Chapter 7

The Election of Abraham Lincoln

THE 1860S OPENED with a presidential election like no other in American history.

In April 1860, Democratic Party delegates flocked to Charleston, South Carolina, to choose their candidate for the presidency at the Democratic convention. Outside the convention hall, the atmosphere was poisonous, as Southern rabble-rousers whipped up crowds against Northerners in general and anyone who opposed the slave owners' agenda in particular. Inside, Northerners made up 60 percent of the delegates, because the size of delegations was based on the electoral votes for each state. [1]

By this time, the political spokesmen for Southern slave owners had hardened significantly on their position, with dire consequences for the Democrats. Most Southerners who attended the convention regarded Senator Stephen Douglas as their diabolical foe. Their ferocious anger had been stoked by his opposition to the Lecompton Constitution, in addition to his so-called Freeport Doctrine, which held that the people of any territory could effectively exclude slavery if they failed to pass legislation and to issue local police regulations. The Freeport Doctrine was supposed to give Douglas some wiggle-room on his position on slavery in both the North and the South. Instead, it made him appear slippery to many Northerners and weak to Southerners.

During the third Lincoln-Douglas debate, in September 1858 in Jonesboro, Illinois, Abraham Lincoln had pointed to the constitutional difficulties with Douglas's Freeport Doctrine. He said: "In the first place, the Supreme Court of the United States has decided that any Congressional prohibition of slavery in the Territories is unconstitutional...Hence they reach the conclusion that as the Constitution of the United States expressly recognizes property in slaves, and from that other constitutional provision that no person shall be deprived of property without due process of law, to pass an act of Congress by which a man who owned a slave on one side of a line would be deprived of him if he took him on the other side, is depriving him of that property without due process of law. That I understand to be the decision of the Supreme Court. I understand also that Judge Douglas adheres most firmly to that decision; and the difficulty is, how is it possible for any power to exclude slavery from the Territory unless in violation of that decision?" [2]

At the convention, Southern Democrats demanded that the party include in its platform support for a federal slave code for the territories. Such a code would guarantee the right of any slave owner to take his slave to any territory of the United States. Under such a code, the U.S. government would be required to provide protection for the owner and his property.

Two months earlier, Jefferson Davis had drafted legislation that he presented to the United States Senate. The draft legislation stated that neither the U.S. Congress nor any territorial legislature could abridge the right of any citizen of the United States to take his slave property to the territories of the U.S. and that his property must be afforded protection by the federal government. "We have sought not to usurp the Territory to our exclusive possession," asserted Davis on the Senate floor. "We have sought that government should be instituted in order that every person and property might be protected that went into it — the white man coming from the North, and the white man coming from the South, both meeting on an equality in the Territory, and each with whatever property he may hold under the laws of his

State and the Constitution of the United States." [3]

Jefferson Davis's proposal in the Senate and the demand in Charleston for a federal slave code proved fatal to the unity of the Democratic Party. If the federal slave code were to be included in the party platform, it would doom the electoral prospects of the party in the North, and thereby wipe out Stephen Douglas's chances of winning the presidency in November. On the other hand, if it was not included, many delegates from the South would walk out of the convention, and the party would split.

When the platform committee — the delegates chosen to draft the party platform — reported to the convention, the point of no return was reached. Each state had one vote, and by a margin of 17–16, the slave states and the territories of California and Oregon adopted a federal slave code similar to the one Jefferson Davis had presented to the Senate. A minority report, crafted by representatives of the free states, advanced popular sovereignty as the way to settle the issue of slavery in the territories. Also added was a clause that committed the party to obey a Supreme Court ruling on the powers of a territorial legislature. This attempt to stiffen the 1856 Democratic Party platform was insufficient in the eyes of Southerners. They would settle for no less than a plank that committed the party to support positive federal enforcement of the rights of slave owners in the territories.

The insistence on the federal enforcement of the rights of slave owners in the territories was partially fuelled by expansionist thinking. This desire for more land was captured in the remarks of the chairman of the platform committee, W. W. Avery, a former North Carolina state senator and the chairman of the platform committee. He said that slave owners would need to be able to count on federal protection when the United States acquired territory to the south in Cuba, Mexico, and Central America. Only then could they safely take their human property to these future slave lands.

Because Southerners felt that they were on the defensive, they were determined to uphold slavery, if necessary by seceding from the Union. The man who gave voice to this point of view most insistently was

Senator William Lowndes Yancey of Alabama, the leading orator in support of slavery. One of the so-called "Fire-Eaters" — fierce advocates of the Southern cause — Yancey was born in Georgia but spent most of his adult life in Alabama. He was part of the extreme pro-Southern wing of the Democratic Party. At the Charleston convention, he proclaimed: "Ours is the property invaded; ours are the institutions which are at stake; ours is the peace that is to be destroyed; ours is the property that is to be destroyed; ours is the honour at stake. We are in a position to ask you to yield. What right of yours, gentlemen of the North, have we of the South ever invaded."

He went on to suggest that the Northern delegates should enjoy the amenities available to them: "I have no doubt, gentleman," he said, "that each of you here enjoys most pleasantly, the hospitalities of this city." These were provided, he pointed out, by the black slaves who waited on them and did their bidding.

"If we beat you [in the struggle over slavery in the territories]," he went on, "we will give you good servants for life and enable you to live comfortably." Then he held out the hope that poor whites would be freed from carrying out menial chores not suited to the "highest order of civilization." Thus they could take their place "amongst the master race and put the negro race to do the dirty work which God designed they should do." In his peroration, Yancey warned Northern delegates: "There will be disunion if we are defeated."[4]

From this point, the Democratic Party proceeded to split. Since Northern delegates outnumbered those from the South, Stephen Douglas's platform was adopted by a vote of 165–138. The delegates from Alabama and Mississippi walked out of the convention. They were joined by all but two of the delegates from Louisiana. Others from South Carolina, Florida, and Texas, as well as portions of the delegations from Arkansas and Delaware, soon followed. More delegates from Arkansas and Georgia walked out the next day.[5]

On the evening of April 30, Yancey and the delegates who walked out of the convention staged an enormous gathering on the streets of Charleston. Bands played, and in the celebratory atmosphere, someone in the crowd shouted: "Three cheers for the Independent Southern Republic." The multitude roared out cheers. Yancey proclaimed that the pen of the historian was now poised to write the story of a new revolution.[6]

Meanwhile, Douglas failed to gain the two-thirds majority he needed to win the Democratic Party's presidential nomination. Despite holding fifty-seven ballots, the convention was unable to nominate any other candidate, and the delegates adjourned to return to their homes.

Six weeks later, Democratic delegates reconvened in Baltimore to take up the task anew. Division was again the order of the day. When a credentials fight broke out over which Southern delegates to seat, Lower South delegates walked out once again, and this time most of those from the Upper South followed them. They were even joined by a few pro-slavery delegates from the North.

Those who walked out — more than one-third of the delegates at the convention — proceeded to hold their own conclave, which endorsed a federal slave code platform. These Southern Democrats nominated John C. Breckinridge of Kentucky, the sitting vice president, for the presidency. Those who remained at the convention in Baltimore went on to nominate Douglas, but they knew perfectly well that with their party divided there was little to prevent the election of the Republican nominee, Abraham Lincoln.[7]

ON MAY 16, 1860, the Republican convention was called to order in Chicago, Illinois, at a gigantic new hall nicknamed the Wigwam. From the outset, William Seward appeared to have the nomination sewn up. But his political weaknesses soon became apparent.

He was seen to represent the extreme anti-slavery wing of the Republican Party; he also suffered from a surfeit of overconfidence. On the issue of slavery, Seward's most famous orations — the Higher Law speech in the Senate and the "irrepressible conflict" speech in Rochester, New York — had given him a reputation for stridency. Party centrists and pragmatists worried that he could alienate voters in the

Lower North. Republicans knew that to win the presidency, their candidate would need to prevail in almost all of the free states.

A lesser, but significant, problem for Seward was his association with Thurlow Weed, the New York State political operative whose wheeling and dealing had tainted him with the whiff of scandal. Republicans were counting on the nation's distaste for the corruption of the Buchanan administration to leverage their chances with voters against Stephen Douglas and the Democrats. In addition, prior to the convention, Seward had decided unwisely to spend much of the year doing a grand tour of Europe.

While Seward was the clear front-runner going into the party convention, he had left room for other candidates to challenge him. Among those with national reputations were Salmon P. Chase of Ohio; Simon Cameron of Pennsylvania; and Edward Bates of Missouri. All three, however, had major political liabilities. That left only one serious potential challenger: Abraham Lincoln of Illinois.

By this time, Lincoln had developed a national reputation. His campaign for the U.S. Senate seat against Stephen Douglas in 1858 had attracted attention far beyond Illinois. The centrepiece of that campaign was a series of seven debates between the two candidates held up and down the length of Illinois. Thousands of people were in attendance at each debate, which reached a national audience through newspaper reports. This was the first age of more or less instant communication over great distances. Daily newspapers, which drew on reports sent by telegraph, informed Americans of major events only a few hours after they occurred. Through this new medium, national reputations could be acquired much more swiftly than in the past.

Despite his House Divided speech, Lincoln was regarded within the party and throughout the country as a moderate on the slavery question, at least in comparison to Seward. When he made the case that he would act to block the establishment of slavery in the territories but would not abolish the institution in the slave states, he was believed, at least in the North.

Lincoln personified the promise free labour held for Americans.

He had, after all, been born in a log cabin and had toiled as a rail splitter on the frontier as a young man. His life path appeared to demonstrate that hard work on farms, in mills, and on the frontier could open the way to professional success — in his case as a lawyer — and to a position of political pre-eminence. Following his much-publicized run against Douglas, Lincoln had made speeches in a number of Midwestern states in 1859. In February 1860, he spoke to a large crowd at the Cooper Institute in New York City and then travelled to New England, where he delivered eleven speeches.

At the Cooper Institute, Lincoln reviewed the positions of the individual Founding Fathers on whether the federal government had the power to ban slavery in the territories. He argued that in 1784, the Congress of the United States — operating under the Articles of Confederation — had prohibited slavery in the Northwestern Territory (present-day Midwest), then the only federal territory. Then, in 1787, under the Constitution drafted in Philadelphia (the current U.S. Constitution), Congress passed a law, well known as the Ordinance of '87, which prohibited slavery in the territory. In 1789, the first Congress, operating under the new (and present) Constitution, passed an act to enforce the ordinance, and President George Washington signed the act into law.

Lincoln went on to note that a few years later the state of North Carolina had ceded to the federal government the territory that became the state of Tennessee, and later still Georgia ceded the territory that became Mississippi and Alabama. While these cessions were made on the condition that the federal government could not prohibit slavery in these territories, Lincoln pointed out that in 1798 Congress provided that no one would be allowed to bring a slave from outside the United States into the newly organized territory of Mississippi. Anyone who did so would be subject to a fine, and slaves thus imported would be freed. And, Lincoln told his audience, when in 1803 the U.S. government purchased the Louisiana Territory from France, Congress "did not, in the Territorial Act, prohibit slavery, but they did interfere with it — take control of it — in a more marked and extensive way than they did in the case of Mississippi." Congress had banned the importation of slaves who had been brought into the U.S. after May 1, 1798, and determined that slaves could only be moved by their owners. Those who violated these regulations would be subject to fines and to the freeing of the slaves in question.

Lincoln's motive for going into such elaborate detail on the issue of federal jurisdiction over slavery was to strike out at Stephen Douglas and undermine his Freeport Doctrine. At the beginning of his address, Lincoln quoted a Douglas speech delivered in Columbus, Ohio, the previous autumn, in which the senator had declared: "Our fathers, when they framed the Government under which we live, understood this question [federal power over slavery in U.S. territories] just as well, and even better, than we do now." Lincoln declared that he fully endorsed the approach of the Founders: "I adopt it as a text for this discourse."

Lincoln was determined to show that he and the members of his party were not revolutionaries, but true adherents to the Constitution and the laws of the Founders.

Turning his attention to the slave owners of the South, Lincoln addressed them rhetorically: "But you say you are conservative — eminently conservative — while we are revolutionary, destructive, or something of the sort. What is conservatism? Is it not adherence to the old and tried, against the new and untried? We stick to, contend for, the identical old policy on the point in controversy which was adopted by 'our fathers who framed the Government under which we live;' while you . . . reject . . . and spit upon that old policy, and insist upon substituting something new." [8]

Nearly four months later, when Republican delegates gathered at the Wigwam in Chicago to choose a presidential candidate, neither Lincoln nor Seward was present. As was the custom, the two candidates remained at home as the balloting got underway. Seward was in Auburn, New York, while Lincoln was in Springfield, Illinois. Each man anxiously awaited the arrival of telegrams that would tell the story.

On the first ballot, Seward, who needed 233 votes to win the nomination, received 173.5 votes. He was vulnerable, at sixty votes short, with Lincoln scoring 102 votes. On the next ballot, Lincoln's total soared to 181 votes, while Seward's count rose to only 184.5. Then came the third ballot. Lincoln's momentum carried him to 231.5 votes, just a couple of ballots short of victory. At this electric moment, the chairman of the Ohio delegation stood on his chair and announced that four delegates had switched their votes to Lincoln.[9] That was it.

Leading Republicans in the Northeast were dumbfounded. For a candidate who remained only partially known to the country at large to win the nomination left people scratching their heads. Newspapers that backed the Democratic Party exulted in the presidential candidate of their foes. "The conduct of the Republican party in this nomination," the *New York Herald* blared, "is a remarkable indication of a small intellect, growing smaller...they take up a fourth rate lecturer, who cannot speak good grammar."

The *Herald* charged that Lincoln's speeches were "illiterate compositions...interlarded with coarse and clumsy jokes." The paper even went on to lacerate the candidate's appearance: "Lincoln is the leanest, lankest, most ungainly mass of legs, arms and hatchet-face ever strung upon a single frame. He has most unwarrantably abused the privilege which all politicians have of being ugly."[10]

Disappointed though they were, William Seward and his supporters threw themselves enthusiastically into the Republican effort. And this support was to be of great importance for Lincoln's presidential campaign.

THE DEEPLY CONSEQUENTIAL election campaign that followed Lincoln's nomination was fought in ways that were both novel and familiar. Four major candidates took the field: Republican Abraham Lincoln, Democrat Stephen Douglas, Southern Democrat John Breckinridge, and the Constitutional Unionist John Bell.

The Constitutional Unionists, made up mostly of a remnant of the old Whig Party, came together to try to halt the demise of the Union. They attempted to finesse the paramount issue of slavery by sidestepping it. In place of a platform, they proclaimed simply that they would "recognize no political principle other than the Constitution...the Union...and the Enforcement of the Laws." [11] When the supporters of the Constitutional Unionists convened to choose their candidate, the wealthy slave owner John Bell of Tennessee, it became evident that most of the delegates were more than sixty years of age. This was a party of old-timers who were trying to avoid the crucial issue of the day. And this fact was not lost on the other parties, whose spokesmen were happy to point it out.

John Bell's supporters were well aware that their candidate could not win the presidency. What they hoped to do was to deny Lincoln the majority of votes in the Electoral College. That way, the election would be thrown into the House of Representatives, where each state delegation would have a single vote, and a compromise candidate could be chosen.

What made the presidential election truly unique is that there were really two separate electoral battles: one in the North and one in the South. In the North, the race was between Lincoln and Douglas, with some votes bled off by Bell. In the South, the front-runner was Breckinridge, who was challenged by Bell and to some extent by Douglas. Lincoln was a non-factor in the South. Indeed, the climate of opinion was so hostile to him and to the Republicans that his few supporters didn't dare to campaign openly for him.

While Lincoln remained at home, receiving guests, as was the practice for presidential candidates, Stephen Douglas actively campaigned in the North and in the border states. He also made forays into the South, where his prospects were poor and where he faced death threats. He addressed public meetings despite the risk to his own personal safety.

Lincoln was not inactive in Springfield. He met with hundreds, if not thousands, of people who came to see him. He conversed with politicians and political operatives who then returned to their regions energized to campaign for him. Although still feeling remorse following Seward's defeat in Chicago, Thurlow Weed travelled to meet Lincoln not long after his nomination. After conversing with the candidate, Weed left feeling prepared to "go to work with a will." He wrote later that Lincoln displayed "so much good sense, such intuitive knowledge of human nature, and such familiarity with the virtues and infirmities of politicians, that I became impressed very favorably with his fitness for the duties which he was not unlikely to be charged upon to discharge." [12]

In the first weeks of the campaign, Lincoln answered the letters that poured in, with the aid of a single assistant, John Nicolay, a twenty-eight-year-old immigrant from Germany. [13] The candidate spent a considerable amount of time in conversation with correspondents from favourable newspapers, who wrote sketches of Lincoln for their home readers. Lincoln was well aware that he needed to overcome perceptions peddled in the Democratic press that he was an ungainly, scarcely human frontier character who could hardly string together a coherent sentence.

One portrait, of the kind that appears in twenty-first-century celebrity magazines, gushed that "ten thousand inquiries will be made as to the looks, the habits, tastes and other characteristics of Honest Old Abe." In this piece in the *Chicago Press and Tribune*, Lincoln was depicted as "always clean, he is never fashionable; he is careless but not slovenly...In his personal habits, Mr. Lincoln is as simple as a child...his food is plain and nutritious. He never drinks intoxicating liquors of any sort...He is not addicted to tobacco...If Mr. Lincoln is elected President, he will carry but little that is ornamental to the White House." [14]

While Lincoln was characterized as a plain, unpretentious man of the people, his wife, Mary, was depicted as a highly cultured woman: "Whatever of awkwardness may be ascribed to her husband," wrote a scribe from the *New-York Evening Post*, "there is none of it in her. She converses with freedom and grace, and is thoroughly au fait in all the little amenities of society." [15]

What was being polished was an image of Abraham Lincoln that endures to the present day: married to a cultivated woman with refined manners was a man who embodied the rising new West. Lincoln was a man of the prairie who had supported himself through physical labour, all the while learning from the people around him. As the campaign progressed, the idea of a president who was born in a log cabin and had worked as a rail splitter grew ever more reassuring to ordinary Americans, who came to identify with Lincoln.

Lincoln was not the first presidential candidate to present himself as a man of the people, unencumbered with fussy manners. Andrew Jackson of Tennessee, the creator of what historians depict as "Jacksonian Democracy," had pitted Western populism against the power of Eastern finance. Unlike Jackson, a military man whose victory over the British in the battle of New Orleans in 1815 had won him a national reputation, Lincoln had earned his stripes in politics. During the campaign, Southern and border state Unionists warned publicly that if Lincoln won the election, the South would secede. Just prior to Election Day, for instance, Senator John J. Crittenden of Kentucky, a key founder of the Unionist Party who had served twice as United States attorney general, gave a speech denouncing the "profound fanaticism" of Republicans who "think it their duty to destroy… the white man, in order that the black might be free… [The South] has come to the conclusion that in case Lincoln should be elected… she could not submit to the consequences, and therefore, to avoid her fate, will secede from the Union." [16]

The Republicans, including Lincoln, dismissed such warnings as scare talk. The same warnings had been issued during the 1856 election campaign, when Democratic candidate James Buchanan had run for the presidency and won. While Lincoln had little choice but to ignore talk of secession, he appears genuinely to have doubted that if he were to win the election there would be a serious crisis. [17]

To prevent Lincoln from winning in enough states, and thereby amassing a majority of votes in the Electoral College, Democrats, Southern Democrats, and Constitutional Unionists met in smoke-filled rooms to come up with fusion tickets (Electoral College candidates who were anti-Lincoln, and not drawn from a single party) to pool their votes. Fusion deals were successfully sealed in New York and Rhode Island. In New Jersey, seven electors presented themselves on a fusion ticket, and in Pennsylvania, a partial fusion ticket linking Douglas and Breckinridge electors was achieved.

The effort to block Lincoln was for naught, however. On Election Day, November 6, 1860, Lincoln won a majority of the vote in New York, Pennsylvania, and Rhode Island. In New Jersey, three fusion electors prevailed and cast the only Northern electoral votes Douglas received. Douglas also managed to carry Missouri. Bell prevailed in Virginia, Kentucky, and Tennessee. Throughout the rest of the South, Breckinridge won all of the electors and carried 45 percent of the region's popular vote, with Bell coming second with 39 percent.

Lincoln won 40 percent of the total popular vote, including 54 percent of the votes cast in the North. He won 180 electoral votes, well above the 152 needed to carry the Electoral College. North of the 41st parallel, Lincoln won more than 60 percent of the popular vote. This region of the North elected three-quarters of the Republican members of the next House of Representatives and of the new Republican senators.[18]

The true extent of Abraham Lincoln's political genius was not generally perceived before he won the Republican presidential nomination in May 1860, and even before he was elected president in November of that year. Political geniuses who preside over transformational change draw immense fire from their opponents. Lincoln was fortunate to remain under the shadow of William Seward and even that of Stephen Douglas until well into the critical year 1860.

The weight of the North had placed the levers of national power in the hands of the Republican Party. Gone was the balance that had prevailed in the past between the representatives of the North and the South.

Although this was by no means clear to Lincoln at the time, the national project of the North had seized control of the United States government. The response of the South was not long in coming. Within weeks of Lincoln's election, the political leaders of the South concluded that coexistence was no longer tenable.

Chapter 8

The Confederate States of America: Jefferson Davis's Project

T HE DESTRUCTION OF the Democratic Party — the one political force that remained in existence in both the North and South — was the first fateful event in the fateful year of 1860. Next followed the nomination of Abraham Lincoln as the presidential standard-bearer of the Republican Party.

Lincoln's election in November 1860 was followed by four agonizing months before his inauguration. During this critical time, the new standard-bearer of the North could exercise no real power, and the hapless Buchanan administration remained in place.

As Buchanan dithered and Lincoln waited for the transition to end, the leaders of the secessionist movement in the South seized their opportunity. Through their control of Southern state governments and the support they received from the slave-owning class, they were able to proceed to secession, displaying great sure-footedness and skill in the process.

In January 1861, Jefferson Davis resigned from the U.S. Senate. He remained in Washington for a week afterward. For part of that time, he was ill and bedridden. Then he travelled south to Mississippi. At Jackson, Governor John J. Pettus, who had just acquired seventy-five thousand muskets to prepare his state for war, met with the former senator. Unlike many Southern politicians, Davis believed that a long and bloody conflict lay ahead. He told the governor: "The limit of our purchases [of weapons] should be our power to pay. We shall need all and many more than we can get, I fear." [1]

While Davis was meeting with Governor Pettus, delegates from across the seven seceding states in the Deep South — South Carolina, Mississippi, Florida, Alabama, Georgia, Louisiana, and Texas — were preparing to descend on Montgomery, Alabama. Their task was to organize a federal state to govern what they saw as a new nation, the Confederate States of America.

Over a period of six days, beginning on February 4, 1861, the delegates to the Confederate Convention drafted a temporary constitution, proclaimed themselves a provisional Congress for the new state, and elected a provisional president and vice president to constitute their government's executive branch. [2] The rapid construction of the exoskeleton of their new state was impressive, especially considering that the main focus at Montgomery was choosing a provisional president.

There was no shortage of potential candidates. William Lowndes Yancey was a potential candidate. Another Fire-Eater was Robert Rhett of South Carolina. Three aspirants from Georgia — Robert Toombs, Alexander Stephens, and Howell Cobb — were also considered. In the end, the overriding concern was to choose a provisional president who would appeal to the states of the Upper South that had not yet seceded.

On February 9, the delegates unanimously elected Jefferson Davis to the post of provisional president. Alexander Stephens of Georgia was selected as provisional vice president. Davis's experience as a former U.S. secretary of war and senator, and his reputation as a sober and moderate secessionist, made him the ideal choice. It would be up to him to woo the states of the Upper South and to knit together the Confederacy to face a bloody war if that became necessary.

The time for compromise had now passed, Davis told his cheering listeners in Montgomery on February 16. "Our only hope," he declared, "is to make all who oppose us smell Southern powder and feel Southern steel." Two days later, on February 18, 1861, the new chief executive was sworn in. In his inaugural address, he calmly stated that the CSA hoped to live in peace, but if necessary the new state "must prepare to meet the emergency and to maintain, by the final arbitrament of the sword, the position which we have assumed among the nations of the earth." He held out the hand of welcome to other states that "may seek to unite their fortunes with ours under the government which we have instituted."[3]

Having chosen its chief executives, the convention settled down to draft the permanent constitution of the Confederacy. On March 11, a month before the war erupted, the constitution was adopted. For the most part, the Confederate Constitution was copied word for word from the U.S. Constitution. The differences, however, were highly significant. In its preamble, the CSA Constitution invoked "the favor and guidance of Almighty God," while the U.S. Constitution omitted the word *God*. And the Confederates used the words "slave" and "slavery" to depict an institution that their forebears in 1787 Philadelphia had obliquely depicted with the word "persons." The CSA Constitution stated explicitly that slavery would be legal in any new territories acquired by the Confederacy; there would be no agonizing debates about where slavery would be legal. The Constitution also declared the right of slave owners to take their slaves with them anywhere within the boundaries of the new country.

On one point, the authors of the Confederate Constitution took pains not to offend the British or the slave owners of the Upper South, particularly those in Virginia: they barred any participation in the importation of slaves from overseas. The leaders of the Confederacy were deeply anxious to win British recognition of their country; with Britain using the Royal Navy to block other countries from engaging in the slave trade, the Confederates decided to avoid coming to blows on the issue.

They were also well aware of the importance of the slave trade within the South itself. Over the decades prior to the Civil War, the slave economy of the South had altered dramatically. The proportion of slaves in the total population of Virginia — the Old Dominion, which had provided much of the leadership of the South in earlier days — was considerably lower than in the Deep South. The Confederacy's ban on importing slaves from overseas helped reinforce Virginia's economic position as a breeder of slaves. The CSA desperately needed Virginia and the other states of the Upper South to have any chance of survival, and the drafters understood this all too well.

Ten days after the adoption of the Constitution, in a speech delivered in Savannah, Georgia, Alexander Stephens tied the fortunes and the moral rectitude of the Confederacy to the proposition that the white and black races were unequal: "The new Constitution has put at rest forever all the agitating questions relating to our peculiar institutions — African slavery as it exists among us — the proper status of the Negro in our form of civilization. This was the immediate cause of the late rupture and present revolution. Jefferson, in his forecast, had anticipated this, as the 'rock upon which the old Union would split.' He was right. What was conjecture with him is now a realized fact. But whether he fully comprehended the great truth upon which that rock stood and stands, may be doubted. The prevailing ideas entertained by him and most of the leading statesmen at the time of the formation of the old Constitution were that the enslavement of the African was in violation of the laws of nature; that it was wrong in principle, socially, morally and politically. It was an evil they knew not well how to deal with; but the general opinion of the men of that day was, that, somehow or other, in the order of Providence, the institution would be evanescent and pass away."

He concluded: "Those ideas, however, were fundamentally wrong. They rested upon the assumption of the equality of races. This was an error. It was a sandy foundation, and the idea of a Government built upon it — when the 'storm came and the wind blew, it fell.' Our new Government is founded upon exactly the opposite ideas; its foundations are laid, its cornerstone rests, upon the great truth that the Negro is not equal to the white man; that slavery, subordination to the superior race, is his natural and moral condition." [4]

Known ever after as the Cornerstone Speech, Stephens's address put in full view the thinking of the Confederate leadership on the issues of race and slavery when their project was being launched.

MANY APOLOGISTS FOR slavery right up until the secession of the Southern states in 1860–61 had made the claim that the wording in the Declaration of Independence, "all men are created equal," was intended to refer only to the white race and did not imply that blacks were the equal of whites. Illinois Senator Stephen Douglas, although himself a solid Unionist, explicitly made this case. Others put it down to the author of the Declaration, Thomas Jefferson, a Virginian and a major slave owner, getting carried away with his rhetoric. Southerners couldn't very well go as far as to claim that Jefferson was not one of theirs, so they insisted instead that his unfortunate choice of wording was his alone and did not reflect the thinking of the other Founders.

What is significant about Stephens's speech is that the justification for slavery was an unapologetic claim that whites were racially superior to blacks. The claim was rooted in nature, not in Scripture. There was nothing culturally "backward" about this position. The closing decades of the nineteenth century and the first half of the twentieth century was the "golden age" of assertions of white and Aryan racial supremacy. This was the era of social Darwinism and assertions of racialism rooted in nature and biology whose extreme manifestation was realized in Nazism and the Holocaust.

The most expansive year of the Confederacy, the one that inspired the greatest optimism among its citizens, was 1861. During the months when state after state seceded from the Union, there was an eruption of euphoria among the whites of the South. People literally danced in the streets. Even in the first months of the war itself, which began in April, and with the stunning victory of the Confederates at the First Battle of Bull Run in July, the citizens of the new country still hadn't realized that they faced a long and bloody conflict and that every white family in the South was to have loved ones among the fallen.

Alexander Stephens's Cornerstone Speech in Savannah needs to be understood within the context of this period of optimism. Later, especially after the South's defeat, Stephens's speech became a liability, an embarrassment. [5] The speech made it difficult for purveyors of what came to be called the "Lost Cause" to claim that slavery was not central to secession and the Civil War. Southerners tried to argue that it had been Northern abolitionists, black Republicans, and those who advocated for higher tariffs who had provoked the war.

To understand Jefferson Davis's project, it is essential to cut through the nostalgia of the post-war South and the myth of the Lost Cause. In 1861, the CSA's economy was dependent on King Cotton and a capitalist class that made huge profits from the labour of its slaves. For this class, slavery was not the remnant of an earlier age. It was a highly productive system that sought to align the South with the global economics of the time.

The Confederate States of America was a modern mid-nineteenth-century nation state project. This is not the viewpoint of most American historians, whether they lean toward the North or the South in their perspectives. For the most part, American historians have analyzed the Civil War in competing narratives that are exclusively American; they rarely compare the national projects of the South and the North to others, such as Germany, Italy, or Canada, that were conceived in the same era.

Pro-Southern historians, such as the renowned Shelby Foote, have been enmeshed in the hugely influential narrative of the Lost Cause. They dwell on the honour, dignity, and military genius of Robert E. Lee, the refinement of antebellum Southern civilization, and what they allege was the mild and comparatively humane character of slavery in the South. What they do not do is to hone in on the hard-nosed, ruthless, and effective capitalism of King Cotton. Northern historians focus on the emancipation of the slaves and the superiority of the free labour system of the North.

There is a theory of history that holds that societies progress in an orderly fashion through a series of socio-economic stages. According to such a view, free labour is a more advanced social stage, which emerges under modern capitalism and succeeds earlier stages, notably serfdom in feudal and aristocratic societies and slavery in ancient societies. In reality, the socio-economic landscape of the world has been littered with numerous projects, some of which have been hybrid forms involving slavery and capitalism or serfdom and capitalism. The secession of the Southern states and the rapid establishment of the Confederate States of America provide evidence of the existence of a highly developed national project in the South. As was the case in Germany and Italy, intellectuals, writers, and educators threw their energies behind the creation of the Confederacy. They believed that the South needed to achieve intellectual independence from the North if the new nation was to be a success.

Southern writers and publishers strove mightily to create the beginnings of a national literature that would allow the South to stand alongside England, France, Germany, and Italy as a culturally distinct people. The drive to establish the conditions for, and the beginnings of, such a national literature was a sign that Confederate nationalists looked to the future of their new country. Theirs was not a nostalgic, backward-looking mindset.

In marked contrast, coming decades later, Margaret Mitchell's *Gone with the Wind* is the best-known work in this genre. In the imaginations of such authors, dashing cavaliers and refined women inhabited antebellum mansions while happy slaves worked the fields. That South was a post–Civil War creation and bore no resemblance to the South of the great slave owners, who were canny businessmen looking out for their profits and their position in the global marketplace. Southern slave-owning capitalists were not aristocrats presiding over a quasi-feudal realm, however much they may have fancied themselves to be just that.

The Civil War, which could equally be called the Southern War of Independence, was a collision between two nation state projects. The Southern slave-owning class was tied economically to Europe, as well as to mill owners in the American Northeast. Their natural adversary was the expansionist Northern capitalist class. As the Northern capitalists grew in power and wealth more rapidly than the Southern slave owners, the latter reached the conclusion that they needed their own exclusive state to protect their interests. While the slave owners had been notably successful in maintaining their place within the federal order for many decades following the American Revolution, by the 1850s they were losing their quest to maintain balance.

Two issues have blocked the recognition of the Confederacy as an authentic nation state project. The first has to do with the taint of slavery. For many historians, the idea that white Southerners would fight so tenaciously to create an independent slave-owning republic is not easily accepted. There has been a long-established approach among some American historians that holds that the failure of the Confederacy to achieve independence can be attributed to serious internal class divisions and the lack of a clear national identity.

This interpretation contends that the Confederacy was a project too narrowly constructed around the interests of the wealthy slave-owning class, a minority of the population. The large majority of white Southerners were yeoman farmers who did not own slaves, and town dwellers who were mostly working class and poor. The argument goes that as the war dragged on and the South paid the price of high casualties, falling living standards, runaway inflation, deprivation due to destruction at the hands of Yankee invaders, and the effects of the naval blockade, increasingly members of the yeoman class came to see the conflict as a "rich man's war and a poor man's fight."

While this case is not without some factual basis, it fails to account for the immense human sacrifice made by white Southerners of all social classes — men and women and the young — to sustain the struggle for independence. The fact is that in all of American history, no American cohort in any armed struggle ever paid a comparable price in blood to that paid by white Southerners on behalf of the Confederacy. Over the course of the four-year war, 75 percent of white male Southerners of military age ended up in the Confederate military, and one-third were either killed or severely wounded.

Non-slave-owning whites gave their lives on a scale that far exceeded the sacrifice of Northerners and completely dwarfed the sacrifice of Americans during the Revolutionary War, the War of 1812, the Mexican War, the Spanish-American War, the two world wars, Korea, Vietnam, Afghanistan, or Iraq.

The second issue is that it has often been more palatable for historians, with the exception of neo-Confederates from the South, to regard the rebel South in sectional and class terms, rather than to comprehend it as a rejection of so much that is American. Overwhelmingly white Southerners — rich and poor, male and female — hated, with a ferocity that leaps out of the historical record, the Yankee invaders who destroyed their towns and farms and looted their property, food, and livestock. This was no brothers' war.

AS THE SOUTH and North were preparing for war, Southern writers, journalists, and thinkers armed themselves to fight a different kind of war — a war of words against their Northern opponents. In Southern newspapers and periodicals, the case was made that the identity of the South was sharply at odds with that of the North. Southern writers rued the extent to which Southerners read Northern newspapers, periodicals, and books, and they deplored the reliance of Southern educators on textbooks published in the North. The identity of white Southerners was shifting. In the event of a major political crisis, they could cease thinking of themselves as Americans, conceive of themselves as Southerners, and bestow their loyalty on the South as their homeland. While Southern whites continued to proclaim their American patriotism, celebrating the Fourth of July and the birthday of George Washington, their nationalism became increasingly contingent on the acceptance of slave ownership within the United States.

Once the Confederacy was established and the war erupted, the views of writers hardened into justifications for Southern secession. The engagement of journalists and other writers against the enemy took two forms: the first was to denounce the North as the home of destructive "isms";[6] the second was to advance the positive case for the new nation and to trumpet the need for a full-fledged Southern culture, nothing less than a voyage of Southern self-discovery. In his influential journal, *De Bow's Review*, James De Bow affirmed that "adhering to the simple truths of the Gospel, and the faith of their fathers, [Southerners] have not run hither and thither in search of all the absurd and degrading isms which have sprung up in the rank soil of infidelity."[7]

Especially repellent to Confederate thinkers were the beginnings of the women's rights movement in the North. "Our women are all conservative, moral, religious and sensitively modest," wrote George Fitzhugh, the writer and self-appointed racial theorist, "and abhor the North for its infidelity, gross immorality, licentiousness, anarchy, and agrarianism."[8]

Odd though the term may be, "agrarianism" was a particular *bête noire* of Southerners. It was an ism that embodied a host of sins, including "levelling" tendencies in the North, such as equal distribution of land and property; notions of mob rule and class war; as well as the idea of dramatically extending the right to vote.

Most abhorred of all the Northern isms, not surprisingly, was abolitionism.[9] Abolitionists threatened not only the profits and the power of the Southern slaveocracy; they also imperilled the social structure of the South, one in which all whites, no matter how poor, could feel themselves superior to the four million slaves.

Some Southerners were prepared to admit that the system of slavery had its flaws, but even these voices were hostile to the North. "We do not pretend that our system of labour is free from its defects," read an article in the *Southern Episcopalian*, published in Charleston, "that our laws are altogether righteous, or our practice all that a Christian could desire. We believe that there are many and important points in which each and all might be improved; but we are certain that the pretensions of Northern fanatics to regulate our domestic slavery are presumptuous, and their remedies of the most pernicious tendency."[10]

Much more fierce were the views of author and minister Joseph C. Stiles: "The social and religious improvement of the man of colour, his all-in-all, awakens comparatively no interest...in the Northern mind, while his personal freedom, which it were murder to put into his hands to-day, the man of colour must have, though it cost the instant over-throw of the universal social order." [11]

George Bagby, the editor of the *Southern Literary Messenger*, went even further in his denunciation of the North and presented a very wide definition of the term "abolitionist": "An Abolitionist is any man who does not love slavery for its own sake, as a divine institution; who does not worship it as the cornerstone of civil liberty; who does not adore it as the only possible social condition on which a perma-nent Republican government can be erected; and who does not, in his inmost soul, desire to see it extended and perpetuated over the whole earth, as a means of human reformation second in dignity, impor-tance, and sacredness, alone to the Christian religion." [12]

At the moment of its inception and for many months afterward, euphoria swept the states of the Confederacy. Jefferson Davis had many reasons to believe that he was presiding over an ascending state. If the Yankees could be held at bay for a time, so that their will to conquer would collapse, King Cotton would prevail.

Chapter 9

A Very Political War

A T 4:30 A.M. on April 12, 1861, forces under the command of
P. G. T. Beauregard — appointed as a brigadier general in the
Provisional Army of the Confederate States of America six weeks
earlier — shelled Fort Sumter, the island fortress in the harbour
of Charleston, South Carolina. Major Robert Anderson oversaw
the small complement of Union troops at the fort. An attempt to
resupply the fort with food and supplies had failed in January, effectively rendering the Union's position hopeless. Batteries at the fort
returned fire; the siege continued until the afternoon of April 13.
After negotiations, Anderson surrendered Fort Sumter the following afternoon.

No casualties resulted from enemy fire during the siege. However,
the one-hundred-gun salute to the United States flag that followed —
Anderson had insisted on this as a condition for evacuating his
force — cost the lives of two Union soldiers who were mortally
wounded when a spark set off the explosion of a pile of cartridges.
The brief battle, which ended with the gentlemanly surrender of the
Union force, provoked waves of patriotic fervour in the South and
the North.

Thus began what would prove to be the world's most terrible war
during the hundred years between the Battle of Waterloo and the

First World War. Before it was over, between six hundred thousand and eight hundred thousand men would die.*

The Civil War occupies a unique place in the hearts of Americans. American historians have published more works on this war than on any other. It represented an unparalleled existential crisis in the history of the Republic, encompassing a struggle over slavery and race; tales of individual heroism, myths, and legends; and spectacles of slaughter and suffering on a titanic scale. It is not surprising that the focus on the Civil War should be so inward-looking in the United States, whether it comes from a Northern or Southern point of view, whether it turns the lens on battles or on political leaders, or on freedmen and their struggles on or off the battlefield. For Americans, the Civil War is *sui generis*, a cataclysm unto itself.

Historians and popular writers have endlessly regaled the American public with stories of the battles and military strategies of the two sides in the Civil War. This book does not aspire to making a contribution to that literature.

Rather, the critical point is to show how the progress of the war was immensely important, not only in the obvious way that victories and defeats determined whether the North or the South held particular cities or pieces of territory. The way the war was going from month to month and year to year had huge implications for the politics of the struggle. All wars are political, but this was a very political war. The fates of two nation state projects were on the line. Politics shaped military strategy to an unusual extent, forcing both sides to adopt military approaches that might have been deemed inappropriate were not the Confederate and Union regimes so subject to the pressures of changing public moods.

The assault on Fort Sumter generated a wave of patriotic outrage in the North. In this volatile moment, Lincoln called up seventy-five thousand soldiers to be supplied by the Northern states. At stake were

---

* The very wide range of estimates is accounted for by the fact that so many Union and Confederate soldiers died hours, days, or even weeks after being struck. Medical care, on both sides, was rudimentary during this deadly conflict.

the states of the Upper South — North Carolina, Arkansas, Tennessee, and Virginia — and the border states of Missouri, Kentucky, Maryland, and Delaware, where slavery existed. Winning over these states to the Confederacy or keeping them in the Union was at the centre of the struggle in the first months of the war.

The Confederate government needed the Upper South, especially the critical state of Virginia, to have any hope of winning Southern secession. For Davis's newly minted regime, it was crucial to make the CSA appear both viable and moderate. From the outset, the Confederates set out to convince Britain and France that the CSA merited diplomatic recognition, which would help secure the adhesion of the states of the Upper South. Well aware that these two powers and other European states were deeply hostile to the institution of slavery, the CSA tried to soft-pedal this issue and instead focused on the new state's control of its territory and the right of its people to determine their own future. Inclusion of the Upper South would bolster this moderate image.

The Lincoln administration was also under immense pressure to underemphasize the issue of slavery at the beginning of the conflict, to keep the Upper South and the border states securely in the Union. In his first inaugural address, Lincoln set out to reassure slave owners, quoting countless speeches he had made over the past year: "I have no purpose, directly or indirectly, to interfere with the institution of slavery in the states where it exists. I believe I have no lawful right to do so, and I have no inclination to do so."

On the volatile issue of the return of fugitive slaves to their owners, he made a solemn pledge, quoting Article IV, Section 2 of the U.S. Constitution: "No Person held to Service or Labour in one State, under the Laws thereof, escaping into another, shall, in Consequence of any Law or Regulation therein, be discharged from such Service or Labour, but shall be delivered up on Claim of the Party to whom such Service or Labour may be due."

"It is scarcely questioned," Lincoln underlined, "that this provision was intended by those who made it, for the reclaiming of what we call fugitive slaves; and the intention of the law-giver is the law. All members of Congress swear their support to the whole Constitution — to this provision as much as to any other. To the proposition, then, that slaves whose cases come within the terms of this clause 'shall be delivered up,' their oaths are unanimous."[1]

The fall of Fort Sumter and the Lincoln administration's response of calling up seventy-five thousand troops pushed four states in the Upper South — North Carolina, Arkansas, Tennessee, and the most important of all, Virginia — to join the Confederacy. Virginia's border ran along the Potomac River, with Washington, D.C. on the northern bank. George Washington was buried in Virginia soil, a stone's throw away from the U.S. Capitol and the White House. Seceding Southerners still claimed Washington as one of their heroes, a man who had set an example in leading a people to political independence. The Confederate government defiantly moved its capital to Richmond, Virginia, so that during the bloody war, the two capitals were separated by a mere one hundred miles.

While enthusiasm for the Southern cause varied from region to region across the vast territory of the Confederacy — the western counties of Virginia and eastern Tennessee were stubbornly pro-Union — white Southerners proved themselves overwhelmingly loyal to their new state and were prepared to fight and die for it. Morale rose and fell over the course of the war. Despite the problem of desertion, which became acute at times, white Southern men of military age demonstrated a remarkable willingness to commit themselves to the Confederate forces, even though they were often poorly armed, clothed, and fed in comparison to their Northern counterparts.

The loss of these four states shifted the Lincoln administration's focus to Missouri, Kentucky, Maryland, and Delaware. With slaves constituting only 2 percent of its population — concentrated in its southern section — Delaware was for all practical purposes a free state. While Missouri was quickly secured for the most part by Union forces, Confederate raiders waged a vicious guerrilla war there. In the years following the war, the hatreds provoked by the conflict continued.

Bandits such as Jesse and Frank James, who were former Confederate raiders, visited mayhem on parts of Missouri, winning folkloric status in the process.

The state government of Kentucky, the birthplace of Abraham Lincoln, sought neutrality at the beginning of the conflict. Anxious to hold on to the state, with its important strategic location between the Ohio River and Tennessee, Lincoln at first chose not to challenge Kentucky's neutral stance. Later, when fierce fighting broke out in Kentucky, the North would control most of the state, while the South held on to a southern corner for a time.

Maryland was absolutely critical to the success of the North. Whoever controlled Maryland and its principal city, Baltimore, would control land access to Washington, D.C. But Maryland was a slave state that harboured a large pro-Southern population. With rebel Virginia just across the Potomac from the national capital, and Maryland surrounding it on three sides, the District of Columbia was vulnerable to Confederate attacks during much of the war.

Early in the war, the Lincoln administration arrested a number of prominent Marylanders who were thought to be sympathetic to the South. The arrests provoked complaints about violations of civil rights and even a court order to free those arrested. The administration ignored the court order. It also leaned heavily on the Maryland state government to prevent it from holding a convention on secession. The Lincoln administration decided it must hold on to Maryland and suppress secessionists in Baltimore, whatever the constitutionality of their actions.

Once the Confederacy expanded north and moved its capital to Richmond, and the Union staked its sometimes uneasy claim to the border states, the two sides grappled with their strategies for prosecuting the war. For both Confederates and Unionists, political and military strategies would remain works in progress throughout the war.

WHILE THE NORTH had enormous advantages should the war be of long duration, the South had critical short-term advantages. To win the war, as Southern leaders repeatedly insisted, all that would be needed was for Southern forces to block Northern campaigns to conquer the seceding states. If the North would simply allow the South to depart, peace would be restored. The North, on the other hand, had to conquer a people implacably hostile to it. The military conquest of a territory is profoundly more arduous than its defence. From start to finish, that was the North's burden.

The Lincoln administration grappled with immense military and internal political challenges in its prosecution of the war. Pure military logic dictated that the North should pursue a war of attrition — a lengthy war in which economic pressure, and not just major battles, would play a huge role against the Confederacy. Winfield Scott, the aging top U.S. general whose career had begun during the War of 1812 — by 1861 he was so obese that he could no longer sit on his horse — unveiled just such a strategy, known as the Anaconda Plan.

The plan was to mount a naval blockade to deprive the Confederates of commerce with Europe, including the ability to import armaments. Then the North would push down the Mississippi River, cutting the western secessionist states of Texas and Arkansas off from the Confederate heartland in the east. Seizing New Orleans, the largest city in the Confederacy, the North would further deprive the CSA of commerce with the outside world.

Anaconda's genius was that it would bring to bear the full weight of the superior manpower and industrial capacity of the North. The problem was that of time and political will. Could the people of the Northern states endure the agonies of a long war and the cost of the immense mobilization of men and *matériel*? From the start, Northern politicians, including Abraham Lincoln and the members of his cabinet, as well as military commanders, felt intense pressure to deal head-on with the Confederacy by invading Virginia and marching on Richmond.

By the 1860s, military technology and tactics were advantageous to defensive warfare. The deployment on a major scale of rifle muskets with a much longer effective range than older smoothbore muskets played to the side that fought defensively. And the increasing resort to field fortifications hugely benefited the defence. [2]

Southern political and military leaders, principally Jefferson Davis and Robert E. Lee, agreed that the Confederate strategy should be defensive in nature whenever possible. Choosing to fight a defensive war, however, proved immensely difficult for Southern strategists. The Southern leadership was intent on holding on to as much territory as possible. The bold move to select Richmond as the capital of the new state meant the Confederacy was bound to fight to retain this critical city, which was within striking distance of the federal armies ranged along the Potomac. The fight to save Richmond dominated much of the war. Over the course of the conflict, Confederate forces suffered tens of thousands of casualties vying for control of northern Virginia.

In recent decades, military historians have often been critical of Southern strategy, insisting that the South would have been more effective had the leadership decided on guerrilla tactics rather than waging a conventional war. Undoubtedly influenced by the outcome of the Vietnam War, in which the Viet Cong fought a brilliant guerrilla campaign that wore down the Americans and their South Vietnamese allies, some historians have suggested that such an approach would have kept Confederate casualties to a much more manageable level and would have drained Northerners of the political will to prevail.

A guerrilla war would have required the South to allow much of its territory and many of its key cities, including Richmond, to be occupied by the enemy. Instead of fighting large set-piece battles, the South would have had to divide its forces into smaller, mobile units to strike the occupiers with punishing raids, occasional major battles, and constant harassment of the North's lines of communications. The Northern armies would have been reduced to occupying cities whose inhabitants detested them, while defending their lengthy rail lines from swift guerrilla attacks.

While acknowledging Lee's tactical prowess as a commander,

historian Alan T. Nolan has made the case that the general's approach was too wasteful of lives, and that a more truly defensive strategy that included well-timed counteroffensives "would have kept its armies in the fields long enough to wear down the North's willingness to carry on the war…Lee's offensive grand strategy, because of the losses entailed, led inexorably, to use his words, to the 'natural military consequences of the enemy's numerical superiority,' that is, surrender.'" [3]

As a hypothetical case, the argument is plausible. However, it is far from convincing. To keep the slave labour system functioning and to sustain the essential support of white Southerners, the option of guerrilla war or of a defensive conventional war was seriously problematic. As historian Gary W. Gallagher has argued: "The overwhelming imperative of maintaining white control in a slave-based society rendered both an overwhelmingly defensive strategy and a guerrilla resistance unacceptable…the evidence supports the conclusion that a more narrowly defensive strategy was not well suited to Confederate expectations and would not necessarily have saved significant manpower or prolonged the war. Lee's aggressive strategy and tactics yielded immeasurably more good than evil for the southern nation. Guerrilla warfare was not a viable option within the Confederate context." [4]

Southerners had a model from which they drew inspiration: the American Revolutionary War. During that war, the British occupied New York, Philadelphia, and other major centres. George Washington's army remained intact, shifting from location to location in the heart of the Thirteen Colonies, ready to punish the British when the opportunity arose, but never committing themselves to defending a particular city if it would have allowed the British to range their superior forces against them. Over the course of the lengthy war, Washington's forces, at times aided strategically by the French on the sea, wore down their superior enemy until the old imperial power was forced to give up the struggle.

From the first, the Southern leadership rejected such an approach, although it was taken up with considerable effect on the fringes of the war, notably along the Missouri-Kansas frontier, where Captain William Quantrill's raiders subjected Northern forces to bloody hit-and-run attacks.*

There were important reasons why the CSA leadership decided on a conventional war and rejected the idea of following in the footsteps of George Washington. The Confederacy housed two deeply divided populations: whites, who had considerable influence on the CSA leadership; and four million black slaves, whose potential behaviour during the war terrified not merely the leadership in Richmond, but the whole of the white population in the South.

Southern whites demanded protection from invasion, and their morale soared whenever the Confederate military won a major battle. But throughout the war, and particularly during its latter stages, desertion was a major problem. Paradoxically, while white Southern men signed up in very large numbers and gave their lives on an unprecedented scale, they were also prone to desert in large numbers, sometimes to return home for a time and then come back to rejoin their regiments.

Those potent facts weighed very heavily on the mind of Jefferson Davis, a military man who would have preferred to lead Confederates in battle rather than to serve as CSA president. Unless white men were willing to join the Confederate military on a scale vastly beyond the

---

* William Quantrill, the son of an Ohio high school teacher, moved to Kansas in 1857 at the age of nineteen. For a time, he taught school, but he gave that up to become a brigand and cattle rustler. At the outset of the Civil War, Quantrill took the side of the slave owners and the South. After serving briefly in a Confederate army unit, Quantrill went on his own to Missouri, where he recruited a small band, originally of ten men. In early 1862, more men, including Jesse and Frank James, joined the outfit. Over the next two years, Quantrill's band, sometimes numbering as many as 450 men, engaged in guerrilla-style warfare, launching raids into neighbouring Kansas against Union forces and pro-Union civilians. In August 1863, he led a large-scale attack on the town of Lawrence, Kansas, which had a population of two thousand people. The guerrillas hunted down men and boys as young as fourteen, killing about 175 of them, often in executions carried out in front of the families of the victims. When they were through, Quantrill and his men rode out of town, leaving most of Lawrence's buildings in flames.[5]

size of George Washington's tiny army during the revolution, the new state simply would not survive.

Then there was the reality of four million slaves. Without slave labour to drive agricultural production, the South was doomed. For white men to fight, slaves had to remain at work, in many cases overseen by white women whose husbands were at the front. But from the earliest days of the conflict, the evidence was clear — given the chance, slaves sought freedom behind Union lines.

The Confederate leaders were also focused on gaining European recognition. If the unsavoury optic of legal slavery was compounded by engagement in guerrilla warfare, the chances of European recognition would be severely diminished. Political leaders in Victorian Britain and in Napoleon III's France placed considerable weight on formalities. They were well aware that the British and French people were appalled by slavery, and as the leaders of imperial powers, they had a strong distaste for guerrilla warriors, who were more often than not the kind of opponents they might encounter in their own empires.

Also running strongly against the notion that the Confederates should fight a defensive conventional war was the effect of commanders' tactics upon military reputations. At the beginning of the conflict, after Lee turned down the invitation to command the Northern forces, he was the most popular Southern general, and much was expected of him. That soon changed when he was dispatched to the front in the mountainous contours of western Virginia, where the terrain and the society were wholly different from those of tidewater Virginia.

The inhabitants of the western counties, where slavery was rare, resented the aristocratic airs of the great landowners farther east. They believed, not without reason, that the state was run on behalf of the privileged — which did not include them. In these counties, most inhabitants opposed secession and supported the Union.

In the summer of 1861, short of men and equipment and saddled with subpar subordinate commanders, Lee oversaw a losing campaign. As a consequence, he was nicknamed "Granny" and was accused by newspaper editors of being too theoretical and impractical as a military leader. In October 1861, Lee's less-than-stellar efforts in western Virginia came to an end. While he had managed to safeguard a vital rail connection from the federals, he had not been able to drive Union forces from their well-entrenched positions. As a consequence, pro-Union morale rose in the region.

The Confederates' weak performance in the western counties of Virginia had very real political consequences. In June 1861, pro-Union delegates convened in Wheeling, in the northwest corner of Virginia, and set themselves up as the "restored government" of the state, labelling the Confederate legislature illegal. They took this step so they could tear western Virginia out of the Old Dominion. To create the new state, its advocates had to cope with Article IV, Section 3, of the U.S. Constitution, which stipulates that a new state can only be established out of the territory of an existing state with the consent of that state's legislature. Obviously, the Confederate legislature of Virginia would provide no such consent. Having claimed to be the restored government of the state, the convention in Wheeling appointed a new roster of state officials, with Francis Pierpont as governor. Enjoying the recognition of the Lincoln administration, this legislature elected two senators, who were duly seated in the U.S. Senate, as were three congressmen from the region.

On October 24, 1861, voters in the thirty-five counties of Virginia west of the Shenandoah Valley and north of the Kanawha River, containing 25 percent of the Old Dominion's white population, elected delegates to a constitutional convention to promote secession from Virginia. Originally conceived as the state of Kanawha, the new state was admitted to the Union as West Virginia, the only new U.S. state created during the war. The socio-economic logic was clear enough: West Virginia had much more in common with Ohio and Pennsylvania than with the rest of the state from which it had seceded.

On his return from western Virginia in October 1861, Robert E. Lee had lost his standing with most of the leadership and opinion makers of the Confederacy. He had, however, retained the confidence of the man who mattered most: President Jefferson Davis. And for Lee, that would make all the difference. Lee's reputation was at a low ebb when the fortunes of war presented him with the opportunity of a lifetime: the command of the Army of Northern Virginia.

ON MAY 31 and June 1, 1862, during the Battle of Seven Pines, General Joseph E. Johnston, commander of the Army of Northern Virginia, was struck by a bullet in the right shoulder and then by a shell fragment in the chest. The wounded general was temporarily replaced by Major General G. W. Smith. But the new commander seemed uncertain about the course he should follow and made a poor impression on Jefferson Davis and Robert E. Lee, who was serving as the president's military advisor. Davis then appointed Lee to command the South's most important army, and it was Davis's most consequential appointment during the war.

Influential critics had been publicly assailing Lee's reputation. Edward A. Pollard, a principal editor of the capital's most important paper, the *Richmond Examiner* — after the war his multivolume *Southern History of the War* chronicled the course of the conflict — said of Lee: "A general who had never fought a battle and whose extreme tenderness of blood induced him to depend exclusively upon the resources of strategy, to essay the achievement of victories without the cost of life." He charged that Lee had blindly lost an "opportunity of a decisive battle in western Virginia" when he made no attempt to pursue the enemy who had so skillfully eluded him. [6]

North Carolina diarist Catherine Edmonston wrote: "I do not much like him, he 'falls back' too much. He failed in Western Va. owing, it was said, to the weather, had done little in the eyes of outsiders in SC. His nickname last summer was 'old-stick-in-the-mud.' There is mud enough now in and about our lives, but pray God he may not fulfill the whole of his name." [7]

These words were written just a few weeks before Lee's great counter-offensive drove the federal forces back from within a few miles of Richmond — they had been so close that Union troops could hear the church bells in the city — and Lee's ascension to mythical status in the South commenced.

In the crucial Seven Days Battles, which began on June 25, 1862, Lee launched a series of attacks against the numerically superior federal forces commanded by General George B. McClellan. In a landscape of hills, woods, rivers, and narrow roads, Confederate tactics — including those of Lee's subordinate Thomas J. (Stonewall) Jackson — were often poorly co-ordinated. Despite these problems, Lee's forces managed to throw the federals off balance.

The battles were also conducted in the minds of the two leading adversaries: Lee and McClellan. Lee was highly fortunate to have McClellan — the dashing young self-styled Napoleon of the North — as his foe. McClellan's great defect was that he habitually overestimated the field strength of the enemy and then blamed the War Department in Washington for failing to provide him with sufficient troops. During the Seven Days Battles, McClellan informed Washington that he was facing two hundred thousand rebels when the real number was about ninety thousand. McClellan failed to follow up on opportunities that presented themselves during battle and decided in the end that he had no choice but to carry out a strategic retreat.

When McClellan ordered a continuation of the Union retreat at the end of the battles, Philip Kearney — one of McClellan's brigadiers and a man who had lost an arm during the Mexican War — shouted that he was disgusted by the retreat. He favoured instead a counter-attack: "Such an order [to retreat] can only be prompted by cowardice or treason...We ought instead of retreating to follow up the enemy and take Richmond."

Lee, who had won a major strategic victory, was well aware that his forces were not in a position to drive forward. The Confederates had paid a very high price: twenty thousand men were wounded or killed, twice the number of casualties suffered by the federals. [8]

The political consequences of Lee's victory were enormous for both the South and the North, which sheds considerable light on the question of the appropriate strategies for the two sides. In the South, morale soared. In practice, if not in theory, Lee's strategic offensive, with its accompanying high casualties, advanced the Confederate cause. And that was the Southern dilemma for much of the war—victories won at the price of staggering casualties.

Lee's victories not only won over the skeptics; they recast him as the South's greatest hero. He "amazed and confounded his detractors," declared the *Richmond Whig*, "by the brilliancy of his genius...his energy and daring. He has established his reputation forever, and has entitled himself to the lasting gratitude of his country." [9]

Edward Pollard, who had earlier been harshly critical, later noted that Lee's triumphs had so transformed his reputation that he "might have had the Dictatorship of the entire Southern Confederacy, if he had but crooked his finger to accept it." [10]

Lee's success drew on the important fact that a very large number of white Southerners had military experience, or at least proficiency in the use of firearms. For the most part, the top Southern commanders were graduates of West Point. During the early battles, the Southern commanders and rank-and-file cavalry and infantry showed more mettle than the armies and commanders of the North.

In the early going, the South made use of its offensive prowess during the critical time when the North was mobilizing its forces. Stonewall Jackson achieved his most glorious victory at the Battle of Chancellorsville on May 2, 1863. Along with Lee, Jackson conceived an audacious plan to counter a Union offensive in Virginia led by General Joseph Hooker. The Confederates divided their army, which was numerically inferior to the Union forces, and Jackson led thirty thousand men around the enemy, striking him unawares on his extreme right flank. The surprise attack panicked the Union troops, who were quickly routed. This brilliant tactical success was Jackson's last. He decided to continue the battle at night, under a full moon. Nighttime battles were extremely rare during the Civil War. Scouting Union lines, Jackson was mortally wounded by Confederate pickets who mistook him and his men for the enemy. It was the war's greatest single loss due to friendly fire.

The deeply religious Thomas Jonathan "Stonewall" Jackson bolstered the morale of Southerners. In death, he served them as the personification of unshakeable determination. It is true that Chancellorsville was a defensive triumph, but it was sufficiently daring to underline that the Confederates were much more motivated by heroic victories than by military caution.*

THE NORTH'S STRATEGIC problems were the inverse of those of the Confederacy. While the South had to wear down its adversary's determination to continue the fight, the North had to conquer the South. And it had to do so in the context of open political struggles over strategy and, indeed, over the goals of the Union's war. Both the South and the North were democracies, or at least partial democracies, at war. In the South, white males had the vote, while white women, and of course slaves, did not. In the North, white males had the vote and again women did not. The Davis administration in Richmond and the Lincoln administration in Washington had to pay attention to public debates, political opponents, newspaper publishers, and voters.

While political parties did not emerge in the South, political factions — groupings supportive of, or critical of, the Davis administration's approach — certainly did. In the North, the Lincoln administration, which had the backing of the Republican Party, had to cope with the Northern Democrats, a party whose leading members had a wide variety of views on the war, its goals, and the extent to which it should be prosecuted. While some fully supported the Union war effort, others backed it to a limited extent. The Lincoln

---

* It was not the case, as Gallagher reminds us, that all Southern commanders adopted an offensive strategy in their military campaigns. The South did indeed include generals in its ranks, notably Joseph E. Johnston, who did hew to the defensive in their campaigns. The consequence of these campaigns was a string of defeats, and bitter recriminations against Johnston from Southern observers.

administration had to face a series of gubernatorial and legislative elections in states that remained loyal to the Union. More importantly, members of the administration knew they would be vitally affected by the midterm congressional elections in 1862 and that the presidential election of 1864 could be decisive in determining the outcome of the war.

As the war dragged on, still others were determined to make peace with the South, which would almost certainly require recognizing the Confederacy as an independent state. Northerners prepared to make peace on Richmond's terms were known as Copperheads.

For Lincoln, the Copperheads posed a deadly threat that could undermine the effectiveness of Union morale and political will. Clement Vallandigham, who was a Democratic congressman from Ohio at the start of the war, waged a highly effective campaign against the Lincoln administration and the Union war effort, sometimes using Canada as a base for his activities. During the first days of the conflict, he made incendiary speeches in opposition to the war in the House of Representatives. By 1862, after his electoral defeat — when new congressional boundaries were drawn, his own district was removed from Congress — Vallandigham spoke at large peace rallies in the North.

Following an inflammatory address at Mount Vernon, Ohio, on May 1, 1863, Vallandigham returned to his home in Dayton. Union General Ambrose Burnside dispatched soldiers to arrest him. The Ohio Copperhead managed to fire two pistol shots before soldiers burst through a doorway and dragged him off to jail. [11]

Vallandigham was charged with treason — a charge that carried a potential death sentence. But Abraham Lincoln decided that there was another way to get rid of him that posed fewer political risks and skirted the constitutional issues raised by the incarceration of an opponent. Under a flag of truce, Vallandigham was taken to the front and released across the line to Confederate General Braxton Bragg. [12]

Vallandigham was not through politicking yet. Outfitted with papers and with his transportation arranged by General Bragg, the

Copperhead travelled to Wilmington, North Carolina, where he boarded a ship to Bermuda that successfully eluded the Northern naval blockade. From there, Vallandigham took a transport vessel to Halifax, where he was welcomed by a crowd that erupted in cheers for Jefferson Davis and the Confederacy.[13]

When he arrived in Quebec City, Vallandigham was received as a distinguished guest. The exclusive Stadacona Club hosted a dinner in his honour. There, Vallandigham met members of the Canadian business and political elite, including John A. Macdonald.[14]

In mid-July 1863, Vallandigham reached the border town of Niagara Falls, an ideal point from which to carry on his political intrigues. He took a two-room suite at Clifton House — a hotel that already buzzed with pro-Confederate goings-on — where he met with Copperheads from across the border. From this base in Canada, he mounted a campaign as the Democratic Party's candidate for governor of Ohio. On October 13, 1863, President Lincoln waited anxiously to receive the results of the mid-term elections. When he learned that Vallandigham had been beaten by the Republican candidate by more than one hundred thousand votes, he fired off a telegram proclaiming: "Glory to God in the highest. Ohio has saved the Nation."[15]

The Ohio Copperhead was defeated, but the efforts of these opponents of the administration were by no means at an end. The fact that so prominent an adversary of the Northern war effort could conduct his activities openly and brazenly from a perch in Canada added to the tension that already existed between the United States government and the Canadian and British governments.

IN ADDITION TO the Copperheads, the Lincoln administration contended with a variety of political challenges throughout the war. Morale rose and sank over the course of the four-year-long struggle. The shifts in mood were directly related to what was happening on the fields of battle. While the North's enormous manpower advantage, superior production of weapons, and more advanced railroad network gave the Union the edge, the critical question was whether Northern morale would hold up until victory was achieved. This is where Lee's stunning victories, though costly to the South, were of immense importance. Lee's triumphs, and the misery of Northerners who watched a string of hapless Union commanders come and go, depressed willingness to continue the war. Periods of low morale in the North enhanced the potential of opposition politicians to challenge the Lincoln administration and perhaps even to limit the president to one term in the White House.

In the spring of 1862, there had been considerable hope that General McClellan could capture Richmond and end the war. McClellan's defeat in the Seven Days Battles plunged the North into doubt. A Northern Republican wrote in his diary: "Things look disastrous... I find it hard to maintain my lively faith in the triumph of the nation and the law." [16]

In a message to state governors, Lincoln's dark feelings were clear even as he sought to rally the country: "I expect to maintain this contest until successful, or till I die, or am conquered... or Congress or the country forsakes me." [17]

The president's immediate response to the bitter setback was to conclude that the Union needed to recruit more troops — reversing the halt in recruitment that had occurred in April — while there was still reason to hope for a great Northern victory crowned by the capture of Richmond.

To camouflage the appearance of panic in the wake of Lee's victory, Secretary of State William Seward journeyed to New York to meet with Northern governors, who acceded to his request to issue a public address to the president, an address that had in fact been written by Seward himself. In the call for new volunteers, which was backdated to June 28, 1861, so that it would appear to predate McClellan's retreat, the governors urged men to enlist, to take up the cause to "follow up" on the "recent successes of the Federal arms" so as to "speedily crush the rebellion."

Lincoln, of course, welcomed the appeal of the governors, which had in fact come from his own administration. On July 2, he called for the recruitment of three hundred thousand new volunteers to prosecute the war "to a speedy and satisfactory conclusion."[18] Governors put out the patriotic call to men to enlist to fight for "the old flag, for our country, Union and Liberty."[19]

Though the Lincoln administration continued to resort to the formulation that the purpose of the Union war was to "crush the rebellion," the conflict became much more than that. To achieve victory, the administration was forced down the path of total war. The struggle became all-encompassing, extending beyond the battlefields to every element of American life. To preserve the Union, Lincoln was compelled to conceive of a new Union. Eventually that came to mean a Union without slavery — a Union in which freed slaves and free blacks would be recruited to fight the enemy.

Chapter 10

Lincoln's Project: Total War

A BRAHAM LINCOLN, THE rail splitter who was born in a log cabin, had seen much of life by the time he became a circuit lawyer in Illinois. He was a natural populist, with tales to tell for every occasion, stories to entertain any audience. He could talk easily with farm labourers, workers, senators, and soldiers. Likewise, he could entertain women and children with fables that conveyed a moral point or were simply eye-opening and amusing. What set him apart from other voluble populists was his enormous capacity to place himself in the shoes of others. In his sad and thoughtful fashion, he was humane. He almost never used his acute wit to denigrate another.

During his political career, which included the most consequential presidency in the history of the United States, Lincoln regularly shouldered the blame when things went wrong. He sheltered subordinates from storms of criticism when they suffered defeats on the field of battle or came up short in their political calculations. He was that rare leader who wanted those around him to be as strong as possible and to be confident in their own capacities. He never offered them up as scapegoats to protect his own reputation.

In the face of an unprecedented national crisis, what were Lincoln's goals? What was the essence of his project for the United States, and how did it evolve over the course of the war? For the past century and a half, the opinions of historians have evolved and continue to change on these fundamental questions. Was the preservation of the Union Lincoln's overriding national objective? Or, especially as the war dragged on, did the crucial goal of his project become the emancipation of the slaves?

In recent decades, the emphasis among historians has shifted from the first objective, the preservation of the Union, to the second one, the emancipation of the slaves, and also to the role played by former slaves in their own emancipation. Not a small reason for this change of perspective has been the increasing difficulty people have had comprehending the preservation of the Union as a sufficient motivation for the immense human cost of the Civil War.

Was all this pain endured solely to keep the Union whole, to prevent a group of states from seceding? To the contemporary mind, this single goal seems vastly insufficient to justify such a toll. Was Lincoln's project basically an orgiastic expression of American nationalism? There must have been much more to it than that, recent analysts have insisted.

An enormous positive consequence of the war, of course, was the abolition of slavery and a first great attempt to assure that the freedmen acquired the full rights of citizenship, including the right to vote. To that end, the Thirteenth, Fourteenth, and Fifteenth Amendments to the Constitution were all passed into law. From the proposition that emancipation was the key goal, the thinking has diverged in two directions: first, that the war was fought to free the slaves; and second, that the slaves fought for and won their own emancipation.

That Lincoln's paramount goal during the first year of the war was the preservation of the Union is indisputable. In his first inaugural address, on March 4, 1861, Lincoln reached out the hand of reconciliation to the seceding states. He reiterated that it had never been, and was not now, his goal to abolish slavery in the states where it then existed. Moreover, he undertook in his address to enforce the Fugitive Slave Act.

If the North had managed to win the war by the late spring of 1862, the preservation of the Union could have been accomplished without the emancipation of the slaves. In the spring of that year, U.S. armies won a string of victories in the western theatre and farther south. In addition, they managed to advance to the doorstep of Richmond, the Confederate capital. As a consequence, the North captured Nashville and Memphis and the vital port of New Orleans, at the mouth of the Mississippi.

Had Richmond fallen, precipitating the collapse of the CSA, the North would have prevailed with slavery still intact in most of the South. By the late spring of 1862, no black military units had yet been raised and deployed.

A Union victory without emancipation was not unlikely before the Army of Northern Virginia, led by Robert E. Lee, changed the course of the war with victories in the Seven Days Battle in late June and early July 1862, which drove the federal forces away from Richmond. This Confederate success was followed up by Lee's victory at Second Bull Run in late August.

Confederate victories raised Southern morale, but they also pushed the Lincoln administration in the direction of total war: a political and military strategy that targeted not only Southern armies but the socio-economic system of the South.

From the moment serious fighting began on July 21, 1861, with the Confederate victories at the First and Second Battles of Bull Run, Northern politicians, the press, and society elites found themselves engaged in debates about how to press the Union war effort forward.

One man who quickly understood that early Union defeats could actually invigorate the anti-slavery cause was Republican Senator Charles Sumner, a fervent opponent of slavery. In a letter to abolitionist leader Wendell Phillips following the Union disaster at First Bull Run, Sumner wrote: "Be tranquil. Never did I feel so sure of the result. The battle and defeat have done much for the slave...I told the President that our defeat was the worst event and the best event in our history; the worst, as it was the greatest present calamity and shame — the best, as it made the extinction of Slavery inevitable."[1]

During the summer of 1862, Lincoln promulgated the idea of gradual and compensated emancipation of the slaves in the border states and the emigration or colonization of freed slaves to Liberia or South America. On July 12, the president delivered a speech in Washington to congressional representatives of the border states, urging them to consider such a course. "I do not speak of emancipation *at once*," he declared, "but of a decision at once to emancipate *gradually*. Room in South America for colonization can be obtained cheaply, and in abundance; and when numbers shall be large enough to be company and encouragement for one another, the freed people will not be so reluctant to go." [2]

A month later on August 14, 1862, Lincoln addressed a Committee of Colored Men at the White House on the subject of black colonization to foreign countries: "You and we are different races," he began with brutal frankness. "We have between us a broader difference than exists between almost any other two races…this physical difference is a great disadvantage to us both, as I think your race suffer very greatly, many of them by living among us, while ours suffer from your presence. In a word we suffer on each side. If this is admitted, it affords a reason at least why we should be separated."

Pointing to the war and "our white men cutting one another's throats," Lincoln said that "without the institution of Slavery and the colored race as a basis, the war could not have an existence."

"It is better for us both [blacks and whites], therefore, to be separated.

"For the sake of your race," he appealed to the free black men in his audience, "you should sacrifice something of your present comfort" to consider the prospect of emigrating to Central America.

"The practical thing I want to ascertain is whether I can get a number of able-bodied men, with their wives and children, who are willing to go." [3]

Lincoln's idea was that if free black men could be persuaded to emigrate, slaves could be emancipated on the understanding that they would leave the United States.

Setbacks for the Union on the field of battle drove Northern decision makers to widen the scope of the war to target the rebels and their
personal property, including their slaves. The U.S. Congress passed
the First Confiscation Act immediately following First Bull Run. Even
though President Lincoln had opposed the bill because he feared its
potential consequences in the border states, he signed it into law on
August 6, 1861. The law authorized the federal government to confiscate the property of persons engaged in the rebellion. Not only did
this allow the government to seize the weapons of citizens who had
exhibited rebellious intentions; it also gave the Union army the right
to confiscate any and all personal property from such citizens. Fugitive
slaves who were captured were to become the contraband of the Union
Army and were not to be returned to their owners.

When wars initially go badly for powerful states, their leaders are
forced to mobilize for a more costly conflict, both in terms of the lives
they are prepared to sacrifice and the treasure they are prepared to
expend. To do this requires a deepening of the war aims of the state
and, where possible, the embracing of new constituencies needed to
prosecute the war. Through that arduous process, emancipation was
put on the agenda.

The South's four million slaves were key to its productive apparatus. Offering freedom to slaves would not only disrupt production; it
would also open a second front behind the battle lines. The prospect
of emancipation threatened the South with slave uprisings, the flight
of slaves seeking liberation under the protection of Union armies, and
ultimately the possibility of freed slaves wearing the Union uniform.

In July 1862, with the Army of the Potomac reeling from Lee's
blows, Congress passed two acts: the Second Confiscation Act, which
aimed to free slaves in the South, and the Militia Act, which allowed
the U.S. Army and Navy to recruit "persons of African descent" to
provide service "for which they may be found competent." [4] The first
act directly targeted the South's socio-economic engine and thus the
ability of the Confederates to prosecute the war. The second determined that African Americans, including former slaves, could join the

United States Army and fight for the liberation of their own people.

Further, on July 13, 1862, following Lee's victory at the Seven Days Battles, which had pushed prospects for a Northern victory to an indefinite future, Lincoln privately told Seward and Gideon Welles, his secretary of the navy, that he planned to issue an emancipation proclamation. In his diary, Welles quoted the president as saying that the idea had "occupied his mind and thoughts day and night" for the past few weeks. Lincoln had concluded that emancipation was "a military necessity, absolutely essential to the preservation of the Union. We must free the slaves or be ourselves subdued. The slaves were undeniably an element of strength to those who had their service, and we must decide whether that element should be with us or against us." Lincoln explained to his colleagues that as commander-in-chief, he had the authority to order that enemy slaves be seized in the same way that he could order that the enemy's railroads should be destroyed.

On the constitutionality of such an order, Lincoln reasoned that "the rebels...could not at the same time throw off the Constitution and invoke its aid. Having made war on the Government, they were subject to the incidents and calamities of war." He concluded: "The Administration must set an example, and strike at the heart of the rebellion." [5]

Nine days later, the president informed the members of his cabinet that he planned to issue an emancipation proclamation. When Lincoln asked for their thoughts, only Postmaster General Montgomery Blair dissented, arguing that the proclamation would result in the Republicans losing control of Congress in the fall elections. Seward intervened, suggesting that the public announcement be delayed until the Union forces had won a major military victory, so that the proclamation would be associated with strength, not weakness. Lincoln acceded to this proposal. [6]

Even though he was committing himself and his cabinet to the historic decision to issue the Emancipation Proclamation, Lincoln continued to prevaricate publicly on the issue of slavery. On August 22, 1862, a month after informing his cabinet that he had decided to issue the proclamation, Lincoln penned an often-quoted letter to Horace Greeley, the editor of the *New York Tribune*, in which he declared: "If there be those who would not save the Union, unless they could at the same time *save* slavery, I do not agree with them. If there be those who would not save the Union unless they could at the same time *destroy* slavery, I do not agree with them. My paramount object in this struggle *is* to save the Union, and is *not* either to save or to destroy slavery. If I could save the Union without freeing *any* slave I would do it, and if I could save it by freeing *all* the slaves I would do it; and if I could save it by freeing some and leaving others alone I would also do that. What I do about slavery, and the coloured race, I do because it helps to save the Union."[7]

In this letter, Lincoln's fundamental priority — saving the Union — is sparklingly clear. As he explained in the letter, with some pedantry, the issue of slavery was a related but subsidiary question. The president let it be known that his stand could change, possibly dramatically, entirely in relation to how freeing the slaves would affect the essential goal of saving the Union.

Although a minority of white Northerners who were genuine abolitionists pursued emancipation as an ethical crusade, the majority came to support it as a war-winning measure — as a way to break the power of the treasonous slaveocracy. Abraham Lincoln's own pursuit of emancipation, and ultimately the abolition of slavery, evolved along similar lines. Although his personal distaste for slavery had existed for decades, emancipation and the recruitment of black soldiers were weapons to be wielded in a time of war.

The Emancipation Proclamation, an executive order, which came into effect on January 1, 1863, was explicitly drafted as a war measure: "Now, therefore, I, Abraham Lincoln, President of the United States, by virtue of the power in me vested as Commander-In-Chief of the Army and Navy of the United States in time of actual armed rebellion against the authority and government of the United States, and as a fit and necessary war measure for suppressing said rebellion, do, on the 1st day of January, A.D. 1863, and in accordance with my purpose so to do, publicly proclaimed for the full period of one hundred days from the first day above mentioned, order and designate as the States and parts of States wherein the people thereof, respectively, are this day in rebellion against the United States the following."

Then followed the list of states and parts of states to which the proclamation would apply.

"And by virtue of the power and for the purpose aforesaid, I do order and declare that all persons held as slaves within said designated States and parts of States are, and henceforth shall be, free; and that the Executive Government of the United States, including the military and naval authorities thereof, will recognize and maintain the freedom of said persons," the proclamation continued. [8]

The proclamation freed not one slave on the day it was issued. It left slavery in place in the border states, Maryland and Kentucky, that had remained loyal to the Union. It did not free the slaves in those parts of the South that were then occupied by Union troops. What it did do was to proclaim that from that day forth, as the Union army advanced into rebel territory, the slaves in such territories would be permanently emancipated.

This was not the first time in American history that slaves had been emancipated during a war. The British launched the first such liberation during the American Revolution. In November 1775, the Earl of Dunmore, governor of Virginia, issued what came to be called Dunmore's Proclamation. For months prior to the proclamation, the governor invited slaves to join his forces. In the proclamation, he declared martial law and asserted that the Patriots were traitors to the Crown. He made a direct offer to slaves: that those who were willing and able to take up arms and to fight on the side of the British would win their freedom.

Virginia's Patriot leaders, many of whom were slave-owning landowners, responded with outrage. In December 1775, the Virginia Convention responded to Dunmore's Proclamation with a warning that runaway slaves who returned to their owners within ten days would be pardoned. Those who failed to return, the Virginians warned, would be severely punished. They faced flogging, being sent to work in the lead mines, or execution. In 1776, Patrick Henry, the Virginia Patriot most famous for his defiant utterance "Give me liberty or give me death," fulminated against Dunmore's Proclamation at the Fifth Virginia Convention. He complained that the Governor was "encouraging insurrection among our slaves, many of whom are now actually in arms against us." The threat of emancipation revealed that the King was "a tyrant instead of the protector of his people." The freeing of slaves by the British drove Henry to favour "an immediate, clear and full Declaration of Independency."*

Dunmore's Proclamation failed to emancipate many slaves. When he left Virginia in 1776, he took about three hundred former slaves with him to freedom.

In 1779, a second attempt to free slaves was more successful. British General Sir Henry Clinton issued the Philipsburg Proclamation. It stated that slaves owned by Patriots were free whether or not they joined the British military. As many as 100,000 slaves — there were about 650,000 in the colonies at the time — tried to escape from their masters to join the British during the Revolutionary War. Most were ultimately unsuccessful; many were returned to their masters when British forces were defeated. At the end of the war, the British transported three thousand former slaves to freedom in Nova Scotia. They constituted the founding cohort of the significant black population of the colony.

During the War of 1812, the British once again offered the promise of freedom to American slaves. In April 1814, Vice Admiral Sir Alexander Cochrane issued an official offer to slaves in the battle at Chesapeake Bay: those who wished to leave the United States with their families would be welcomed on board British ships. They would have the choice of enlisting in the British forces or of being transported to British territory as free settlers. About four thousand slaves

---

* The War of Independence, which began in April 1775, had been underway for over a year when the Patriots issued the Declaration of Independence in July 1776.

gained their freedom this way. At the end of the war, the Americans demanded the return of the former slaves. When the British refused, the United States government insisted on a clause in the Treaty of Ghent of December 1814, providing monetary compensation for the loss of the slaves. The British did pay compensation to the United States for the slaves who had been lost by American masters.

During these wars, the British used emancipation for much the same purpose that Lincoln did — as a war measure intended to undermine the operations of the enemy. Freeing the slaves disrupted the enemy's economic activities. More than that, it visited fear on white slave owners and their communities, where slave rebellions were dreaded above all else.

By 1863, THE Lincoln administration freed slaves not only to rob the South of a crucial labour force but also to recruit fit young black males into the Union military.

In his attitude to African Americans and his political stance on slavery, Lincoln's positions evolved, not least as circumstances changed. In 1858, during his unsuccessful senate race against Stephen Douglas, he declared the following to an audience in Charleston in southern Illinois:

"I will say then that I am not nor ever have been in favour of bringing about in any way the social and political equality of the white and black races — that I am not nor ever have been in favour of making voters or jurors of negroes nor of qualifying them to hold office, nor of intermarrying with white people; and I will say, in addition to this, that there is a physical difference between the white and black races which I believe will for ever forbid the two races living together on terms of political and social equality." [9]

When Lincoln uttered these words, he was well aware that he was speaking in southern Illinois, a region of the state with close ties to the South — a region whose population included many people sympathetic to the institution of slavery. Given the declaratory nature of his remarks, it is more reasonable to conclude that he was setting forth basic propositions that would appeal to the majority of Republican voters in Illinois and across much of the North: he expressed opposition to slavery while holding to the view that the white race was superior to the black race.

Lincoln was America's poet president. In our age, when many of the celebrated phrases spoken by presidents have been conceived by speech writers, it is hard to imagine a leader who devoted endless hours to crafting the words he was to deliver. Lincoln did consult colleagues about important addresses or declarations. But his words were his own.

Among the most famous words he spoke were those in the Gettysburg Address, delivered on the afternoon of November 19, 1863, at the enormous soldiers' cemetery on the edge of the terrain on which the momentous battle had been fought four months earlier. Americans generally believe that the meaning of the Address, which for generations has been memorized by schoolchildren, is a settled question. But interpreting the speech is central to identifying Lincoln's fundamental goals during the Civil War.

The thesis of Garry Wills's Pulitzer Prize–winning book, *Lincoln at Gettysburg: The Words That Remade America*, is that Lincoln's 272-word address changed the meaning of the American Republic, with consequences for the whole world. Wills claims that in the Gettysburg Address Lincoln "performed one of the most daring open-air sleights-of-hand ever witnessed. Everyone in that vast throng of thousands was having his or her intellectual pocket picked... They walked off... into a different America. Lincoln had revolutionized the Revolution, giving people a new past to live with that would change their future indefinitely."[10] Wills is asserting that Lincoln was transforming the meaning of the Declaration of Independence, imbuing it with a much broader sense of freedom that would certainly extend to include the ending of slavery.

The passages at the beginning and the end most explicitly set out the values on which the Republic was established and must be based in the future: "Four score and seven years ago, our fathers brought forth on this continent a new nation, conceived in liberty and dedicated to the proposition that all men are created equal. Now we are engaged in a great civil war, testing whether that nation, or any nation so conceived and so dedicated, can long endure…

"…we here highly resolve that these dead shall not have died in vain — that this nation, under God, shall have a new birth of freedom — and that government of the people, by the people, for the people shall not perish from the earth." [11]

Lincoln's address is a brief and deeply powerful prose poem. To me, it seems logical that a straightforward reading of it — and Lincoln was consistently straightforward in his speeches and writings — leads to the inescapable conclusion that Lincoln was advancing his essential cause, the saving of the Union, in the celebrated oration.

At Gettysburg, Lincoln did not mention the emancipation of the slaves as a goal of the federal government. He did include two passages that can be interpreted as references to emancipation. The first is the phrase "all men are created equal." That famous phrase, however, is taken directly from the Declaration of Independence, written in 1776, principally by Thomas Jefferson, a slave owner who did not favour the abolition of slavery. In that moment of Enlightenment fervour when the American Revolution erupted, philosophers, publicists, and political leaders were perfectly capable of proclaiming that all men were created equal while actually believing that this proposition was subject to a long list of qualifiers. The phrase could be used by men who simultaneously believed that blacks were inferior to whites, that women were inferior to men, that the poor were inferior to the rich, or that the well educated ought to wield more political power than the poorly educated. Such a proposition could be uttered by those who held, as Hobbes did, that what made humans equal in a fundamental sense was their common mortality. Thinkers or leaders who came at the question this way could support the utility of slavery or could advocate allowing only property owners to elect legislative bodies.

The second phrase in Lincoln's address that is pregnant with possibility is "a new birth of freedom." Does this point to a broadening of the whole concept of freedom to embrace the emancipation of the slaves, or does it refer to the words that immediately follow: "and that government of the people, by the people, for the people shall not perish from the earth"? That concluding phrase echoes the earlier passage in which Lincoln proposes that the Civil War was a test of whether any nation "conceived in liberty... can long endure."

What Wills interprets as transformative is more reasonably interpreted as a powerful reiteration of Lincoln's belief in the necessity of preserving the Union. The administration's evolving position on slavery continued to be driven by what it regarded as the more fundamental question of the survival of the Union.

The burden of the address was to point back to the work of the founders, which passed down to subsequent generations a basic proposition and a test. The new nation was "conceived in liberty," and the Civil War was testing whether "any nation so conceived and so dedicated can long endure." There is no evidence to support the view that Lincoln had a hidden agenda at Gettysburg, or as Wills colourfully puts it, "that everyone in that vast throng of thousands was having his or her intellectual pocket picked." [12]

If then, the Address is about saving the Union — and that was the essence of Lincoln's project — what did the project entail? Why was the project so compelling that it commanded the political backing of Northerners throughout the war? Why were tens of thousands of men willing to die for the cause, forcing the Southern states back into the Union through the means of raw conquest?

Saving the Union was a cause that appealed to white Northerners because it promised the average citizen the prospect of upward mobility through hard work. In the minds of Northerners, the United States promised liberty and democracy to the whole of the population in a way that no other country did. In 1860, the cause of democracy in Europe was not a bright one. In France and Prussia, autocratic monarchies had succeeded in stamping out the liberal promise of 1848. While the cause of gradualist democratic advance was making headway in Britain and in the British North American colonies, Americans thought little about Canada and continued, not without reason, to regard Britain as an imperial power in which the upper classes wielded most of the power.

To white Northerners, the key constituency of Abraham Lincoln and the Republican Party, the president's pledge in the Gettysburg Address of "a new birth of freedom" that would be the sustained by a "government of the people, by the people, for the people" held out the promise that America would not be allowed to become the preserve of powerful vested interests. It would remain a democracy in the image of the Founders.

What did white Americans, who constituted the overwhelming majority of people in the free states, have in mind when they rallied around the cause of the preservation of the Union? In the mid-nineteenth century in the North, the term "Union" was very closely tied to the concept of nation. The Union was not a bloodless, formal entity conceived merely around the details of the U.S. Constitution and the division of powers between the federal government and the states. The Union conjured up an image of the American nation, which was already understood by people in exceptionalist terms. The Union was home to the liberty conceived by the Founders and paid for in blood during the Revolutionary War. No other nation on earth embodied liberty for the people as a whole in the way the United States did.

What made the Union special came to the fore when Americans contrasted their condition with that of Europeans. In the decade following the failed revolutions of 1848, Americans firmly believed that their land was the true repository of liberty, in contrast to Europe, whose people lived under the rule of kings, emperors, aristocrats, and entrenched upper classes. Only in America could a poor man, often an immigrant, lift the members of his family from the labouring class to the propertied class through sheer hard work. This was the version of the American Dream that drew Northerners together to form the Republican Party in the 1850s.

It was a populist, capitalist, free-labour dream, a vision of personal betterment for the deserving, and it stood in sharp contrast to the perceived values of the slave-owning South. To those who valued the Union, the South was the land of the hated and feared slaveocracy. Most Northerners saw the slave owners as a class of powerful and greedy men who were intent on spreading slavery in the new territories of the United States. The mass of the Northern population believed that the interests of the slave owners were inimical to their own.

Attitudes to slaves and to blacks in general were mixed among Northern whites. By today's standards, they were profoundly racist. It was generally assumed in the North as well as the South that whites were innately superior to blacks. While an increasing and important minority of Northern whites espoused abolitionist views and were deeply opposed to slavery, the majority were ambivalent. They had sharply negative opinions of slave owners, but they also feared a huge influx of freedmen in the event of the abolition of slavery. White Northerners were divided on whether blacks should have the right to vote or even be allowed to migrate to their states.

Certainly Lincoln did not exclude emancipation of the slaves from the vision he offered at Gettysburg. But the essence of his appeal was to white Northerners and their hopes for the Union once the great rebellion (as the Civil War was often called by contemporaries) was crushed.

THE DESCENT OF the conflict into the horrors of total war proceeded as the North set out to destroy the economy and the social order of the South. Not only would the North raise ever larger armies; it would also seek to shatter the capacity of the foe to supply and sustain its own armies. This meant, among other things, tearing up Southern rail lines.

Total war reached its zenith with Union General William Tecumseh Sherman's notorious March to the Sea, following his capture of Atlanta on September 2, 1864.

The whole of Sherman's army had been brought forward to Atlanta, then set out in mid-November across Georgia to its objective, the port of Savannah. Once out of Atlanta, Sherman's troops lived off the land, sending out foraging parties to confiscate vegetables, poultry, livestock, and other supplies from local farmers and towns. The forty-mile-wide stretch of territory devastated by Sherman remained scarred for decades after. While the immediate objective was to keep his army supplied, the broader goal was to destroy the capacity of the region to contribute to the Confederacy war effort. Beyond that, the terrible assault was intended to teach white Georgians the lesson that resistance to the Union would provoke far more than battles and casualties at the front. It would strike people in their homes and would destroy their means of sustenance.

In his post-war memoirs, Sherman candidly set out his army's approach as all of its units reached Atlanta to prepare for the March to the Sea: "On the 12th of November the railroad and telegraph communications with the rear were broken, and the army stood detached from all friends, dependent on its own resources and supplies. No time was to be lost; all the detachments were ordered to march rapidly for Atlanta, breaking up the railroad *en route*, and generally to so damage the country as to make it untenable to the enemy." [13]

Once the South seceded, the North set out to quash Southern independence. A new nation, a new Union, a new capitalism was on the rise.

Chapter 11

The War Threatens Canada

FROM THE MOMENT the Confederate War of Independence was launched, the Canadian position on the continent was gravely imperilled. Canadians and the people of the Atlantic provinces were divided in their sentiments about the Civil War. Most of them opposed slavery. George Brown, a strong and principled opponent of slavery, used the pages of the *Globe* to drive home the message that slavery was an evil institution. A few other major newspapers took the pro-North stance of the *Globe*: the *Herald* and *Le Pays* in Montreal, the *Morning Freeman* in Saint John. On the other hand, newspapers in Canada, New Brunswick, Prince Edward Island, and Newfoundland tended to be sympathetic to the South.[1]

Most of the daily and triweekly newspapers, whether they leaned Tory or Reform, took the Southern side. The *Montreal Gazette* and the *Toronto Leader*, for instance, welcomed the news that Lee's Army of Northern Virginia had invaded the North in June 1863. When subsequent news arrived that the North had achieved a great victory at Gettysburg, Southern-leaning newspapers in British North America downplayed the significance. The *British Colonist* in Halifax, for example, stated: "The Yankee press has such a monstrous talent for lying that it would be gross folly to believe, in all its minutiae, anything which it publishes."[2]

British North Americans could not help observing a people much like themselves in the Southerners — a small population fighting to free themselves from the North with its burgeoning population and economic might. British North Americans feared that the rising American military power could threaten Canada. The enormous Union army could be mobilized should tensions between the United States and Britain explode. And even if the United States did not seize the most populous British possessions to the north, American forces could readily occupy the lands northwest of Canada that now constitute the prairie provinces and the northern territories — land that would be essential if a great British North American state was to be created.

Canadians were acutely aware that any war between the United States and Britain would immediately trigger a U.S. invasion of Canada. For years, the politicians in Canada and the Atlantic provinces had batted around the subject of British North American union. Colonial leaders knew that a political union would certainly open the way for the construction of the strategically vital rail link between Canada and the Maritimes.

Canadian political leaders also comprehended the most important reality of all, which was that the British were anxious to avoid a land war against the United States and were increasingly determined to leave the defence of British North America to the colonial regimes themselves. When war erupted in the United States, the members of the government of the Province of Canada, headed by Étienne Taché (Canada East) and John A. Macdonald (Canada West), realized that Canada was virtually defenceless. Fewer than five thousand British regulars — the heart of the defence force — were stationed in the province.

In September 1861, when the Civil War had been underway for five months, the Taché-Macdonald ministry addressed a minute on the state of Canada's defences to Viscount Monck, who held the positions of governor of Canada and governor general of British North America. The minute pointed out that no modern artillery was available in the province and that the supply of rifles numbered a meagre fifteen thousand; it asked for Britain to supply Canada with one hundred thousand rifles and additional artillery batteries and further expressed the hope that the provincial legislature would "organize an efficient force to be drawn from the ranks of the sedentary militia." Britain responded speedily by sending thirty thousand rifles, artillery ammunition, greatcoats, and blankets. [3]

The government of Jefferson Davis understood that Confederate national interest would best be served by widening the war to draw Britain and France into the struggle. If the Lincoln administration could be provoked into war with Britain, Canada would be the battleground, as it had been during the War of 1812.

The Confederates had several cards to play to lure the British and French onto their side. The first one was King Cotton. The political, military, and business leaders of the South were convinced that the French and the British would recognize their new state because they needed its cotton.

One of the Lincoln administration's first acts was to mount a blockade of Southern ports, which struck a direct blow at cotton exports. The measure was purportedly to collect tariffs on imported goods. This was no small issue at a time when the main revenue sources of the U.S. federal government were tariffs and excise duties. The blockade and the tariff were as much about the solvency of the federal government as they were about winning the war. Since the CSA had established its own, low tariff regime, failure to blockade Southern ports would have enticed much American trade to pass through the South and end up sold into the Northern states without the higher U.S. tariff being collected.

The tariff had been a major irritant between North and South on the eve of the Civil War. The industries of the North, whose most important political voice was the Republican Party, demanded high tariffs to protect them against British imports. Industrialists also wanted tariff revenues to help fund the construction of railroads, among them a transcontinental railroad. The knitting together of the American national market was the highest item on the North's economic agenda.

Beyond their concerns about a shortage of cotton, political leaders in Britain and France could see solid advantages in recognizing the South. Limiting the rising power of the United States was an attraction in itself. European imperial powers had a tangible interest in forming partnerships with weak states that presided over the large-scale production of primary products. Many in the English upper classes found the South and its hierarchical society appealing compared to the brash, capitalist, democratizing North, which was already becoming a threat to the world's leading economic power. But British society had deep class divisions of its own, and most British workingmen, who enjoyed rising influence through their trade unions and their votes, sided fiercely with the democratic North and the anti-slavery struggle. To a remarkable extent, this was true of workers in the Midlands whose jobs depended on cotton manufacturing.

The Lincoln administration had to insist to European powers that the war was an American affair. U.S. Secretary of State William Seward initially assured foreign diplomats that the rebellion would be short-lived and that the seceding states would soon return to the Union. British and French diplomats waved this argument aside and told Seward and other American political leaders that the CSA could not be so summarily dismissed.

On May 13, 1861, the British government issued the Queen's Proclamation of Neutrality, declaring that "whereas hostilities have unhappily commenced between the Government of the United States of America and certain States styling themselves the Confederate States of America...we, being at peace with the Government of the United States, have declared our Royal determination to maintain a strict neutrality in the contest between the said contending parties."[4]

That same evening, Charles Francis Adams, Lincoln's new ambassador to Great Britain, arrived in London. Five days later, in an interview with British Foreign Minister Lord John Russell, Adams stated: "I must be permitted to express the great regret I had felt on learning the decision to issue the Queen's Proclamation, which at once raised the insurgents to the level of a belligerent State...I then alluded more especially to the brief report of the Lord Chancellor's speech on Thursday last, in which he had characterized the rebellious portion of my country as a belligerent State and the war that was going on as *justum bellum*." [5]

While Adams put the case to Lord Russell in diplomatic language, in Washington the mood was far from diplomatic. The Lincoln administration was outraged that any foreign state, especially Great Britain, would treat the war as anything other than an internal rebellion. For Seward and Lincoln, Britain's recognition of the Confederacy as a belligerent was a highly negative development. Not only was belligerent status a step along the way to the recognition of the CSA as a sovereign state; it also meant that the Confederacy could immediately borrow funds from England and that its ships could visit British ports. [6]

Then, out of the blue, came a sudden crisis in Anglo-American relations that put Canada in potential danger.

ON NOVEMBER 8, 1861, the USS *San Jacinto*, under the command of Captain Charles Wilkes, intercepted the RMS *Trent*, a British mail vessel en route to Southampton, England, from Havana, Cuba. Following a symbolic show of force, the Americans seized James Mason and John Slidell, two Confederate diplomats travelling to Britain and France to press the case for the recognition of the CSA. Mason's and Slidell's secretaries were captured as well, while their families were left on board the *Trent* to continue their voyage to England.

Captain Wilkes was playing with fire. An American warship interfering with the free passage of a British vessel on the high seas was an affront that the world's leading sea power could not ignore. The tone the British would adopt in the affair was evident from the moment the Americans boarded the *Trent* and prepared to take the Confederates prisoner. Richard Williams, the Royal Navy commander of the *Trent*, addressed these words to Lieutenant D. MacNeill Fairfax, who led the American boarding party: "In this ship I am the representative of Her Britannic Majesty's Government, and in the name of that Government,

I protest against this illegal act — this violation of international law — this act of piracy, which you would not dare to attempt on a ship capable of resisting such aggression."[7]

The *San Jacinto* made for the United States with the prisoners on board. Once ashore, Mason and Slidell and their two secretaries were imprisoned in Fort Warren, near Boston. Across the North, people rejoiced and morale soared. For patriotic Americans, who had watched eleven states secede from the Union and then endured the indignity of the stunning defeat of Union forces at Bull Run, the capture of Mason and Slidell was brilliant news. Gideon Welles, the secretary of the navy, wrote to Captain Wilkes to approve the course of action he had taken. In his report, Secretary Welles noted: "The prompt and decisive action of Captain Wilkes on this occasion merited and received the emphatic approval of the Department."[8]

The U.S. House of Representatives adopted a resolution that expressed the thanks of Congress to the captain of the *San Jacinto* "for his brave, adroit and patriotic conduct." The House also passed resolutions requesting that President Lincoln order that Mason and Slidell be incarcerated as convicted felons, in retaliation for the similar treatment meted out to two U.S. colonels who had been captured at Bull Run and imprisoned for the jailing of the crew of a Confederate privateer for piracy.[9] Northerners were more than happy to savour the poke in the eye Captain Wilkes had delivered to John Bull.

Britons and British North Americans were infuriated by the capture of the *Trent*, a vessel that had been sailing between two neutral ports. Declaring that the United States had violated international law — the same rights of innocent passage on the high seas the U.S. had espoused in the past — the British demanded the release of the four Confederates and a public apology from Washington.

When the news reached England, delegates from Canada, New Brunswick, and Nova Scotia were in London, lobbying the imperial authorities to provide aid for the construction of a railway between the Maritimes and Canada.[10] While British North Americans favoured the railway as an economic link, they also regarded it as strategically important for their defence in the event that an incident like the *Trent* Affair could touch off hostilities with the United States.

The capture of Mason and Slidell created a major political problem for the Lincoln administration. With Wilkes seen as a hero and the British portrayed as imperial bullies, it would be very difficult for Washington to give way to British demands without a major loss of face. Initially, the prevailing opinion in the Lincoln cabinet, including that of the president himself, was that the U.S. could not hand over the captured Confederates to the British.

Secretary of State William Seward was against the view that the U.S. needed to hang tough even if it meant war with Britain. From the beginning, he set out to avoid war. On November 30, 1861, Seward wrote to Charles Francis Adams that Captain Wilkes had not been acting on the instructions of the United States government when he had halted the *Trent* and seized Mason and Slidell. The note set out the ground upon which Seward planned as graceful a diplomatic retreat as possible.

Meanwhile, the British stated their case in no uncertain terms. In two dispatches instructing Lord Lyons, the British minister (ambassador) at Washington, on how to proceed, Foreign Minister Lord Russell set out the British demands. In the first dispatch, he began by stating that the British were prepared to believe that the "naval officer who committed this aggression was not acting in compliance with any authority from his Government." From there, the foreign minister grew much tougher, insisting that the "Government of the United States must be fully aware that the British Government could not allow such an affront to the national honour to pass without full reparation."

Then came the demands: "Her Majesty's Government therefore trusts that when this matter shall have been brought under consideration of the Government of the United States, that Government will, of its own accord, offer to the British Government such redress as alone would satisfy the British nation, namely, the liberation of the four gentlemen, and their delivery to your Lordship [Lord Lyons] in order that they may again be placed under British protection, and a suitable apology for the aggression which has been committed."

In the second dispatch, issued the same day, Lord Russell instructed Lord Lyons that "should Mr. Seward ask for delay in order that this grave and painful matter should be deliberately considered, you will consent to a delay not exceeding seven days. If, at the end of that time, no answer is given, or if any other answer is given except that of a compliance with the demands of Her Majesty's Government, your Lordship is instructed to leave Washington with all the members of your Legation, bring with you the archives of the Legation, and to repair immediately to London." [11]

With its strict timetable, the second dispatch could only be construed as an ultimatum. Well aware that he had placed the Lincoln administration in a very awkward position, Lord Russell added a private letter to Lord Lyons, the purpose of which was to soften how the British demands were received in Washington: "The despatches which were agreed to at the Cabinet yesterday, and which I have signed this morning," he wrote, "impose upon you a disagreeable task. My wish would be that at your first interview with Mr. Seward you should not take my despatch with you, but should prepare him for it, and ask him to settle with the president and the cabinet what course they would propose.

"The next time you should bring my despatch and read it to him fully.

"If he asks what will be the consequence of his refusing compliance, I think you should say that you wish to leave him and the President quite free to take their own course, and that you desire to abstain from anything like menace." [12]

Heightening the pressure on the Lincoln administration, the government of France agreed with the British and its minister in Washington. France's ambassador, Henri Mercier, told the U.S. government that unless it backed down, Washington faced the near-certainty of war with Britain and even the strong possibility of war with France. [13]

North of the border, members of the Canadian government,

notably John A. Macdonald, took stock of the situation. Especially alarming was the recent positioning of American troops along the border. As the Anglo-American crisis neared its climax, it happened that Canadian Finance Minister Alexander Galt was in Washington, dealing with commercial matters connected with the Reciprocity Treaty.[14]

Galt met with Seward and later wrote to his wife that the secretary of state "did not impress me much; seemed fidgety, and out of temper." Galt dined twice with Lord Lyons, the British ambassador to Washington, who was formally in charge of Canada's relations with the United States. He attended Lincoln's State of the Union address, and on December 4, he met with Lincoln at the White House.[15] Galt told the president that the positioning of troops along the border with Canada and the inflammatory tone of many Northern newspapers was alarming to Canadians. Lincoln replied reassuringly that the Mason-Slidell affair "would be gotten along with." On the matter of the positioning of U.S. troops at the border, Lincoln remarked: "We must say something to satisfy the people."[16]

Galt wrote in a memo to Macdonald: "The impression left on my mind is that the President has…no hostile designs upon Canada…I cannot, however, divest my mind of the impression that the policy of the Govt is so subject to popular impulses that no assurance can be, or ought to be relied upon under present circumstances…the idea is universal that Canada is most desirable for the north, which its unprepared state would render it an easy prize."[17]

By late December 1861, Seward had made up his mind that the prisoners would have to be surrendered; Lincoln, on the other hand, had not yet reached that conclusion. On December 21, the president shared his view with Senator Orville Browning: "The question was easily susceptible of a pacific solution, if England was at all disposed to act justly with us, and suggested that it was a proper case for arbitration."[18]

As secretary of state, Seward was more in tune with the fury in Britain and the French support for the British side in the *Trent* Affair than were the president and other cabinet members. As the crisis developed, Seward had been receiving numerous letters and reports from Europe. One letter that he took very seriously was from his long-time political ally Thurlow Weed, who had been acting as Seward's unofficial representative in Europe. Weed was in Paris when the news of the seizure reached the French capital. He reported to Seward: "If the taking of the rebels from under the protection of the British flag was intended, and is avowed, and maintained, it means war." [19]

On December 24, Seward also was shown two letters received by Senator Charles Sumner, written by two British members of Parliament: John Bright and Richard Cobden. Bright and Cobden were pro-Union liberal free traders. Cobden's message was that the Lincoln administration should release the prisoners and should work to develop a more adequate system of belligerent rights. Bright wrote: "At all hazards you must not let this matter grow to a war with England. Even if you are right and we are wrong, war will be fatal to your idea of restoring the Union." [20]

At 10:00 a.m. on Christmas day, the Lincoln cabinet met at the White House to consider the crisis. Seward laid before the members of the cabinet the British foreign secretary's position and then read them the draft of his own response. He made the case that the captain of the *Trent* knew that the Confederate diplomats were enemies of the United States and that they were carrying enemy dispatches with them to Europe. Seward asserted that Mason and Slidell and the documents they held were "contraband of war" and that Captain Wilkes was on solid legal ground when he searched the British ship.

Then Seward said that he believed Captain Wilkes had erred by permitting the British ship to resume its voyage to England. The proper course would have been to take the *Trent* into port, where the issues could have been settled in court. Failing to do that, Wilkes had violated not only international law but American norms, which Jefferson, Madison, and Monroe had upheld in the past.

Seward's draft argued: "If I decide this case in favour of my own government, I must disavow its most cherished principles, and reverse and forever abandon its essential policy." The secretary of state concluded that the four Confederate prisoners ought to be "cheerfully liberated" to Lord Lyons, who should indicate "a time and place for receiving them." [21]

Lincoln and the members of his cabinet also heard letters from Adams, the American minister in London, and from Weed and Senator Sumner, who was present at the meeting at the request of the president. Sumner read aloud the letters from Cobden and Bright. Seward set his case out with clarity and force, but he was met, as Attorney General Edward Bates recorded in his diary, with "great reluctance on the part of some members of the cabinet — and even the President himself." As Bates recollected, Lincoln expressed concern about "the displeasure of our own people — lest they should accuse us of timidly truckling to the power of England." [22]

As always, Lincoln had his finger on the pulse of Northern opinion. The day after the cabinet meeting, John Parker Hale, a Republican senator from New Hampshire, declared publicly: "Not a man can be found, who is in favour of this surrender [of Mason and Slidell and their secretaries], for it would humiliate us in the eyes of the world, irritate our own people, and subject us to their indignant scorn." [23]

Seward had shown the president and his cabinet colleagues how they could back off while retaining a fair degree of self-respect, but it was a tough sell. Bates wrote in his diary: "To go to war with England now is to abandon all hope of suppressing the rebellion." He added that the British "would sweep us from all southern waters and our trade would be utterly ruined and our treasury bankrupt." While conceding that he believed that Seward was correct on the law, cabinet colleague Salmon Chase's notes revealed that he had not yet decided on his own position. He wrote that giving in to the British would be "gall and wormwood."

"Rather than consent to the liberation of these men, I would sacrifice everything I possess," Chase concluded. [24]

During this crucial discussion, William Seward's son Frederick arrived at the White House, bringing with him a letter from French Foreign Minister Édouard Thouvenel, which members of the cabinet were anxious to see. In the letter, Thouvenel agreed with Seward that by failing to bring the *Trent* into port, Wilkes had indeed violated international law. The foreign minister wrote that if belligerent powers could halt neutral ships at sea and carry off what they regarded as contraband, "we would be right back to the vexatious practices of earlier days against which no other power has protested more strongly than the United States."

France took the view that the United States should release the Confederate prisoners. "One would search in vain," Thouvenel reasoned, "to find in what interest, for what objective, [the United States] would risk provoking a rupture with Great Britain by a contrary attitude."[25] Thouvenel's letter allowed Seward to argue cogently that any thought of asking France to mediate the dispute made little sense, since the French government had already come down on Britain's side on the legal issues.

Before the meeting broke up, the best evidence shows that Lincoln had a conversation with Seward in which he said that he was working on an alternative draft reply to the British, laying out the case for continuing to hold the prisoners and proposing the matter be arbitrated. If this version of events is correct, it meant that Lincoln and some of his cabinet colleagues still needed to be convinced of the necessity of releasing the Confederates.[26]

At the decisive meeting on December 26, however, the president and the members of the cabinet "all yielded to the necessity, and unanimously concurred in Mr. Seward's letter to Lord Lyons, after some verbal and formal amendments."[27] After the meeting, Frederick Seward wrote that when his father mentioned to the president that he had been proposing to present his own draft, Lincoln had smiled and replied: "I found I could not make an argument that would satisfy my own mind, and that proved to me your ground was the right one." Other versions of the conversation between the two don't have Lincoln making this pithy comment, but they agree on the substance.[28] Lincoln decided that the United States had to back down on the matter of the prisoners. He concluded that what was of supreme importance was the war to preserve the Union. The United States could not afford a simultaneous war against Britain.

The United States government informed the British that it was releasing Mason and Slidell, and their secretaries, which it proceeded to do. The diplomats resumed their journey to Europe, where despite their best efforts they ultimately failed to win diplomatic recognition for the Confederacy.

WHILE NEGOTIATIONS ON the *Trent* Affair were underway, the British sent eight thousand soldiers to the Maritime provinces and Canada to guard against a possible American invasion. The dispatch of the troops revealed both the strengths and weaknesses of the Canadian position. Sending troops across the North Atlantic in mid-winter delivered a message to Americans that the British intended to stand by their possessions on the continent. The expedition also reassured Canadians that they would be defended in the event of war. On the other hand, eight thousand soldiers (in addition to the British regulars already in British North America and the much-neglected and under-strength local militias) were hardly sufficient to thwart a full-scale American invasion.

Most of the transport ships carrying the British soldiers failed to reach the Gulf of St. Lawrence and the river before the waterway froze over for the winter. In January 1862, about seven thousand soldiers had to be landed in the Maritimes and then transported in sleighs across northern New Brunswick to Rivière-du-Loup, on the St. Lawrence River.[29] Offsetting the rigours of the extreme cold and stormy winter was the enthusiastic effort of New Brunswick farmers to assist the British regulars during their journey. The farmers provided comfortable sleds to carry the troops, who were warmly clad, many of them outfitted with sheepskin coats and fur caps. Alerted by bugle calls, the local populace came out to welcome the warriors enthusiastically.[30]

Despite the warm reception, the affair was warning enough for the future. The absence of a railway linking the great interior province of Canada to the Maritimes, particularly in winter, was a glaring strategic weakness. It pointed to the reality that during the great war raging to the south, the British North American provinces were living politically and militarily in the past. Unless they could figure out ways to come together for defence and for a common political and national future, each of them could be swallowed up by the United States.

In the aftermath of the *Trent* Affair, the number of British regulars stationed in British North America was eventually increased to seventeen thousand. It remained at about this level until 1867 — two years after the end of the American Civil War, and the year of Canadian Confederation — when the number of regulars was again sharply reduced.[31]

In January 1862, John A. Macdonald, who had assumed the position of minister of militia affairs in addition to his post as attorney general, headed up a legislative commission on military preparedness. The other members were Canadian politicians George-Étienne Cartier, Alexander Galt, and Sir Allan MacNab, and Colonel Thomas Campbell, C.B. (representing the provincial militia forces) and Colonel Daniel Lysons, C.B. (a British regular officer). The goal was to strengthen the militia and to make Canada a tougher target against a potential U.S. invasion. Halting a full-scale invasion by the ever more powerful Union army might be out of the question, but Canada could at least harden its borders to make it clear to the United States that Canadians controlled their territory and would resist an incursion from the south.

The commission, which reported on March 15, 1862, came down strongly in support of the view that the Canadian militia had to become the central pillar upon which the defence of the province would rest. The report declared that Canada needed an active militia force of fifty thousand men and a reserve militia of the same strength. The homegrown forces should be made up of volunteer militia corps to be enrolled in the cities and battalions of regular militia to be enlisted in rural districts. These forces were "to be taken as nearly as practicable in equal proportions from the male population...between the ages of 18 and 45."[32] The commission recommended that the active militia should be raised through a system of volunteering to be supported as necessary by a ballot (a draw of names from all those eligible).

When Macdonald moved the adoption of the commission's propos-als in the provincial legislature, the opposition assaulted the proposals. On May 20, 1862, the militia bill was defeated in the House, leading to the fall of the Taché-Macdonald government, which was replaced by a ministry headed by Reformer John Sandfield Macdonald and mod-erate Rouge Louis-Victor Sicotte.[33]

The new government survived for only one year, at which time it was replaced by a ministry, this time headed by John A. Macdonald and George-Étienne Cartier. What the short-lived government did manage to achieve, however, was to shoot down ambitious plans for substantially improving the province's defences.

While the governments of the British North American prov-inces hailed the stationing of more British regulars on their soil, the British soldiers themselves often created problems. They frequently attempted to desert their posts near the U.S. border to seek a bet-ter life for themselves in the United States. British sentries had to be posted in New Brunswick, and in Kingston and Toronto in Canada West, to prevent soldiers from deserting. And the Union army was eager to attract British regulars; these were well-trained soldiers, and they were quickly welcomed into Union army regiments.[34] This was an old issue for the British. During the years prior to the War of 1812, when Isaac Brock was building up British forces to resist a possible American attack on Canada, British regulars often deserted to the U.S. On one occasion, the British secretly sent troops across the bor-der at Niagara and captured a number of deserters and mutineers. In March 1804, seven of those captured were executed.[35]

During the Civil War, the stream of deserters ran in both direc-tions. While British deserters headed south, Americans intent on avoiding military service went north. On some occasions, agents of the U.S. government and Union soldiers covertly crossed the border to hunt down deserters and return them to the United States. When these incidents became publicly known, they provoked tension between the United States and British North American authorities, as well as the British government.[36] The governments of the British North American provinces refused to send the thousands of American deserters back to the United States.

Over the course of the war, it is estimated that between thirty-three thousand and fifty-five thousand British North Americans headed south and joined the Union army.[37] They had a variety of motives for fighting. Some deeply opposed slavery. Others sought excitement and adventure, and the great conflict on Canada's doorstep seemed to promise a larger experience than was available at home. Not inconsequential in their thinking, those enlisting were paid a bounty to do so. Many of the British North Americans who enlisted were already living in the United States when they joined the Union forces, and their motives were similar to those of their American neighbours.[38] A few hundred men from the British North American provinces joined the Confederate army to fight on the side of the South — the fact that the vast majority of men from north of the border who participated in the Civil War did so on the side of the Union does not negate the existence of pronounced pro-Southern feeling in much of British North America.

The *Trent* Affair had shown just how great the danger from the South could be. In December 1863, another incident rattled nerves, especially in Nova Scotia, and demonstrated the extent of pro-Southern sympathy in Halifax. Early that month, a group of Confederates and their Maritime supporters seized the *Chesapeake*, a steamer that took passengers back and forth between New York and Portland, Maine. The csa government in Richmond had issued a letter of marque to those who took command of the ship. They hoped to turn the vessel into a Confederate commerce raider.

On the afternoon of December 17, 1863, the people of Halifax and their leaders witnessed the worrying spectacle of two American warships, with a third ship in tow, entering their harbour. The U.S. vessels had tracked down the *Chesapeake* in British North American waters and had captured her. Tension in the provincial capital eased when Captain A. G. Clary of the uss *Dacotah* handed over the captured ship to Nova Scotian officers.

Anger among Nova Scotia government ministers was reignited, however, when they learned that among those seized onboard the *Chesapeake* and locked in irons below deck were three Nova Scotians. When one of them, George Wade, was released at the harbour, Halifax authorities were waiting to arrest him for piracy for his involvement in the seizing of the *Chesapeake*. But Haligonians sympathetic to the Confederacy crowded the wharf. During his brief moment of liberty before he was to be taken into custody by the Halifax police, Wade leapt into a small boat that was then rowed away by two fishermen. As the police constable attempted to ready his pistol to fire, pro-Southerners blocked him and Wade made good his escape.

Some of the U.S. citizens who had been aboard the *Chesapeake* were arrested in Saint John and charged with piracy. At the end of their trials, which lasted nearly three months, the magistrate's court ruled that they should be extradited to the United States. This ruling was overturned on appeal on the ground that the accused had been involved in an act of war, and the prisoners were discharged. The outcome of the trial was highly popular in Saint John and Halifax.[39]

The risk of war alerted Canadian political leaders to the potential perils British North Americans faced and to the need to shore up defences as much as they could. The *Trent* Affair injected a cold dose of reality: the British had no appetite for a war to defend Canadian territory from the United States. It alerted Canadian leaders to the fact that they needed to come to terms with each other if a wider British North American union was to have any chance of success.

Chapter 12

George Brown Changes Course

E CONOMICS AND POLITICS aligned to propel Canadians on the boldest venture in their history: the road to Confederation.

With a total population of three million people by the 1860s — equivalent to that of the Thirteen Colonies when they declared their independence from Great Britain in 1776 — the British North American provinces, in many respects, were well positioned to launch a country of their own. But not only was the Province of Canada geographically remote from the Atlantic provinces; furthermore, its internal politics was at an impasse due to the sectional issues that divided its French- and English-speaking inhabitants. The obstacles were at least as great as those that confronted the Americans when they drafted their second Constitution in Philadelphia in 1787.

One vastly important difference between the 1780s and the 1860s was the revolutionary new technology of the telegraph, which gave British North Americans front row seats as observers of the Civil War. The telegraph fed copy to daily newspapers, allowing them to publish accounts of developments in the war within hours of their occurrence. Canadians and Maritimers watched in deep unease as hundreds of thousands died next door. Over the first three days of July 1863, the Battle of Gettysburg, the greatest single battle of the war, was fought in Pennsylvania, a northern state that bordered Canada across Lake Erie.

The pressure was on British North American political leaders to rise above partisan antagonisms and parochialism to come together to form a new political union that could cope with the storms sweeping the continent. Resolving the deadlock in the Province of Canada, let alone pursuing the dream of British North American union, would require political leadership of the highest order. Fortunately, British North Americans had in their midst a political leader as shrewd and far-sighted as any in the history of the continent: John A. Macdonald.

The triumvirate that drove the Canadian project included the chief political leaders of Canada West and Canada East, George Brown and George-Étienne Cartier respectively. These two leaders were implacably opposed to one another on the issue of political structure. There was a way out, of course — the way eventually taken. That was the resort to federalism, which could combine Rep by Pop in a federal government with the creation of two separate provinces, one in each half of the existing province.

The third member of the triumvirate, John A. Macdonald, played the indispensable role of devising and launching the Canadian nation state project. Macdonald stood head and shoulders above his peers as a master politician. Even though he is often and unfairly relegated to the status of a skilled and somewhat unsavoury political operative, Macdonald was the visionary behind the Canadian federal union. He presided over the creation of the crucial political party of the nineteenth century, the Conservative Party (formally the Liberal-Conservative Party), shepherded Confederation to fruition, brought the West into Confederation (a deeply flawed exercise in the way it rode roughshod over the rights of native peoples and the Métis), and saw the building of the transcontinental railway to completion. No other figure in Canadian history comes close to equalling Macdonald's achievements.

In the politics of the province, George Brown, the voice of Canada West and the Reformers, demanded Rep by Pop, while George-Étienne

Cartier, leader of the Bleus in Canada East, could not accept this proposed change. Since the late 1850s, a simple and implacable barrier blocked progress between the two: Brown was not prepared to give up the demand for electoral reform and Cartier could not give way to Brown without undermining the political position of French Canadians in the province.

For a breakthrough to be achieved, George Brown would have to make the first move. As it happened, Brown had been evolving politically, although that internal process, which would soon prove critically important, was not yet publicly evident. Until he was prepared to combine Rep by Pop with the idea of federalism, he remained a principal barrier to finding a solution.

Much more acceptable to French Canadians, meanwhile, was the concept of the Double Majority, but the problem with that concept was that it could worsen the province's already serious political conundrum. In practice, when potential coalition partners (Tory-Bleu or Reform-Rouge) increased their support in one section of the province, they tended to lose it in the other.

These were the realities that made Brown the political figure who had a greater chance of overcoming the deadlock than any other. That is, he could do this if he could convince his opponents that he genuinely sought reform and was no longer a rabid foe to be avoided.

In June 1864, in what was doubtless the most important moment in his political career, Brown approached the Conservatives with a proposal for a major new political initiative. This proposal transformed Canadian politics.

After suffering a bruising defeat in the 1861 election, which cost him his seat in the legislature, Brown had been downcast, depressed, and ill. A voyage to England and his native Scotland — he had not been across the Atlantic for a quarter of a century — changed him. On a visit to the Edinburgh home of his friend Thomas Nelson, Brown became truly and deeply smitten with Nelson's young sister Anne. The hardbitten bachelor in his mid-forties fell hard. In November 1862, the two married, and a more pensive, less harshly judgemental Brown emerged. Despite marital bliss and preoccupation with his wife, their new baby, and furnishing their new home in Toronto, Brown did not relinquish his passion for politics. In March 1863, he won a by-election in South Oxford and returned to the legislature. [1]

By 1864, conditions had changed both inside the province and externally as a consequence of tension between Britain and the war-torn United States. And Brown had indeed evolved. He was now willing to adopt a vision and a program that suited the wider needs of the province and that took the French-Canadian position fundamentally into account. On March 14, 1864, Brown delivered a speech in the legislative assembly during its session in Quebec City. [2] He spoke in a calm, even-handed manner, arguing for the appointment of nineteen members of the assembly to a select committee on constitutional reform.

To demonstrate that he sought backing that extended beyond the Upper Canadian Reformers, who were sure to support him, he offered an olive branch to his political opponents. His motion included a lengthy quotation from a letter written to the colonial secretary in 1858 by Alexander Galt, George-Étienne Cartier, and John Ross, three members of the Tory-Bleu ministry that had then been in office, in support of the concept of a British North American federation. [3]

It was clever of Brown, the great tribune of the Canada West Reformers, to associate his initiative with one made in the past by his adversaries. In his speech, he did not push his own preferred option to the fore. He said, instead, that he would consider any proposals with an open mind.

Not surprisingly, his long-standing foes remained leery of the "new" George Brown. George-Étienne Cartier expressed amusement that Brown had come so belatedly to recognize the wisdom of the 1858 Conservative proposals. For his part, John A., the master of the rapier, took pleasure in satirically noting that Brown had turned away from his panacea of foregone days — Representation by Population. In a letter to his wife Anne, Brown wrote: "John A. was especially mean and contemptible." [4]

Four days after Brown's speech, the floundering Reform-Rouge government, headed by Sandfield Macdonald and A.-A. Dorion, resigned. It was replaced by a Tory-Bleu government, headed nominally by Sir Étienne Taché. The two powerhouses in the ministry were John A. Macdonald and George-Étienne Cartier. As had been the case with its predecessor, the new government faced the prospect of razor-thin majorities for the adoption of its measures, and the likelihood that it too would collapse before too long.

On March 31, 1864, the House adjourned until May, leaving Brown's constitutional initiative hanging in the air. On May 19, eight days after he arrived back in Quebec City, Brown was able to speak to his motion once more. He held his fire and refrained from responding to Cartier and Macdonald with personal vindictiveness for the cheap shots they had taken at him in March. While Macdonald, Cartier, and Galt, along with important Reformers, voted against Brown's motion to set up the committee on the constitution, the government did not oppose it.

To his delight, Brown's motion was adopted by the surprisingly wide margin of 59–48. The following day, the committee held its first meeting,[5] where it set up a subcommittee whose task was to come up with propositions to serve as the basis for discussion.

On June 14, 1864, with the new government already struggling to maintain its perilously small majority and the House session about to end, George Brown reported on behalf of his committee. The brief, and quite general, report dispensed with the ineffective or wholly impossible constitutional remedies that had nonetheless been a part of the political conversation for years. Getting these concepts off the table was essential in any serious attempt to grapple with the dead-lock that held Canada in its grip. Dismissed was the Double Majority, Representation by Population, and the simple dissolution of the province into its two halves. That left the way open for the option the committee strongly endorsed: a federal system. Exactly what type of federal state should be established, the report wisely did not say, thus avoiding the very real danger of driving away potential supporters because of disagreements over a particular scheme.

Summing up the report, Brown told the House: "A strong feeling was found to exist among the members of the committee, in favour of changes in the direction of a federative system, applied either to Canada alone, or to the whole British North American Provinces; and such progress has been made as to warrant the committee in recommending that the subject be again referred to a committee at the next session of parliament." [6]

What gave the report its critical, even historic, importance was the bearer of the message and its timing: George Brown, who had been the strident voice of one section of the province for so long, was now favouring a proposal aimed at serving the common good. Then there was the ideal timing. Yet another ineffectual Canadian government — this one Tory-Bleu — was at the helm and faced the prospect of being brought down by a motion of no confidence, as had happened so often to ministries of both stripes in recent years. Leading politicians of all persuasions were weary of this and many were open at least to the possibility of a new initiative. In addition, there was the ever looming reality of the great war to the south. Canadian political leaders understood that the position of the province on the continent was exceedingly vulnerable. A new and much more effective Canadian state was needed, hopefully a state that could secure the northern half of the continent for British North Americans.

Following Brown's report there came something all too wearily customary in Canadian politics: the defeat in the House of yet another government. But what came after that was entirely novel, and it opened the way for the transformation of the northern half of the continent.

When Brown sat down at the end of his report, Minister of Finance A. T. Galt stood to move the assembly into committee of supply, the standard procedure allowing the members to debate the province's finances. This was the appropriate moment for an Opposition member to move a non-confidence amendment, and that is what A.-A. Dorion, leader of the Canada East Rouges, proceeded to do. The amendment censored the current government for a financially dubious transaction undertaken by Galt when he served as finance minister in a former government in 1859. It was a thin basis for bringing down a government, but in the highly partisan, deadlocked politics of the day, it was typical fare. The Dorion amendment passed by a vote of 60–58.[7]

The government was thereby defeated on a clear vote of confidence. Cabinet ministers decided to go to the governor general, Viscount Monck, to seek the dissolution of the assembly and new elections. But that was not the end of it. Brown approached two assembly members who were supporters of the defeated government: Conservatives J. H. Pope and Alexander Morris. Brown told his two political opponents that the present governmental crisis should be seized as an opportunity to settle once and for all "the constitutional difficulties between Upper and Lower Canada." He went further, telling Pope and Morris that he himself would be ready to work promptly with the current ministry or any other that would deal with the constitutional issue so as to finally settle it. Realizing the import of what Brown was saying, his two interlocutors asked if they could pass it along to John A. Macdonald and A. T. Galt. Brown readily assented.[8]

On the afternoon of June 15, Macdonald rose in the House and said very briefly that in light of the serious position now faced by the ministry following the adverse vote the previous evening, he and his cabinet colleagues had decided that they had to communicate with the governor general. Reform leader John Sandfield Macdonald rose at once to demand fuller enlightenment on what the members of the government intended.[9] Then Brown rose and delivered a message with a very different tone. While he agreed with Sandfield in requesting more information, he adopted a notably sympathetic tone toward the government: "In the position of great gravity in which the honourable gentlemen opposite were now placed," he declared, "they should be allowed every fair opportunity to consider what course they should pursue." In addition to another election, he suggested intriguingly that the members of the government might want to consider other possible ways to cope with the political stalemate.[10]

By this time, John A. Macdonald had already heard from Pope and Morris. Six days later, on June 22, following a historic week in

Canadian politics, Macdonald reported what had happened over the course of that week, including a brief exchange he himself had had with Brown following his speech: "On Thursday [June 16] at 3 P.M., just before the Speaker took the Chair, Mr. John A. Macdonald said to Mr. Brown, while standing in the centre of the Assembly Room, that he had been informed of what he, Mr. Brown, had stated, and he wished to know if Mr. Brown had any objections to meet Mr. Galt [and himself] and discuss the matter? He replied, certainly not.

"Mister Morris accordingly arranged an interview with Mr. Brown, and on Friday, the 17th June, about one P.M., Messrs. Macdonald and Galt called on Mr. Brown at the St. Louis Hotel." [11]

The three mid-Victorian gentlemen sat in Brown's room, and in this prosaic setting they reached a compact that changed the course of Canadian history. The conversation, not surprisingly, began rather stiffly. Macdonald and Brown were the two leading political personalities in Canada West, and their rivalry had an all-too-personal taint to it. When they got down to business, Brown asked in what capacity the two had come to see him. As Macdonald later reported: "They replied they were charged by their Colleagues formally to invite his aid in strengthening the Administration with a view to the settlement of the sectional difficulties of Upper and Lower Canada." [12]

Brown told his two political foes that for personal reasons he was not in a position to enter any administration. He noted that given the long-standing enmity between himself and some members of the current administration, it would be shocking to the public were he to be included in a cabinet with them. He did say, more hopefully, that there was now an opportunity to deal with the fundamental issues facing the province and that such an opportunity "might never occur again." Brown, Macdonald reported, told his two visitors that if the administration were prepared to announce publicly that it was ready to take steps to resolve the governmental crisis and address the underlying concerns of Upper Canada with respect to representation, he would heartily co-operate with them. Macdonald responded that in his view, for this to happen it would be essential for Brown to become a member of the cabinet so as to assure the members of the Opposition and the public of the earnestness of the administration. [13]

In response, Brown stated that other members of the Opposition could bring the same assurances to the public as he could and that "his position had been such for many years as to place a greater bar in the way of his entering the Government than in that of any other Member of the Opposition." [14]

Macdonald probed further to find a way around Brown's apparent reticence. Would Brown be prepared to be publicly identified with the negotiations to reorganize the governing of Canada? And would he be ready to travel on a mission to present this approach to members of the governments of the Atlantic provinces or to England, or to both? [15]

To this Brown replied, and Macdonald and Galt agreed, that for the present, personal questions should be put aside and an attempt should be made to find a formula to overcome the sectional problem in Canada.

As Macdonald later reported: "Mr. Brown asked what the Government proposed as a remedy for the injustice complained of by Upper Canada, and as a settlement of the sectional troubles. Mr. Macdonald and Mr. Galt replied that their remedy was a Federal Union of all the British American Provinces; local matters being committed to local bodies and matters common to all to a General Legislature constituted on the well understood principles of Federal Government." [16]

In response to the sweeping idea promulgated by his two guests, Brown laid out his stock political idea — Representation by Population — as the way out of Canada's constitutional deadlock. This was old ground, and Macdonald and Galt countered with their often-repeated answer that Canada East would never accept Rep by Pop.

The negotiation could have ended there, but the two sides — Brown on one, Macdonald and Galt on the other — needed each other if any breakthrough were to be achieved. "After much discussion on both sides," Macdonald later reported, "it was found that a compromise might probably be had in the adoption either of the Federal principle for all the British North American Provinces, as the larger question, or for Canada alone, with provision for the admission of the Maritime Provinces and the Northwest Territory, when they should express the desire."

Ever the champion of his own section of the Province of Canada, Brown expressed the view that the Canadian federation should be created first so that when negotiations began with the Maritime provinces, "the interests of Upper Canada would in no case be overlooked." [17]

Enormous ground had been gained at this meeting. All three men had agreed that the way ahead would be based on the federal principle in one form or another.

LATER THAT DAY, when the assembly met, Macdonald rose to tell the members that the governor general had agreed to a dissolution of the House, and then revealed that a discussion with the member for South Oxford, George Brown, promised a possible way ahead. At this point, many of the members erupted in loud cheering. First one member of the legislature and then a host of them rushed across the floor to shake Brown's hand. The Rouge members from Canada East looked on in surprise and dismay. Events had passed them by.

Over the next few days, the details of the agreement between Brown and the government members were hammered out. Appropriately, George-Étienne Cartier, the key French-Canadian leader, joined the conversations, as did other members, including Étienne Taché. On the Reform side, Brown had to bear the weight of negotiating on his own.

First there was the question of whether Brown and his backers would support the ministry without joining it at the cabinet table, or whether a new coalition ministry would be formed. The Conservatives were determined that they should form a new government and that Brown had to sit on its cabinet. When Brown agreed to this, he tried to drive a hard bargain on the matter of cabinet representation for the Reformers. He argued that six of the twelve ministers should come from the Reform-Rouge side of the House. This was a non-starter, because A.-A. Dorion and the Rouges opposed the new government platform and had no intention of participating in it. Brown backed off and offered another position, which held that four of the six ministers from Canada West's half of the cabinet should be drawn from his Reformers. That would leave John A. Macdonald with only two members.

Macdonald refused the demand and insisted that he must have three Canada West Tory seats in the cabinet. He was firm as well in demanding that he himself must retain the position of senior minister from Canada West. When Brown finally agreed to Macdonald's position on both matters, the shape of the cabinet table in the new government was resolved. Further discussion determined that a federal state would be the goal of the new government. While Brown leaned toward beginning the federal experiment in Canada alone, Macdonald and his allies insisted on including the Atlantic provinces. And Macdonald got his way. [18]

With negotiations completed on June 20, the results were presented to the Tory-Bleu and the Reform caucuses the following day. Tory-Bleu members were easily convinced. A sizeable minority of the Reformers preferred the idea of the caucus supporting the government from the outside. Most, however, agreed that it was preferable to have their members at the cabinet table. Final arguments and last-minute negotiations continued long into the night and the next morning.

On Wednesday, June 22, the assembly was not called into session until 4 p.m. When the House did begin its deliberations, a new era in Canadian history had truly begun. In English and in French, Macdonald and Cartier announced the formation of what came to be known as the Great Coalition government. George Brown, appropriately enough, delivered the key address. He explained to the House that over the course of the talks he had kept his Rouge allies from Canada East fully informed. He had tried, without success, to bring them on board. He explained that in the last analysis, the political deadlock in the province had forced him to take the step he had taken. "Mr. Speaker," he declared, "party alliances are one thing, and the interests of my country are another." [19]

With the establishment of the Great Coalition, the most pressing question was whether the governments of the Maritime provinces and Newfoundland could be sold on a British North American Federation or whether they would stick to the scheme of Maritime Union, which they were already contemplating.

In 1864, Brown broke the mould of Canadian politics with his proposal that political foes should make common cause to establish a country north of the war-torn United States. He alone could do it. As the most powerful sectional leader in Canada West, Brown held the key to constitutional advance. The same, of course, was true of George-Étienne Cartier in Canada East.

AMONG FRENCH CANADIANS, Cartier was the majority leader. He was also critically important in linking the Tory-Bleus to the Roman Catholic Church and to the most powerful business forces in Montreal: those who ran the railways and the banks.

In the critical year of 1864, no deal could be done to reconfigure Canadian politics without Cartier. During the years when George Brown and his supporters had pushed for Representation by Population, Cartier was on the defensive. But he was determined to hold his ground. To do otherwise would have been political suicide. He was fully conscious of the fact that the French Canadians were a minority people within Canada and British North America as a whole. Conceding the idea of representation based solely on population within the unitary state of Canada was completely unacceptable.

Thus came the years of deadlock. Only when George Brown effectively backed down in 1864 by going over to a fully federal solution could progress be made. To this Cartier could agree.

The enormous gain for French Canadians in the deal that underlay the Great Coalition government was the separation of the Province of Canada into its two halves. The eastern half, the future Quebec, would have a massive French-Canadian majority. It would become — however it was depicted — the homeland of the French-Canadian people. On the other hand, within the new federal state, whether it included only

Canada or all of British North America, Representation by Population would prevail in the federal House of Commons. Within this larger state, French Canadians would be permanently reduced to a minority.

In the eyes of the Rouges of Canada East, George Brown's erstwhile partners, the new state would not offer enough protection to French Canada. As a consequence, the Rouges stayed out of the Coalition. Nonetheless, with virtually all of Canada West and the majority party in Canada East, the Coalition enjoyed a commanding position in the legislature that would be needed in the tough negotiations and politicking to be done with the Maritimers and the British government.

What made the Canadian nation state project a work of genius is that it involved not only a coming together but also a separation. This is something that is too often neglected by historians. The federal state would extend beyond the two halves of the Province of Canada, but within Canada, there was to be a separation between those two halves: Quebec and Ontario were to be distinct provinces, the successors to Canada East and Canada West. Quebec was to be a powerful sub-national state and the launch pad for future attempts to establish it as a sovereign national state separate from Canada.

Transformative political projects customarily involve collaboration among political leaders who are rivals or opponents. In the Canadian case, it required a partnership between men who detested each other. While Macdonald and Cartier enjoyed each other's company and had a long and close working relationship, George Brown and John A. Macdonald did not speak to each other for years.

It is easy to picture Brown as the more hidebound of the two, an unbending man of fixed principles. Macdonald, on the other hand, can readily be portrayed as a clever operator whose beliefs were slippery and subject to change. There is enough truth in these characterizations to account for why the two men were not comfortable with one another. But they leave out much that is important. Both Macdonald and Brown were patriots. They adhered to a common belief in a future in which Canada could survive as a sovereign country next door to the United States. While they valued different aspects of the British

system of government, neither ever doubted the continuing necessity of the British connection for Canada. Both found their bedrock
in their attachment to Canada, and that allowed them to collaborate
at a critical historical moment.

Chapter 13

Confederation:
The House Macdonald Built

THE CIVIL WAR to the south motivated Canadian political leaders to form the Great Coalition to establish a federal union of British North American colonies. John A. Macdonald, George-Étienne Cartier, and George Brown knew that if they didn't work together, the seething conflict between Confederates and Unionists could engulf the British North American provinces. There was only one chance to create a federation that had the potential to span the continent, and Macdonald and the others took it, in the greatest high-stakes gamble in Canadian history.

The political leaders first met in Charlottetown, the capital of Prince Edward Island, in early September 1864 and then in Quebec City in October 1864. At Charlottetown, delegates from Prince Edward Island, New Brunswick, Nova Scotia, and Canada agreed to proceed with the concept of a broader British North American union in place of a union solely among the Maritime Provinces. At Quebec City, the delegates of the provinces worked out the details of how the federal union would function.

In the late summer of 1864, the residents of the small town of Charlottetown could be forgiven for thinking that the arrival of a travelling circus — no circus had come to PEI for more than twenty years — would be the seminal event of their summer. On August 30,

1864, the same day that the Slaymaker and Nichols' Olympic Circus opened its performances to the public, the first of the delegates arrived from Nova Scotia to attend the conference of Maritime political leaders who were to meet to consider the idea of a Maritime political union. The next day, the delegates from the other Maritime provinces came ashore.

On September 1, an impressive, almost warlike steamer, the *Queen Victoria*, appeared in the harbour. On board were eight ministers of the Canadian government — the most prominent among them Macdonald, Cartier, and Brown — and their secretaries. Their arrival prompted both pomp and farce.

W. H. Pope, the provincial secretary of the PEI government, had the task of extending an official greeting to the guests from distant Canada. The best he could do was to commandeer a rather dilapidated flat-bottomed rowboat to take him out under the power of a muscular fisherman. On board the ship, the Canadians were outfitting themselves in their most elegant wardrobes. When they were ready, two craft were dropped over the side of the *Queen Victoria* to take the delegation ashore. Pope, in the rowboat, led the odd little flotilla to the Charlottetown docks.

The Canadians proceeded to upstage the official conference that had been convened to consider Maritime Union. The Maritimers briefly called their conference into session and then put aside their own agenda to unofficially consider the broader scheme of a general British North American federation. Significantly, the "unofficial" meetings began with the personal introduction of the eight Canadian delegates to the fourteen participants in the Maritime conference. Few of the Canadians and Maritimers had actually met prior to this occasion.[1]

Four Canadian ministers — Macdonald, Cartier, Brown, and Galt, the Coalition minister of finance — laid out the plan for an immediate British North American union.[2] Tellingly, just as the discussions in Charlottetown were getting underway, the Confederates were abandoning Atlanta to the army of General William Tecumseh Sherman.

The first two Canadian speakers, Macdonald and Cartier, proved to be extremely effective in combination. Macdonald laid out the case for a strongly centralized union, and Cartier, whose overriding concern was to protect the particularity of French Canada, demonstrated to the Maritimers that local customs and jurisdiction could exist in the proposed federation. Both went a long way toward winning over their opposite numbers. Although the Maritimers were broadly favourable to the idea that a general federation of the territories of British North America should someday be undertaken, the issue was whether the time was now right. [3]

The day after Macdonald and Cartier laid out the broad case, Galt spoke on the proposed financial arrangements for the federation. The federal government would assume the debts of the participating provinces. Subsidies, based on population, were to be paid by the federal government to the provinces. Then Galt detailed the revenue sources that were to be made available to both levels of government. With Galt's formidable, highly competent presentation completed, the Canadians invited the Maritimers to join them on board the *Queen Victoria* for a luncheon. At that event, much buttressed by free-flowing champagne, both Brown and Cartier spoke of the great prospects for the new union.

As Brown recorded: "Cartier and I made eloquent speeches — of course — and whether as a result of our eloquence or of the goodness of our champagne, the ice became completely broken, the tongues of the delegates wagged merrily, and the banns of matrimony between all the provinces of B.N.A. having been formally proclaimed and all manner of persons duly warned then and there to speak or forever after to hold their tongues — no man appeared to forbid the banns and the union was thereupon formally completed and proclaimed!" [4]

The following Monday, George Brown addressed the meeting on how the proposed Lower and Upper Houses of the federal government were to function, what was to be the division of powers between the federal government and the local governments (the provinces), and how the judiciary should be set up. [5] Everyone present was well aware that Brown had been the tireless advocate of Rep by Pop and that this doctrine would inevitably be the principle upon which representation in the elected Lower House of the Canadian Parliament would be based. On the matter of representation in the appointed Upper House, Brown proposed that this chamber (the future Senate) should have sixty members: twenty from Canada West, twenty from Canada East, and twenty from the Maritime Provinces. The principle suggested in this case was that there should be equal representation for each region within the new federation. This would to some extend offset the weight of population as the basis for representation in the Lower House. It was also intended to put aside any notion of equal representation for each province, not surprising among political leaders who believed that states' rights and equal representation for each state in the American Senate had fatally undermined the viability of American federalism. [6]

Brown's was the last of the four set-piece Canadian speeches at the conference. The next day, the delegates gathered for a last time. At this session, the tone was more conversational, with Maritime delegates asking questions and raising concerns about the details of the proposal. Some of the concerns, such as the precise formula for representation in the Upper House, were to dog the Confederation project in the future. But for now, there was general support among those present for a British North American union.

The following day, the Maritimers assembled without the Canadians to once again consider their original idea of a regional union, or a unit to be included within the Canadian proposal. Both possibilities came to naught when the delegates from tiny Prince Edward Island made it clear that they were not prepared to give up their status as a political entity with a capital city. The road was open, therefore, for the Maritime provinces to participate in the Confederation undertaking. In the end, the path for the Maritimes would prove to be strewn with obstacles that came perilously close to derailing Confederation.

From Charlottetown, the delegates moved on for a brief session in Halifax, where the idea of a Maritime Union was abandoned in favour of the pursuit of a general British North American federation. The delegates decided that the details were to be hammered out at a subsequent conference, to be convened in Quebec City the following month. At a public dinner in Halifax, on September 12, 1864, John A. Macdonald, in the company of the delegates from the Charlottetown Conference, toasted the capacity of a British North American federation to defend itself. Significantly, he compared British North America to the Confederacy: "I believe we shall have at length an organization that will enable us to be a nation and protect ourselves as we should. Look at the gallant defence that is being made by the Southern Republic — at this moment not much more than four millions of men — not much exceeding our own numbers — yet what a brave fight they have made" — and then, for balance — "notwithstanding the stern bravery of the New Englander, or the fierce *elan* of the Irishman."

Then he went on to warn British North Americans to learn from the mistakes made by the Americans when they established their own system of government decades earlier: "The dangers that have arisen from this system we will avoid if we can agree upon a strong central government — a great central legislature — a constitution for a Union which will have all the rights of sovereignty except those that are given to the local governments. Then we shall have taken a great step in advance of the American Republic."[7]

QUEBEC CITY WAS the overwhelmingly logical setting for the next step in advancing the project of union. The city was historically, politically, and geographically central to the northern half of the continent, and the first substantial French-Canadian settlement on the continent. It was also where a brief battle in 1759 brought down the edifice of New France. For French Canadians, the Battle of the Plains of Abraham was the most tragic, never-to-be-forgotten event in their history. For the majority party of the French Canadians, led by George-Étienne Cartier, the Confederation project was a hugely important wager on the future, and it was only appropriate that its details should be worked out in their historic capital.

The setting, high above the river that opened Canada's way into the heart of the continent, was overpowering. The St. Lawrence and the Great Lakes formed the highway that connected European states and investors to the primary products of the Canadian hinterland. At Quebec, the delegates could palpably feel both their own historic past and the prospects for a future country that would one day span the continent.

On October 10, 1864, delegates from Canada, New Brunswick, Nova Scotia, and Prince Edward Island, as well as two observers from Newfoundland, began deliberations that were to continue until October 27 to establish the constitution for the proposed British North American union. The overarching issue was the division of powers between the federal government and the local or provincial governments. John A. Macdonald supported a legislative union that would place the major levers of power in the hands of the central government. Cartier, along with delegates from the Maritimes, came down on the side of a federal union in which the provinces would exercise substantial power. For Cartier and other francophone delegates from Canada East, the power to be exercised by the future Province of Quebec was a matter of the greatest importance. Maritimers, who wished to counterbalance Canada West, which was to be the most populous region in the new federation, lined up with Cartier to favour local or provincial governments that would exercise real power.

On the evening of October 9, the delegates, in some cases accompanied by wives and sons and daughters, came together to fete their mutual undertaking. The next morning, the delegates assembled in the rather prosaic legislative building in Quebec City, in the reading room of the Legislative Council. (Within a few years, the building was to become a post office.) Through the windows, they had a view that was anything but prosaic, the mighty river and the trees on its banks still ablaze with autumn colour.

Sir Étienne Taché, the elderly titular head of the Canadian coalition government — he had not attended the Charlottetown Conference — was elected chairman of the conference, and he opened the meeting with a few general remarks. It was agreed that the meetings would be held in secret. The following morning, the delegates unanimously agreed that Canada, as a consequence of its historic division between Upper and Lower Canada, would have two votes, and that each of the Maritime provinces would have one vote. [8] This was accepted readily enough, since the Maritimers would still have the majority of votes at the conference.

Two weeks earlier, the Canadian government had attempted to counter some concerns in the province that the Confederation project was being pushed ahead in almost total secrecy. A semi-official document that broadly summarized the proposals, and that made clear that everything was subject to change at the Quebec Conference, was published in the *Montreal Gazette* and *Le Courrier du Canada* and extensively reprinted in other newspapers. [9]

John A. Macdonald rose to move the resolution on which the work of the conference would be based. Using the words of the Maritimers at Charlottetown the previous month, Macdonald's resolution read: "That the best interests and present and future prosperity of British North America will be promoted by a federal union under the Crown of Great Britain, provided such union can be effected on principles just to the several Provinces." [10] New Brunswick Premier Samuel Leonard Tilley seconded the resolution. Immediately, Cartier rose to lend his enthusiastic support to the motion. [11]

The morning after the resolution was moved, Macdonald spoke to it. The principal point of his address was to drive home his conviction that the central government must be endowed with the key levers of power. He remarked that states' rights — the reservation to each state of all sovereign powers — "save the small portion delegated" to the central government was what he termed the "primary error" of the constitution of the United States. "We must reverse this process," he concluded, "by strengthening the general government and conferring on the provincial bodies only such powers as may be required for local purposes."

Macdonald's speech, which was strongly applauded, was followed by the rapid and unanimous passage of the motion he had moved the previous day.[12]

Agreement on the broad nature of the project by no means meant that there would be a consensus as to its details. On October 13, with generalities out of the way, strong disagreement emerged on the question of representation in the Upper House. The Maritimers went along with the idea that the federal parliament would have two houses, an elected Lower House (House of Commons) and an appointed Upper House (Senate). But Macdonald's proposal on the Upper House, that there should be an equal number of seats for each of the three regions — Canada West, Canada East, and the Maritimes — drew the ire of the delegates from the eastern provinces. This was because at the Charlottetown Conference, the term "Maritimes" had referred to Nova Scotia, New Brunswick, and PEI, but at Quebec Macdonald was including Newfoundland.

The debate on the makeup of the Legislative Council continued heatedly for the rest of the day and on to the next day, when Samuel Leonard Tilley and Nova Scotia delegate R. B. Dickey moved an amendment to Macdonald's motion to the effect that Upper Canada would have twenty-four members, Lower Canada twenty-four members, and the four Maritime Provinces thirty-two members among them. Other amendments were considered and moved. The Maritime objection to Macdonald's plan was that it would provide roughly for Representation by Population for the Upper House, which was also to be the basis for representation in the Lower House. This, they contended, made for unfair Upper House representation for smaller provinces already heavily outnumbered in the elected Lower House.

For a few days, it seemed possible that the heated debate over representation in the Upper House could derail the conference. Finally, the Canadians decided to go along with a proposal from Charles Tupper, premier of Nova Scotia and future prime minister of Canada, to resolve the issue. Tupper moved that Nova Scotia, New Brunswick, and PEI be treated as the Maritime region, which would then have an equal number of Upper House seats with the other regions, Canada

West and Canada East. Under Tupper's plan, Newfoundland would be offered additional seats. Despite strong opposition from PEI, which was to get four seats in the Legislative Council while Nova Scotia and New Brunswick each acquired ten, the Tupper proposal was adopted.[13]

Next came Macdonald's proposal that members of the Upper House be appointed for life by the Crown, on the advice of the federal government. For some delegates — Canada and PEI had recently held elections for their Upper Houses — this was a retrograde step that harkened back to the pre-democratic ways of the British North American past. Two Reform delegates who were associates of George Brown — William McDougall and Oliver Mowat, the future premier of Ontario — made the case that members of the Upper House should be elected. Brown parted company with his fellow Reformers on this matter and sided with Macdonald. After further debate, advocates for an appointed Upper House carried the vote.[14]

On the critical issue of representation in the Lower House, George Brown presented the Canadian government's proposal that Canada East should have sixty-five members in the Lower House, and that representation in the other provinces should be adjusted proportionally with respect to population in relation to Lower Canada's sixty-five seats. Using the censuses of 1861 for each province as his guide, Brown explained that this formula would give Canada West eighty-two seats, Nova Scotia nineteen, New Brunswick fifteen, Newfoundland seven, and PEI five. What was new in this proposition was the idea of using Lower Canada as the constant against which the populations of other provinces would be measured for representation, and the suggestion that the Lower House be called the House of Commons. The number of seats was to be adjusted in the future according to changes in population as recorded in the decennial census.[15]

After a brief discussion about whether the 1861 census figures should be used or estimates for 1866, it was agreed that an eighth seat would be added for Newfoundland, to take account of population growth since the last census in the province, which had been in 1857. Brown's proposition was then adopted and the total number of seats reckoned at 194.[16]

Thus the issue of the composition of the two houses of Parliament was dealt with, but not without provoking the wrath of one of the delegations. The Prince Edward Islanders — already divided between those generally for Confederation and those generally against, and between Conservative and Liberal political rivals — were further alienated by the realization that the Island would have only a tiny number of seats in both houses. But they had not voiced these concerns, and so the conference was surprised when they voted against Brown's motion, sending an unmistakable signal that the Island could well absent itself, at least initially, from the Confederation project.

As it turned out, the Island would stay out of the union in 1867, joining six years later when Canada offered the province special terms: the purchase of farmlands from British absentee owners, which made PEI farmers owners rather than tenants; and a long-term commitment to subsidize the cost of transportation between the Island and the mainland.*

Meanwhile, at the 1867 conference, some delegates made a last-ditch attempt to bring PEI back into the fold by offering the province a sixth seat in Parliament, but this idea was brushed aside as unprincipled meddling with the whole concept of representation. The Islanders were left disaffected and alienated.

One last issue remained to be decided before the conference could wind up, and it was a major one: the division of powers between the federal government and the local or provincial governments. It was quickly agreed that the Crown representatives in each of the local governments would carry the title lieutenant-governor, and that the federal government would appoint these officials. But when Brown suggested that the local governments should be simple, single-chamber affairs, more akin to municipalities than to legislatures, Cartier objected and received the backing of Maritime delegates. On this matter, a resolution, which was passed unanimously, decided that each

---

* A subsidy that continues in the twenty-first century with Ottawa's contribution to the price of the "fixed link," the Confederation Bridge that now connects PEI to New Brunswick.

local legislature would determine its own structure. This opened the door to what was to follow after Confederation: the establishment of provincial governments operating as parliaments that increasingly accrued powers as the decades passed. Along with this resolution, delegates agreed to the proposition that the power of local legislatures to determine their own way of operating be granted "with a view of reducing the expenses of the local governments." [17]

On October 21, John A. Macdonald presented a lengthy, detailed resolution on the powers that were to be exercised by the federal government. His resolution included general clauses in addition to a long list of specific and enumerated areas of jurisdiction. This formula was to prove highly problematic for the government of Canada in subsequent decades: courts would often try to limit the powers of the federal government to the enumerated powers and severely downplay the significance of the general clauses.

Macdonald's goal was to place residual power in the hands of the federal government and to limit local or provincial governments to a list of specified areas of jurisdiction. His motion commenced with the proposition that the federal government should have the power "to make laws for the peace, welfare, and good government" of the country* and concluded with the proposal that the federal government should exercise the authority to legislate "generally, respecting all matters of a general character, not specially and exclusively reserved for the local governments and legislatures." The list of specific powers for the central government was spelled out between these two general clauses. [18]

The tone of the debate that followed Macdonald's motion was positive. The idea that the key economic powers, especially with respect to railways and harbours, should be in the hands of the central government was widely accepted. The motion passed easily.

The next day, Galt rose to present the crucially important financial details that were a part of the Canadian proposal. The plan involved granting the federal government the power to raise revenues through

---

* Later, the key phrase was altered to: "peace, order, and good government."

any form of taxation it chose, whether direct or indirect (at the time, "indirect taxes" principally meant customs and excise duties). Because the federal government was to assume the burden of the total debts of the provinces, it had to have broad taxing powers. So, Galt proposed, the public assets of British North America — principally railways, canals, harbours, and steamboats — should be transferred to the central government. [19]

The issue of how the provincial governments were to be funded, and the matter of how to evaluate the assets of the provinces that were to be turned over to the federal government, led to rancorous and protracted debate. When the next session began on Monday, October 24, with neither of these matters resolved, another volatile question was thrown into the mix. It might have been thought that with the passage of Macdonald's motion on the issue, the federal government had been granted residual powers. That proved not to be the case, however.

E. B. Chandler, a former first minister of New Brunswick, rose to argue that the powers of the provincial governments should not be specified and enumerated, and that residual power should go to the provinces and not the federal government. His intervention reopened this issue, which was potentially highly divisive. The Canadians had reasons to be concerned that this decentralist intervention could garner considerable Maritime backing. Saving the day for the Canadian scheme was Charles Tupper of Nova Scotia.

"Those who were at Charlottetown," Tupper declared, "will remember that it was fully specified there that all the powers not given to the local should be reserved to the federal government...Mr. Chandler says that it gives a legislative instead of a federal union. I think that a benefit...If it were not for the peculiar condition of Lower Canada, and that the Lower Provinces have not municipal systems such as Upper Canada, I should go in for a legislative union instead of a federal...If Conference limit the powers of the general legislature, I feel that the whole platform is swept away from us." [20]

In this seminal debate, John A. Macdonald delivered his second-lengthiest speech of the Quebec Conference. He was determined to defend the Canadian project against any possible weakening, built as it was around the necessity of making the central government paramount in its power. In a passionate appeal, he warned the delegates not to forget that the principal weakness of the U.S. Constitution had been to grant the residual powers to the states: "Mr. Chandler would give sovereign power to the local legislatures just where the United States failed... We should concentrate the power in the federal government and not adopt the decentralization of the United States."[21]

Between them, Tupper and Macdonald managed to quash the decentralist revolt so that no provincial delegation voted in favour of a motion to entrust the residual power to the provinces.

On Tuesday, October 25, the delegates finalized the matters of the division of powers and the financial settlement. By then the fire had gone out of the assemblage. Instead of a heated struggle, as could have been anticipated, the delegates, having already come down on the side of a strong, centralized federation, reached agreement without too much difficulty. Oliver Mowat presented the Canadian proposal outlining the specific areas of provincial jurisdiction. The most important amendment to his motion came from Thomas D'Arcy McGee, an immigrant from Ireland and a member of the Great Coalition cabinet: a caveat that provincial control of education be modified to protect "the rights and privileges which the Protestant or Catholic minority in both Canadas may possess as to their denominational schools at the time when the Constitutional Act goes into operation."[22] Following some debate, Mowat's motion carried.

The federal government would exercise the power of disallowance over provincial legislation, and the lieutenant-governors, who were to be appointed by the federal government, would have the power to reserve provincial legislation for review by the federal government. These practices, important for the Canadian future, were drawn from the experience of the British Empire in its relations with its self-governing colonies. And with the American war blazing next door, British North American leaders were at pains to rely on British precedent and experience.

During the evening session on October 26, Galt moved a resolution, which was carried by the delegates, on the critical issue of language. The motion declared: "Both the English and the French languages may be employed in the General Parliament and its proceedings, and in the Local Legislature of Lower Canada, and also in the Federal Courts and in the Courts of Lower Canada." [23]

Then Galt presented to the conference a resolution on the subject of the financial arrangements for the new federation. Although altered in wording from his earlier resolution on the subject, the substance remained the same. Canadians, New Brunswickers, and Nova Scotians went along with the proposal, leaving only the delegates from PEI in disagreement. By this point, the delegates from Canada had grown increasingly tired of the Islanders' protests.

As the conference drew to a conclusion, two resolutions were passed that held immense importance for the future. The delegates committed the new union to the construction of the Intercolonial Railway that would link Canada to the Maritimes. With the threat from the south very much on the minds of political leaders, the rail link was critical both for commercial and strategic reasons. The second resolution pointed the way to a continental future for the new country: it provided for the admission to the federation of Rupert's Land (the prairies and the north), as well as British Columbia and Vancouver Island. [24]

Over the course of the conference, with some sessions going all day and on into the late hours of the night, the delegates had drafted a plan for the launch of a new North American country that one day could extend from the Atlantic to the Pacific and north into the Arctic. Together the motions that were adopted constituted the seventy-two resolutions. In the coming months, this package would have to be endorsed by the provincial legislatures. Then they would have to be taken to London for the final drafting of the British North America Act, which, when passed by the British Parliament, would bring the new federation into existence.

None of this would prove easy.

Chapter 14

Debating Confederation

WITHIN THE COALITION government and at Charlottetown and Quebec, John A. Macdonald emerged as the pre-eminent leader. In the speeches he made to sustain morale and keep the project moving forward, and behind the scenes, drafting and amending resolutions, Macdonald was the Master Builder. Indeed, most of the critical resolutions passed at Quebec were originally in Macdonald's handwriting, a graphic illustration of the indispensable role he played.[1] At the Charlottetown and Quebec conferences, he was in his element. He was, as well, a gifted performer on the hustings during an election campaign. But in the intimate confines of a conference with a number of political leaders thrown together for a period of days, he excelled. Both on the floor and in private encounters when the conference was out of session, he drew others to him, won them over to his vision, and honed the needed compromises on matters of detail that kept the agenda advancing.

No other British North American politician was nearly as effective as Macdonald. It is, therefore, noteworthy that he has come to be seen by the present generation of Canadians as something of a slick operator and a periodic drunk who made under-the-table arrangements with American railway promoters. There is more than a little truth in this characterization, as attested by John A.'s bouts with alcohol and by the Pacific Scandal of the early 1870s. Despite his flaws, Macdonald was a gifted, far-sighted political leader whose charisma and steadfast vision attracted others. Given his gigantic achievements over a forty-year period, it is surprising that Macdonald remains so relatively underrated.

Macdonald had good reason to be pleased at the end of the Quebec Conference. His concept of a centralized federation, as remote as possible in its essentials from the American model, had prevailed. The road ahead to July 1, 1867, and the launch of Confederation would, however, take longer and require yet more political labour than Macdonald could have anticipated. Creating a new nation within an empire from a group of colonies — something that had never been accomplished before — would require skills in inspiring the broad public and political leaders as well as mastery in the dark arts of compelling compliance. Macdonald excelled at all of these, making him quite unique among the three leaders who oversaw the launching of nation state projects on the North American continent.

The next step was to present the seventy-two resolutions to provincial legislatures.

The debate on the resolutions was held three and a half months after the Quebec Conference adjourned. In February 1865, when the Union Army of the Potomac, under the command of Ulysses S. Grant, was opening the final assault on Petersburg, the gateway to Richmond, Canadian political leaders debated the pros and cons of the proposed Confederation in the legislature of the Province of Canada. By this time, events south of the border had entered a new phase. As late as September and October 1864, it remained possible for outside observers to believe that the Confederate States of America could endure.

Things changed abruptly on the afternoon of October 19, 1864, while the Quebec Conference was in session. Confederate raiders, who had crossed the border into Vermont from Canada East, launched an assault on the town of St. Albans. The attackers robbed the banks; wounded two citizens, one of them fatally; destroyed property; and then fled north, crossing the border back into Canada. News of the

cross-border raid infuriated Northerners and the Lincoln administration. General John A. Dix, the commander of U.S. forces on the
northeastern frontier, issued an order to his men to pursue the attackers "into Canada if necessary and destroy them."

The impetuous order, which remained in force for nearly two
months, created the possibility of clashes at the border. Such clashes,
although local in nature, carried the risk of igniting conflict between
the United States and Great Britain. Secretary of State William Seward
was well aware of where General Dix's order could lead, but he was
feeling the wrath of angry public opinion and congressional pressure
to reinforce American defences at the northern border.[2] When the
St. Albans raid took place, Seward was still concerned about an incident that had taken place a month earlier, when Confederate agents
seized two commercial vessels on Lake Erie, hoping to use them to
attack a federal prison on Johnson's Island. That attempt failed, and
the secretary of state subsequently resisted any plan to increase U.S.
naval strength on Lake Erie, mindful that the U.S. had signed a treaty
with Britain following the War of 1812 that limited naval forces on the
Great Lakes.[3]

As if the incident on Lake Erie and the St. Albans raid were not
enough, on November 1, Seward received a telegram from the United
States consul in Halifax, stating that a plot was afoot to set major fires
in Northern cities a week later, on Election Day. Seward responded
with telegrams to big-city mayors, warning them of the menace.[4]

The threatened assault on Northern cities did not materialize, and
on November 8, 1864, Abraham Lincoln was elected to a second term
as president of the United States. Lincoln's victory swept aside the hope
among Confederates that if the Democrats won the White House,
peace might still be possible on the basis of a separate existence for
the Confederacy. Just as it was becoming ever more clear that British
North America would have to deal henceforth with a powerful and
victorious United States, American opinion turned anti-Canadian as
a result of the St. Albans raid.

The raiders were arrested in Canada and placed on trial. On

December 13, 1864, much to the consternation and even shock of the prosecutors and members of the Canadian government, the presiding magistrate, C.-J. Coursol, ruled that due to a defect in the Canadian extradition law, his court did not have jurisdiction in the case. He released the raiders, and they walked out of the courtroom. The $84,000 they had stolen from the banks in St. Albans was surreptitiously handed over to an agent of the Confederate government. [5]

American newspaper editorials erupted in fury. The *Chicago Tribune* called on the United States to dispatch troops to Montreal "or any other place where the St. Albans pillagers may have taken refuge, to take them out and hand them over to a Vermont jury, to be dealt with according to the law." General Dix responded by reiterating his previous order to take action, if necessary, by crossing the border into Canada. On December 17, President Lincoln revoked the order. [6] He did this not to lessen the tension with Canada and Britain, but to deal with it more effectively and to prevent a headstrong general from determining the course of events. The same day Lincoln restrained General Dix, his administration issued an order requiring all British North Americans to present passports when visiting the United States.

Meanwhile, members of the United States Congress were turning their attention to the abrogation of the Reciprocity Treaty. In the early years of the agreement, reciprocity had been popular both in the United States and British North America. During the Civil War, as relations grew strained between the United States and Great Britain, American politicians grew increasingly hostile to the trade agreement, claiming that it favoured British North America to the detriment of American interests. As a consequence of the Civil War, a boom market opened in the United States for British North American exports, making reciprocity more important than ever to commerce north of the border. On December 13, 1864, the very day that the St. Albans raiders were released from a Canadian court, the House of Representatives voted to abrogate the treaty. A month later, on January 12, 1865, the United States Senate also voted for abrogation. [7] This meant that the

Reciprocity Treaty would expire in March 1866, one year after the new bill was signed into law in Washington.

While British North Americans could hope that relations would improve and that the U.S. could be talked out of abrogation or into a new trade deal, the threat of the end of free trade pushed the British North American provinces more decidedly into a union among themselves. For the first time in their history, Canadians were forced to adopt an economic strategy that was much less dependent on either the old mercantilist relationship with Britain, which had ended almost two decades earlier, or the more recent free trade relationship with the United States.

On February 6, 1865, John A. Macdonald, in his role as attorney general of Canada West, rose in the provincial legislature to spell out his views on the Confederation project. In this unusually important speech, Macdonald set out his overarching perspective on the critical issues. He critiqued what he saw as the basic flaws of American federalism. He stated that he preferred the strongest possible union for British North America, but explained why he had abandoned his preference for a legislative union in favour of a federal system with a powerful central government. He stressed the point that the new union must maintain the recognition of the French Canadians as a "nationality." He warned that British North Americans needed union so they could prepare for their mutual defence at a time of great crisis on the continent.

Macdonald's assessment of the American system of government began with a few suavely positive generalities before it became bitingly critical: "It is the fashion now to enlarge on the defects of the Constitution of the United States, but I am not one of those who look upon it as a failure. I think and believe that it is one of the most skillful works which human intelligence ever created...To say that it has some defects is but to say that it is not the work of Omniscience, but of human intellects. We are happily situated in having had the opportunity of watching its operation, seeing its working from its infancy until now...We can now take advantage of the experience of the last seventy-eight years, during which that Constitution has existed, and I am strongly of the belief that we have, in a great measure, avoided in this system which we propose for the adoption of the people of Canada, the defects which time and events have shown to exist in the American Constitution."

Macdonald laid out precisely what was wrong with the American system: "They commenced, in fact, at the wrong end. They declared by their Constitution that each state was a sovereignty in itself, and that all the powers incident to a sovereignty belonged to each state, except those powers which, by the Constitution, were conferred upon the General Government and Congress."

Macdonald then outlined how the Confederation proposal before the House remedied this fundamental flaw: "We have strengthened the General Government. We have given the General Legislature all the great subjects of legislation. We have conferred on them, not only specifically and in detail, all the powers which are incident to sovereignty, but we have expressly declared that all subjects of general interest not distinctly and exclusively conferred upon the local governments and local legislatures, shall be conferred upon the General Government and Legislature." [8]

On why he had been convinced to abandon his preference for a legislative union in favour of a federal union, Macdonald stated: "I have always contended that if we could agree to have one government and one parliament, legislating for the whole of these peoples, it would be the best, the cheapest, the most vigorous, and the strongest system of government we could adopt. But, on looking at the subject in the Conference [the Quebec Conference], and discussing the matter as we did, most unreservedly, and with a desire to arrive at a conclusion, we found that such a system was impracticable."

To drive home this point, Macdonald examined the case of French Canada and the perennially sensitive issue of the relations between the two Canadas. He made the point that even if Upper Canada (Canada West) had won its long struggle for Representation by Population, in his view this would not "have been for the interest of Upper Canada."

His reasoning on this point was telling and vividly portrayed his perspective on English-French relations in Canada: "For though Upper Canada would have felt that it had received what it claimed as a right," he declared, "and had succeeded in establishing its right, yet it would have left the Lower Province with a sullen feeling of injury and injustice. The Lower Canadians would not have worked cheerfully under such a change of system, but would have ceased to be what they are now — a nationality, with representatives in Parliament, governed by general principles, and dividing according to their political opinions — and would have been in great danger of becoming a faction, forgetful of national obligations, and only actuated by a desire to defend their own sectional interests, their own laws, and their own institutions." [9]

Consummate politician as he had become by 1865 — younger than Davis and Lincoln at the height of their powers — Macdonald was well aware that he had to make the case that this was a moment to be seized, that such a propitious time for Confederation might never recur. Despite the election of an anti-Confederation government in New Brunswick, the moment was right because events were aligned so as to make possible a union that included the English and French Canadians and the Maritimers. A propitious moment, yes, and furthermore one that needed to be grasped because of the severe dangers that threatened from the south.

In one powerful passage, Macdonald drew together the twin strains of opportunity and danger: "If we do not embrace this opportunity the present favourable time will pass away, and we may never have it again. Because, just so surely as this scheme is defeated, will be revived the original proposition for a union of the Maritime Provinces, irrespective of Canada; they will not remain as they are now, powerless, scattered, helpless communities; they will form themselves into a power, which, though not so strong as if united with Canada, will, nevertheless, be a powerful and considerable community, and it will be then too late for us to attempt to strengthen ourselves by this scheme, which, in the words of the resolution, 'is for the best interests, and present and future prosperity of British North America.'

"If we are not blind to our present position, we must see the hazardous situation in which all the great interests of Canada stand in respect to the United States. I am no alarmist. I do not believe in the prospect of immediate war. I believe that the common sense of the two nations will prevent a war; still we cannot trust to probabilities." [10]

Opportunity against the backdrop of mortal risk — Macdonald was unique in his ability to convey this urgent message to British North Americans during this critical time.

The day after Macdonald spoke, his close partner in French Canada, George-Étienne Cartier, addressed the House. Cartier's speech carried great weight because he led the Bleu Party, the party with the largest number of French-Canadian members in the House. In his acceptance of the Confederation project, Cartier was making a major concession on behalf of the French-Canadians, and in return he was gaining something of immense importance for their future: as a province separate from Ontario, Quebec would become a French-Canadian homeland, a state with great potential for the future and vast implications for the future of the new Dominion of Canada.

"The consequence of representation by population would have been that one territory would have governed another," declared Cartier, "and this fact would have presented itself session after session in the House, and day after day in the public prints. The moment this principle had been conceded as the governing element, it would have initiated between the two provinces a warfare which would have been unremitting."

Cartier praised the potential for Confederation, asserting that the project would not be diminished by the presence of people in Canada of different ethnic groups: "Objection had been taken to the scheme now under consideration, because of the words 'new nationality.' Now, when we were united together, if union were attained, we would form a political nationality with which neither the national origin, nor the religion of any individual, would interfere.

"It was lamented by some," Cartier continued, "that we had this diversity of races, and hopes were expressed that this distinctive feature would cease. The idea of unity of races was utopian — it was impossible.

"Distinctions of this kind would always exist," he affirmed, reassuring French Canadians that their nationality would continue within the framework of a larger "political nationality."

"Dissimilarity, in fact, appeared to be the order of the physical world and of the moral world, as well as of the political world," Cartier reasoned. "But with regard to the objection based on this fact, to the effect that a great nation could not be formed because Lower Canada was in great part French and Catholic, and Upper Canada was British and Protestant, and the Lower Provinces were mixed, it was futile and worthless in the extreme. Look, for instance, at the United Kingdom, inhabited as it was by three great races.

"Had the diversity of race impeded the glory, the progress, the wealth of England?" he asked rhetorically. "Had they not each contributed their share to the greatness of the Empire? . . . In our own Federation we should have Catholic and Protestant, English, French, Irish and Scotch, and each by his efforts and his success would increase the prosperity and the glory of the new Confederacy." [11]

Not only did Cartier predict that the success of the proposed Confederation would be enhanced by its diverse peoples; he also warned of the potential consequences of the U.S. Civil War for British North Americans: "Confederation, was, as it were, at this moment almost forced upon us. We could not shut our eyes to what was going on beyond the lines, where a great struggle was going on between two Confederacies, at one time forming but one Confederacy. We saw that a government, established not more than 80 years ago, had not been able to keep together the family of states which had broken up four or five years since. We could not deny that the struggle now in progress must necessarily influence our political existence. We did not know what would be the result of that great war — whether it would end in the establishment of two Confederacies or in one as before. However, we had to do with five colonies, inhabited by men of the same sympathies and interests, and in order to become a great nation they required only to be brought together under one General Government. The matter resolved itself into this, either we must obtain British American Confederation or be absorbed in an American Confederation." [12]

The final leader of the triumvirate at the heart of the Great Coalition government to speak was George Brown. He held the position of president of the council. Brown addressed the House the day after Cartier. He began with his stormy, years-long campaign for Rep by Pop: "I cannot help feeling that the struggle of half a life-time for constitutional reform, the agitations in the country, and the fierce contests in this chamber — the strife and the discord and the abuse of many years, — are all compensated by the great scheme of reform which is now in your hands.

"Here is a people composed of two distinct races, speaking different languages, with religious and social and municipal and educational institutions totally different; with sectional hostilities of such a character as to render government for many years well-nigh impossible; with a Constitution so unjust in the view of one section as to justify any resort to enforce a remedy. And yet, sir, here we sit, patiently and temperately discussing how these great evils and hostilities may justly and amicably be swept away forever."

As Macdonald and Cartier had, Brown raised the pressing issue of defence: "I am in favour of the union of the provinces, because, in the event of war, it will enable all the colonies to defend themselves better...

"In the conversations I had, while in England, with public men of different politics — while I found many who considered that the connection between Canada and England involved the Mother Country in some danger of war with the powerful state upon our borders, and that the colonial system devolved heavy and unreasonable burdens upon the Mother Country — and while a still larger number thought we had not acted as cordially and energetically as we ought in organizing our militia for the defence of the province, still I did not meet one public man, of any stripe of politics, who did not readily and heartily declare that, in case of the invasion of Canada, the honour of Great

Britain would be at stake, and the whole strength of the Empire would be unhesitatingly marshaled in our defence." [13]

The debates in the Canadian legislature in the winter of 1865 were noteworthy not only for the important addresses delivered by the members of the triumvirate: opponents of Confederation, although the minority in the House and divided among themselves, pointed out weaknesses in the project, and some of the points they made resonated in the politics of the dominion in the decades to come.

One of the most effective of the opponents was A.-A. Dorion. In the past, Dorion had considered both Rep by Pop and federalism; in the winter of 1865, however, he aligned himself squarely against the Confederation project. As he began his address on February 16, he remarked that he would have preferred to deliver his speech in French, but since so many of the members of the Assembly did not understand French, he would speak in English. He made the case that Confederation was to a considerable extent a project undertaken on behalf of the railways, that the proposed system of government was deeply illiberal, and that the institutions and culture of the French Canadians were far from sufficiently protected under the scheme.

Dorion cited the example of the Grand Trunk Railway and its ambitions over many years to build the Intercolonial Railway to link Canada to the Maritime Provinces. Efforts to construct the rail line fell through, one after another, because the Grand Trunk would not proceed without what it regarded as sufficient funding from the public purse.

"Some other scheme had to be concocted for bringing aid and relief to the unfortunate Grand Trunk," declared Dorion. "And the Confederation of all the British North American Provinces naturally suggested itself to the Grand Trunk officials as the surest means of bringing with it the construction of the Intercolonial Railway. Such was the origin of this Confederation scheme. The Grand Trunk people are at the bottom of it.

"The whole scheme, sir, is absurd from beginning to end. It is but natural that gentlemen with the views of honourable gentlemen opposite want to keep as much power as possible in the hands of the Government — that is the doctrine of the Conservative party everywhere — that is the line which distinguishes the Tories from the Whigs — the Tories always side with the Crown, and the Liberals always want to give more power and influence to the people. The instincts of honourable gentlemen opposite, whether you take the Hon. Attorney General East [Cartier] or the Hon. Attorney General West [Macdonald], lead them to this — they think the hands of the Crown should be strengthened and the influence of the people, if possible, diminished — and this Constitution is a specimen of their handiwork, with a Governor General appointed by the Crown, with local governors also appointed by the Crown; with legislative councils [the future Senate], in the General Legislature, and in all the provinces, nominated by the Crown; we shall have the most illiberal Constitution ever heard of in any country where constitutional government prevails."[14]

Dorion concluded his pointed and effective speech with a passage on the fate of French Canadians under the proposed Confederation. He warned that the federal union could be the first step toward a much more centralized system:

"Honourable members from Lower Canada are made aware that the delegates [to the Quebec Conference] all desired a Legislative union, but it could not be accomplished at once. This Confederation is the first necessary step towards it. The British Government is ready to grant a Federal Union at once, and when that is accomplished the French element will be completely overwhelmed by the majority of British representatives. What then would prevent the Federal Government from passing a set of resolutions in a similar way to those we are called upon to pass, without submitting them to the people, calling upon the Imperial Government to set aside the Federal form of government and give a Legislative union instead of it? Perhaps the people of Upper Canada think a Legislative union a most desirable thing. I can tell those gentlemen that the people of Lower Canada are attached to their institutions in a manner that defies any attempt to change them in that way. They will not change their religious institutions, their laws and their language, for any consideration whatever. A million of inhabitants may seem a small affair to the mind of a philosopher who sits down to write out a constitution. He may think it would be better that there should be but one religion, one language and one system of laws, and he goes to work to frame institutions that will bring all to that desirable state; but I can tell honourable gentlemen that the history of every country goes to show that not even by the power of the sword can such changes be accomplished." [15]

Over the succeeding decades, Dorion's words were to be quoted many times by Quebeckers who believed that English Canadians were pushing for too centralized a union and were abandoning the spirit of the federal union to which they had committed themselves in the 1860s.

Confederation — the house Macdonald built — was very much a product of the political and economic forces of its time. The original Confederation was far from sovereign, enjoying what we can rather call "home rule." The imperial government in London continued to preside over Canadian foreign and defence policies. And for decades after 1867, the governor general, a British aristocrat, appointed by the British government, enjoyed significant political influence in Ottawa.

Under the leadership of John A. Macdonald, the constitutional house in which the nation state of the north would reside had been constructed.

Chapter 15

Surrender and Assassination

A s BRITISH NORTH Americans were launching their federal union, the Confederate States of America was going down in defeat. In the autumn of 1864, when political leaders met at Charlottetown and later at Quebec, the Confederacy was being cut to pieces.

As early as April 1862, Admiral David Farragut had led a Union fleet and federal troops in a successful assault that resulted in the capture of the vital port of New Orleans. On July 4, 1863, federal forces under the command of Major General Ulysses S. Grant captured Vicksburg, Mississippi, the victory coming one day after the Union's success in the crucial three-day Battle of Gettysburg in Pennsylvania. With Vicksburg under federal control, command of the Mississippi fell to federal forces. This severed the states of Arkansas, Louisiana, and Texas from the heart of the Confederacy. In early September 1864, General Sherman's forces captured Atlanta, and in mid-November his army set out to Georgia, cutting a swath of destruction en route to Savannah. By then, Jefferson Davis's hope for a political settlement with the North had been shattered by Abraham Lincoln's re-election on November 8.

Lincoln spent much of the war in a frustrating and agonizing search for a commanding general who could take the fight to the enemy and give no quarter. In March 1864, with the authorization of Congress, Ulysses S. Grant was promoted to the rank of lieutenant general. Having won laurels in the western theatre of the war, most notably in his triumph at Vicksburg, Grant would now command all the armies of the Union.

Critics, especially Southern sympathizers, would later charge that Grant was nothing but a butcher who was prepared to throw wave after wave of Union soldiers at the enemy, whatever the cost in casualties. Once he took on the fight against Robert E. Lee, Grant never let up. The climactic chapter in the war, with Grant face to face against Lee, came in the fight for Petersburg, the vital rail hub south of Richmond. In response to setbacks, Grant threw in ever more troops and brought up ever more artillery. He was determined to pound the weaker Confederate forces into submission. He had the men and the supplies to do it.

The Confederates fought on doggedly during the lengthy battle, which started on June 9, 1864, and ended on March 25, 1865. Over nine months, the two sides faced each other in a campaign of trench warfare that was vastly different from the Civil War's earlier and much more mobile battles. Indeed, the battle for Petersburg foreshadowed the trench warfare on the Western Front in the First World War. In the sharing of romantic tales about the great campaigns of the war, Americans rarely talk about Petersburg. Squalid and deadly and far from romantic was that battle.

The stakes for the Confederacy could not have been higher. If Grant's Union forces captured Petersburg, the supply lines to sustain Lee's army and the city of Richmond would be ruptured. By November 1864, after five months of hard fighting, the trench lines between Petersburg and Richmond had stretched to almost twice the distance between the two locations, which as the crow flies is about twenty miles. Lee's men fought on in miserable conditions, short of food and attired in ragged clothing. In contrast to the well-supplied Union forces, the Confederate men often preferred to go barefoot rather than wear the pitiful half-cured-leather bits of footwear provided by their government.[1]

While the slogging match around Petersburg continued, political events were moving swiftly. Lincoln interpreted his re-election as a mandate from the people to abolish slavery once and for all. In January 1865, the Republicans, under the direction of the president and making use of the lobbying skills of Secretary of State William Seward, strove to push a Thirteenth Amendment to the Constitution, which would abolish slavery permanently, through the House of Representatives. To achieve this, a two-thirds majority of votes would be needed. Lincoln was well aware that on March 4 a new Congress would be seated and that the Republicans would have three-quarters of the seats. He wanted, however, to win the vote with the support of at least some Democrats.

During the politicking in advance of the vote, most Democrats refused to support the proposed amendment, and their party remained officially opposed to it. A few Democratic congressmen, however, took the view that if their party was to prepare itself for the future, it needed to back the abolition of slavery. An additional dozen or so lame-duck Democrats, who could be crucial to the outcome of the vote, were heavily lobbied by Seward and other Republicans, who offered them or their relatives government jobs or other favours.

On January 31, when the historic roll call was held, the vote was 119 for the amendment with 56 opposed. Thus, by a margin of only two votes, the two-thirds majority was reached. When the result of the vote was announced, spectators in the gallery, including many African Americans, joined the cheering of the Republicans on the floor. African Americans had only been allowed in the galleries beginning in 1864. Outside, there were celebrations in the streets, and cannons fired a one-hundred-gun salute.[2] From the House, the amendment would go to the Senate and from there to state legislatures. Three-quarters of the state legislatures would need to ratify the amendment for it to come into force. The amendment was declared ratified on December 18, 1866.

In addition to that huge step on the way to the abolition of slavery, there were efforts to achieve a negotiated peace; on both sides, political leaders were feeling public pressure to seek a way to end the war. The most remarkable of these attempts was a meeting on February 3, 1865, at Union-controlled Hampton Roads, Virginia, onboard Abraham Lincoln's steamer the *River Queen*. In attendance for the U.S. government were William Seward and the president himself; attending for the Confederates were Vice President Alexander Stephens, Assistant Secretary of War John A. Campbell, and Senator Robert M. T. Hunter of Virginia. Although this was the highest-level meeting between the two sides during the entire war, the conference lasted only four hours and nothing of substance was accomplished.

Even though the tone of the meeting was frank and, at times, friendly, the Southerners were not prepared to accept the basic conditions for peace laid out by Lincoln and Seward: that the Confederates lay down their weapons and return to the Union. Lincoln was quoted later as having replied to Stephens's question on whether there was "no way of putting an end to the present trouble" with the direct answer that "there was but one way he knew of, and that was, for those who were resisting the laws of the Union to cease that resistance."[3] While the two representatives of the federal government were at pains to assure the other side that the people of the South would enjoy their constitutional rights as American citizens, they were unbending in their insistence that the war would not end without the complete restoration of the Union. Moreover, Lincoln insisted that the South must accept the actions Washington had taken on the issue of the emancipation of the slaves and the confiscation of the property of Southerners.

Lincoln and Seward did display some tentative flexibility on exactly when the abolition of slavery would take effect. But while they claimed they were not seeking unconditional surrender, they were firm in denying any future existence to states outside the Union. On this question, Lincoln's position had always been that the membership of states in the American Union was perpetual, and that the war amounted to an illegal rebellion against the United States.

Alexander Stephens tried to lure Lincoln and Seward away from the question of the war between the South and the North by bringing up the issue of France's intervention in the internal affairs of Mexico. In 1862, Emperor Napoleon III had taken advantage of the American Civil War to meddle in Mexican affairs by installing Maximilian of Hapsburg, the archduke of Austria, as emperor of Mexico. Stephens proposed that the Confederacy and the United States should send a combined force to Mexico to remove this interloper who had been imposed on the nation to the south. Lincoln and Seward were not drawn, however. The restoration of the Union was the only thing that mattered to them.*

Following the meeting on board the *River Queen*, the conclusion was clear. The war would continue.

A MONTH LATER, on March 4, 1865, Abraham Lincoln delivered his second inaugural address. The morning of Inauguration Day began with pelting rain and high winds. The inclement weather cleared just before the swearing-in at noon. A crowd of thirty thousand to forty thousand people, many of them African Americans, had assembled for the event.[4] Lincoln's address was brief and sombre in tone. He focused not only on the imperative to bring the nation together at the conclusion of a titanic struggle but also on the evil legacy of slavery:

"Fondly do we hope — fervently do we pray — that this mighty scourge of war may speedily pass away. Yet if God wills that it continue, until all the wealth piled up by the bondsman's two hundred and fifty years of unrequited toil shall be sunk, and until every drop of blood drawn with the lash, shall be paid by another drawn with the sword, as was said three thousand years ago, so still it must be said 'the judgments of the Lord, are true and righteous altogether.'"[5]

On March 25, 1865, Petersburg finally fell to Union forces, leaving Richmond indefensible. On April 2, Lee's Army of Northern Virginia

---

* Following the conclusion of the Civil War, under American pressure, the French gave up their intervention in Mexico. In the struggle that ensued, Maximilian was unable to hang onto power. Mexican forces captured him. The would-be emperor was court martialled and executed by firing squad in June 1867.

withdrew from the capital, along with Jefferson Davis, the president of the rapidly disintegrating Confederacy.

Then came one of the most poignant spectacles of the war. On April 4, accompanied by African-American Union soldiers, Abraham Lincoln walked through the streets of the still smouldering city that had been the heart of the Confederacy. By the side of the tall president, who was wearing his signature black silk hat, was his young son Tad. While most white residents of Richmond remained in the background, inside their homes or in their doorways, the street was soon filled with African Americans, the former slaves. One woman came up to Lincoln and said: "I know that I am free for I have seen Father Abraham." When a black man fell to his knees before him, Lincoln said, "Don't kneel to me. That is not right. You must kneel to God only, and thank Him for the liberty you will enjoy hereafter." [6]

Before his visit to Richmond was completed, Lincoln went to the house that had served as the Confederate White House. He even sat down at Davis's desk and remained there for a few moments, as though trying to put himself inside the psychological space of the man he had fought for four years. Meanwhile, Union soldiers helped themselves to trophies from the disintegrating Confederacy.

Lee's army, a remnant of its former self, reduced to a complement of thirty-five thousand underfed and poorly equipped men, was on the run from its federal pursuers. Over the next few days, it fought its final battle near Appomattox Court House. On April 9, Lee realized that his position was hopeless. Following an exchange of messages, a meeting was arranged between Lee and Grant to be held at the residence of Major Wilmer McLean, just beyond the court house.

Handsomely attired in a fresh general's uniform despite the sorry state of his men, Robert E. Lee rode up to the house on his grey steed, Traveler. Inside, the six-foot-tall Lee waited for about half an hour for the arrival of his Union counterpart, the much shorter Ulysses S. Grant. Grant wore a private's uniform, with his mud-spattered trousers stuffed into muddy boots. As Grant approached — at nearly forty-three, he was fifteen years younger than his foe — Lee stood up to greet him.

Recalling the event later, Grant wrote of Lee: "He was a man of much dignity, with an impassable face, it was impossible to say whether he felt inwardly glad that the end had finally come, or felt sad over the result and was too manly to show it. Whatever his feelings they were entirely concealed from my observation; but my own feelings, which had been quite jubilant on the receipt of his letter, were sad and depressed. I felt like anything rather than rejoicing at the downfall of a foe who had fought so long and valiantly, and had suffered so much for a cause though that cause was, I believe, one of the worst for which a people ever fought."[7]

Before getting down to the business at hand, the two men chatted amiably about the time they had fought on the same side in the war against Mexico years earlier. Then they turned to the terms of the surrender of the Army of Northern Virginia. It was to be an honourable surrender. Officers were permitted to retain their side arms, and once the men had stacked their other firearms, they were allowed to return to their homes.

The day after he signed the surrender with Grant, Lee issued a final general order to his men. He stated plainly: "The Army of Northern Virginia has been compelled to yield to overwhelming numbers and resources… With an unceasing admiration of your constancy and your devotion to your Country, and a grateful remembrance of your kind and considerate generosity for myself, I bid you all an affectionate farewell."[8]

Following the capitulation at Appomattox, Confederate forces in the other theatres of war surrendered one by one. Unlike Lee, who had surrendered and was free to go where he liked, Jefferson Davis continued to flee, accompanied by an ever smaller retinue of men. His ordeal was to continue long after the death of Abraham Lincoln. Finally, separated from the members of his family, the former CSA president was captured in Georgia by federal troops on May 10, 1865. He was imprisoned at Fort Monroe in Virginia, at first in shackles, to be released after two years without trial. He lived to be eighty-one, spending much of the rest of his life writing extensively to justify the cause of the Confederacy.[9]

The dream of an independent Southern state was effectively dead. But rage on behalf of the South was far from at an end. The well-known actor John Wilkes Booth recruited a group of would-be assassins whose goal was to murder leading figures in the administration, including the president, Vice President Andrew Johnson, and Secretary of State William Seward. Wilkes, who was born in Maryland, had become a Southern sympathizer and had grown to hate Lincoln and what he stood for. On April 11, 1865, the president delivered the last speech of his life from a White House balcony. He addressed the question of the Reconstruction of the Union. Wilkes was in the crowd below, and he turned to a companion and said of Lincoln's speech: "That means nigger citizenship. Now, by God, I'll put him through. That is the last speech he will ever make." [10]

Three evenings later, on Good Friday, April 14, President Lincoln and his wife went to Ford's Theatre in Washington to see a performance of the English comedy *Our American Cousin*. As had usually been the case during his years in office, the president was only lightly guarded. In comparison with later occupants of the White House, and considering the volatility of the times, the protection of Abraham Lincoln was shockingly weak.

Midway through the Civil War, Lincoln told Noah Brooks, a reporter who worked for newspapers in New York and San Francisco and later authored a biography of Lincoln: "I long ago made up my mind that if anybody wants to kill me, he will do it." [11] Remarkably, during the summers of his presidency, Lincoln often stayed at a country house two or three miles from the city and rode unaccompanied on horseback to and from this house. [12] During the summers, William Seward also travelled that road unattended. In a letter written in 1862, he expressed the opinion that "assassination is not an American practice or habit, and one so vicious and so desperate cannot be engrafted into our political system." [13]

During the third act of the play at Ford's Theatre, John Wilkes Booth had no difficulty entering the box where the Lincolns sat. He shot the president in the back of the head, shouting, "*Sic semper tyrannis*" (thus ever to tyrants) as he leapt to the stage.

On the evening Lincoln was shot, Lewis Powell (also known as Lewis Payne), a Confederate veteran, broke into the home of William Seward while the secretary of state was dozing. Following a fight with Seward's son Frederick in the upstairs corridor, Powell burst into the bedroom with a pistol in one hand and a knife in the other. The intruder slashed at Robinson, Seward's male nurse, and pushed the secretary of state's daughter Fanny aside. He grabbed Seward, holding him down with his left arm and slashing his face and neck with the knife in his right hand. Robinson assaulted Powell from behind, yanking him away from Seward. Fanny's brother Augustus ran into the room in his nightshirt in response to his sister's screams. Powell lunged at Robinson and Augustus, cutting both of them, and then he fled down the stairs and out of the house.

Although bloodied, Seward was not mortally wounded, as the doctor who arrived within a few minutes was able to reassure the members of the household. [14]

John Wilkes Booth, who broke his leg in his leap to the stage after shooting Lincoln, was able to make good his escape from Ford's Theatre. He rode away on a getaway horse held for him outside the theatre by an associate. For the next week, Booth hid in the woods and swamps of southeast Maryland. Then he made it into Virginia with a companion. The pair were spotted by a platoon of New York cavalry and were pursued onto a farm, where they sought shelter in a tobacco shed. Booth's companion surrendered, but Booth stayed put in the shed even after it was set on fire. Shot through the neck, he died shortly after being pulled out of the shed. [15]

On July 7, 1865, four of Booth's co-conspirators, including Lewis Powell, were hanged in front of a crowd of about a thousand people at Fort McNair in Washington, D.C.

THREE HOURS AFTER Lincoln died, Vice President Andrew Johnson was sworn in as president. Johnson had served as a governor and a U.S.

senator from Tennessee. He was selected as Lincoln's running mate for the presidential election of 1864, in place of Hannibal Hamlin of Maine, who had served as vice president during Lincoln's first term. A Democrat who supported the war effort of the North and a Southerner who had stood with the Union, Johnson was seen as a logical choice to make the Lincoln ticket an expression of national unity.

As president, Johnson was a disaster. From his first moments in the White House, the Republicans in Congress saw him as an interloper, a Southerner who would never be one of their own. Johnson's vision of how the Reconstruction of the Union should proceed was markedly different from the vision of the Republicans in Congress. His idea was that Southern states should be readmitted to a full functioning status within the Union relatively painlessly. With the exception of certain groups of Southerners who, because of the prominent role they had played in the Confederacy, were not amnestied, citizens of Southern states who took an oath of allegiance to the United States were to be allowed to hold conventions to amend their state constitutions so they could once again govern themselves. Once they had abolished slavery and had revoked the legislation by which they had seceded from the Union, they could again elect state legislatures and governors, as well as electing members of Congress. The problem, and it was an enormous one, was that white Southerners soon passed codes stripping blacks of political rights and selected many men who were formerly prominent in the Confederacy as their political leaders. Furthermore, not one of the Southern states reconstructed in this fashion granted the franchise to blacks.

While Johnson was prepared for this type of Reconstruction, many others, especially those who came to be known as the Radical Republicans, were not. In the thinking of these political leaders, the triumph of the Union had come at an enormous cost. They were not prepared to let Southerners, among them those who had led the Confederacy, off so lightly. The congressional elections of 1866 resulted in a sweeping Republican victory in the Northern states, which gave the Radical Republicans large enough majorities in both the House and the Senate to override presidential vetoes. Under the leadership of Thaddeus Stevens, a Republican member of the House of Representatives from Pennsylvania, and Charles Sumner, a Republican senator from Massachusetts, they succeeded in largely pushing the president to the sidelines and exercised more power than any Congress in American history. These Republicans were determined to move ahead with their agenda, which included safeguarding the civil and political rights of the newly freed.

The final showdown with Andrew Johnson came when the House of Representatives passed articles of impeachment, charging the president with the commission of High Crimes and Misdemeanors. The main charge centred on Johnson's contention that the Tenure of Office Act was unconstitutional. Acting on this premise, the president ordered Edwin Stanton to resign as secretary of war, which Stanton refused to do. This sent the issue to a trial in the Senate, which began on March 5, 1868. If the Senate convicted Johnson on any of the articles of impeachment — a two-thirds vote was required for this — he would be removed from office. The trial proceeded for almost three months. On three of the articles, the Senate voted 35 to 19 for a conviction, one vote short of the two-thirds needed to oust the president. Following the third vote, the pro-prosecution side gave up and the charges were dismissed.

In 1867, during the height of their power, the Radical Republicans proceeded with a much more comprehensive agenda to transform the South than Johnson had pursued. In addition to the Thirteenth Amendment that had abolished slavery, they successfully drafted and pushed through the Fourteenth and Fifteenth Amendments. The Fourteenth Amendment (proposed on February 1, 1866, and declared ratified on July 28, 1868) defined citizenship for Americans, taking this matter out of the jurisdiction of state governments. The Amendment barred any attempt by the states to abridge citizenship rights on the basis of race. The Fifteenth Amendment (proposed on February 27, 1869, and declared ratified on March 30, 1870) stated: "The right of citizens of the United States to vote shall not be denied or abridged by the United States or by any State on account of race, colour, or previous condition of servitude." In 1867, Congress ousted civilian governments in the South and set up five military districts across the states of the former Confederacy. Congress placed effective power in the units of the U.S. Army that were sent south as an occupying force. New elections were held in Southern states. For these elections, military commanders established the rules, which allowed freed slaves to vote, while those who had occupied prominent positions in the Confederacy were temporarily denied the franchise and were barred from running for office. In ten Southern states, new governments took office. In these Republican governments, freedmen were allied with white Southerners who supported Reconstruction, as well as with whites and blacks who arrived from the North and played a role in the process.*

The newly formed Southern governments undertook far-reaching reforms, including the establishment of public school systems. Across the South, blacks were elected to state legislatures as well as to the U.S. Congress. In the years following 1869, two African Americans were elected to the U.S. Senate, both from Mississippi, and twenty were elected to the House of Representatives. After 1876, this number declined rapidly. By 1902, there were no blacks left in Congress.[16]

From the start, white paramilitary organizations, most prominently the Ku Klux Klan, were formed to counter the new governments in the South and the participation of blacks in politics. The Klan and other similar bodies terrorized freedmen to prevent them from voting and to put a stop to political organizing among African Americans. For a time in the early 1870s, Ulysses S. Grant, who won the presidential elections of 1868 and 1872, used federal troops to block the KKK. In the latter years of Grant's second term, however, conservative white Southerners, many of them prominent former Confederates, regained

---

* Later, when conservative white Southerners had regained political control of their states, and Northerners had lost their political appetite for continuing to require the transformation of the South, the Southerners who had backed the new governments were denounced as "scalawags" and those who had come south to work with them were called "carpetbaggers."

control of their states. By the time Republican Rutherford B. Hayes
became president in 1877 — following the disputed election of the previous autumn, in which his opponent, Samuel Tilden, had prevailed
in the popular vote — Reconstruction was finished. That year, the last
occupying forces of the U.S. army left the South. By then, the elites in
the burgeoning capitalist society of the North had made their peace
with the elites of the South, who had come back from their shattering
defeat to reassert control over their region.

Debates about how to interpret the era of Reconstruction — a subject beyond the scope of this book — have raged ever since that time.
The general consensus of mainstream American historians has been
that Reconstruction was a failure, that the new reforming governments in the South, which included whites and blacks, were poorly
administered and wasteful. They make the case that a major motivation among Northern Republicans for insisting on the political rights
of newly freed slaves was to ensure that the South did not become a
region that would be swept by the Democratic Party in congressional elections, thus threatening the Republican hold on the House and
the Senate. Reconstruction is associated with the corruption that was
prevalent during the presidential terms of Ulysses S. Grant. [17]

On the other hand, other historians make the case that during the
brief spring of Reconstruction, African-American children attended
public schools for the first time. In South Carolina, for instance, by
1876, seventy thousand black children were going to school; none
had attended before. In addition, fifty thousand white children were
attending school, up from only twenty thousand in 1860. During the
same years, black educators and political leaders made their presence
felt, putting the lie to the widespread notion that the former slaves
were unprepared to take their places in the life of the larger society. [18]

The Northern victory in the Civil War put an end to the nation
state project of the South. But with the end of Reconstruction, a
new dark age descended on the African Americans. A reign of terror would consign black Southerners to suppression, segregation,
and marginalization for over three quarters of a century. While the

Thirteenth Amendment did end legal slavery, the Fourteenth and Fifteenth Amendments failed to ensure the full rights of citizenship for African Americans.

The federal government, a shining light in defence of the Union and what it stood for during the Lincoln presidency, entered a long period of declining relevance in the latter decades of the nineteenth century. The new age saw the rise of great corporations and trusts, thrusting men like John D. Rockefeller, Andrew Carnegie, and J. P. Morgan to greater influence than any president from the death of Abraham Lincoln to the accession of Theodore Roosevelt, a vice president who became president following the assassination of William McKinley in 1901.

WHEN ABRAHAM LINCOLN died at 7:22 a.m. on the morning of April 15, 1865, Secretary of War Edwin Stanton famously said: "Now, he belongs to the ages." The Lincoln saga thus began at the moment of his death. It would soon mature to include the chapters of his life as a kind of scripture, punctuated by his greatest orations, most notably the Gettysburg Address and the Second Inaugural Address. The Lincoln vision remained in the consciousness of many Americans even during long periods when administrations that shared few of the values of the late president held office. That vision could be called upon from one generation to the next by reformers who were determined to remake the United States as a country in which the rights of ordinary citizens, regardless of race, would play a genuine role in political decision making. In 1963, at a great demonstration in Washington, D.C., when Martin Luther King, a future martyr, shouted the words of the Declaration of Independence and the Gettysburg Address that "all men are created equal," he was calling on America to live up to the full meaning of those two sacred documents.

Chapter 16

Keeping the Americans at Bay: The *Realpolitik* of Confederation

B Y THE SPRING of 1865, when the Civil War ended, the members of the Canadian government were keenly aware that the threat from the south had not disappeared with the demise of the Confederacy. Indeed, the victory of the North left the government in Washington, D.C., much freer to take action against British North America should a crisis arise. Behind the scenes, the Canadian government was already engaged in the dark arts of espionage. Spying, preparing for war, countering military incursions, and political diplomacy were all weapons deployed to keep the Americans at bay as British North American leaders worked to launch their new federal state.

With John A. Macdonald, as attorney general for Canada West, overseeing the process, Canada set up a spy ring that kept a close eye on the Irish Republican Brotherhood (IRB) in the United States. Established in Dublin in 1858, the IRB was dedicated to ending British rule in Ireland and creating an Irish republic. The strategy of the IRB depended heavily on mobilizing support for the cause from the tens of thousands of Irish immigrants who had moved to the United States in recent decades, much of the migration driven by the terrible famine that struck Ireland in the late 1840s. There were very substantial Irish populations in New York, Boston, Chicago, Cincinnati, and other Northern cities. In addition, a large number of Irishmen had enlisted in the Union army during the Civil War, so that by the end of that conflict, thousands of Irish veterans had undergone military training.[1]

Canada also had thousands of Irish migrants, some of whom were drawn to the cause of Irish freedom. In 1858, Michael Murphy, who ran a tavern in Toronto, established the Hibernian Benevolent Society. He attended the first national Fenian (Irish nationalist) convention in the U.S. in 1863, at the height of the Civil War. The American Fenians publicly debated the option of invading Canada to further the Irish cause, a contentious idea that split the Fenian movement. To the pro-invasion wing, the provinces to the north of the United States were British targets of convenience. If a piece of British North America could be seized, these Fenians believed, it could be held as a bargaining chip to pressure Britain for Irish independence.

One Fenian ditty ran:

We are the Fenian brotherhood,
Skilled in the arts of war,
And we're going to fight for Ireland,
the land that we adore.
Many battles we have won,
along with the boys in blue,
and we'll go and capture Canada,
for we've nothing else to do.[2]

In March 1866 — publicly, at least — Michael Murphy rejected the Fenian faction that preached assaults on British North America. He told those who participated in Toronto's annual St. Patrick's Day parade that Hibernians were loyal to Canada as well as to Ireland. The following month, a rather poorly manned Fenian assault on Campobello Island, New Brunswick (adjacent to Maine), was easily blocked. Despite his claims of loyalty to Canada, Murphy and other Canadian-based Fenians were arrested in Cornwall, Canada West, while travelling to Portland, Maine, to join the Fenian attack.[3]

Faced with the threat of incursions from south of the border, and of support for Fenians in major Canadian cities and towns, the Canadian government recruited agents to spy on those suspected of membership in the organization. By the time of the first Fenian incursion, John A. Macdonald had engaged Gilbert McMicken, a former customs agent, to set up the Western Frontier Constabulary, whose task would be to keep a close eye on those who might participate in an attack. While it is unclear whether he was born in England or Scotland, McMicken migrated to Canada in 1832 and established a business that specialized in cross-border trade. His first-hand knowledge of border communities in Canada and the United States, and his knowledge of local politics, made him just the man Macdonald needed for the job.

Beginning in 1864, McMicken oversaw a team of at least fifteen undercover agents, who filed numerous reports from places such as Detroit, Buffalo, London, Brantford, and Sarnia, based on their surveillance of groups considered capable of threatening Canada. McMicken's battery of agents continued to expand after the conclusion of the Civil War; by 1870, about fifty operatives worked on both sides of the border. [4]

The most serious Fenian assault occurred in the early hours of June 1, 1866, when between one thousand and thirteen hundred armed men crossed the Niagara frontier. A major battle was fought at Ridgeway, where members of the Canadian militia confronted the invaders and were eventually driven off. Thirteen Canadians died from wounds suffered in the battle, and eight Fenians were killed. On the morning of June 3, when the Fenians realized that reinforcements would not reach them from New York State and that large numbers of Canadian militia and British regulars were closing in on them, they retreated across the river to Buffalo. There, they surrendered to the U.S. military.

A few days later, a small Fenian force occupied points in Canada East along the U.S. border. The following day, Canadian militiamen appeared, and the Fenians surrendered to them. In May 1870, a Fenian force operating in Vermont crossed the border into what had become by then the Province of Quebec. In the Battle of Eccles Hill, Canadian militiamen — the Canadians had been tipped off about the attack by a double agent in the Fenian ranks — quickly drove off the Fenians, suffering no casualties in the encounter.

Closely linked to the Fenian campaign was the assassination of Thomas D'Arcy McGee in Ottawa on April 8, 1868. After leaving Ireland and eventually arriving in Canada, McGee had abandoned Irish republicanism to become a political ally of the Conservatives. Initially elected to the legislative assembly from Montreal as a Reformer, McGee shifted his allegiance to the Bleus in Canada East, where he rallied the support of Montreal's Irish Catholics for the party of George-Étienne Cartier.[5]

McGee was a Father of Confederation who had a lyrical sense of the country he was helping to create, which extended well beyond matters of the respective powers of federal and provincial governments. In 1860, in a parliamentary debate on the subject of a Canadian federation, well before the Confederation scheme was conceived, McGee said: "I see in the not remote distance one great nationality, bound, like the shield of Achilles, by the blue of the ocean.

"I see it quartered into many communities, each disposing of its own internal affairs, but all bound together by free institutions, free intercourse, free commerce.

"I see, within the round of that shield, the peaks of the western mountains and the crests of the eastern waves. The winding Assiniboine, the five-fold lakes, the St. Lawrence, the Ottawa, the Saguenay, the St. John, the Basin of Minas, by all these flowing waters in all the waters they fertilize. In all the cities they visit in their courses, I see a generation of industrious, contented moral men, free in name and in fact — men capable of maintaining, in peace and in war, a constitution worthy of such a country."[6]

Prior to being gunned down outside his dwelling on Sparks Street in Ottawa, Thomas D'Arcy McGee had been the object of death threats from Fenians. Patrick James Whelan, an Irish nationalist who worked as a tailor in Ottawa, was arrested and charged with the murder. He was convicted — he always staunchly denied that he was guilty — and hanged in 1869, at the last public hanging in Canada. A number of people connected to Whelan were arrested, and then the net was spread wider and dozens of people with Fenian sympathies were rounded up. In response to the Fenian threat, the government suspended habeas corpus, thus removing a legal roadblock that could have prevented the mass arrests.[7]

In October 1871, the final Fenian attack was mounted against the frontier settlement of Pembina, Manitoba. The hope of the Fenians, that they would be met favourably by the Métis of the region, was dashed when Métis leader Louis Riel sided with Canada and helped suppress the minor incursion.

DURING THE YEARS when John A. Macdonald oversaw the spy network, he was continually involved in the broader question of the defence of British North America and later the Dominion of Canada. In one high-profile case, he had to deal with an undertaking of the imperial government in London that he found exceptionally aggravating.

In September 1863, while the American Civil War raged, Sir John Fox Burgoyne, the inspector general of imperial fortifications, dispatched Sir William Francis Drummond Jervois, an army officer and military engineer with a rank of lieutenant colonel, to Canada to report on the state of the territory's defences. Twice in late 1863, Jervois visited the United States, travelling to Boston and Portland, Maine. In both cases, he set out in a rowboat, disguised as an artist, and made sketches of the defences of the harbours. Back in Canada, he reached the conclusion that hostilities between American and British forces on British North American soil were quite likely. He advised that fortifications in Halifax, Quebec City, and Montreal be improved and that British troops be concentrated in the latter two cities. He further concluded that west of Montreal, Canada was indefensible.

The contents of his report, formally submitted in February 1864, became publicly known somewhat earlier.[8] Not surprisingly, Macdonald and other members of the Canadian government were furious at the contention that Canada West was indefensible. In

Macdonald's opinion, the consequence of the report had been to generate "a panic" in Canada West.[9]

While the British government was prepared to fund improvements to the fortifications in Quebec City, it hoped to persuade the Canadian government to fund similar improvements in Montreal. Jervois was once again sent to Canada in the summer of 1864. Members of the Canadian government met with him in October, at the time of the Quebec Conference. In November, the British officer produced a second and more optimistic report. He pointed to the potential benefits of work on fortifications as far west as Hamilton in Canada West and suggested that deploying a naval fleet on Lake Ontario, supported from Kingston, would be useful. He wrote about what he called "General Winter" (a reference to the aid Canada would receive from the climate in a winter campaign), which could bring on a stalemate in combat with the United States. Finally, he concluded that the dominance of the British fleet in the Atlantic could make victory against the United States attainable.[10]

In May 1865, Macdonald received a confidential memorandum drawn up by the members of the Defence Committee of the imperial government. The memo outlined the steps they supported for the defence of Canada based on the second report of Lieutenant Colonel Jervois. The first name on the list of those who drafted the memorandum was that of General John Fox Burgoyne, who had originally sent Jervois on his mission.

The memorandum amounted to no less than an imperial overview of how to manage the defence of Canada in the event of a war with the United States. Enumerated were the proposals for fortifications in Quebec City and Montreal, and the lesser fortifications farther west at Toronto and Hamilton. Kingston was to be the major naval base for the defence of Canada West. If possible, armour-plated naval vessels were to be deployed in operations on the St. Lawrence River and Lake Ontario.* Much emphasis was placed on the need for Canada to

---

* Such vessels had already been used both by the Union and Confederate navies in the Civil War, and their deployment had signalled to the world that naval warfare had entered a new era.

raise a very substantial militia, since the number of British regulars was far short of that needed to thwart an American land invasion. Improvements to canals, internal waterways, and the construction of strategically useful railways were proposed as measures to be undertaken in subsequent years.

Anyone reading the document would conclude that the imperial strategists were counting on the Royal Navy to take the fight to the Americans; were moderately confident that Quebec City, and perhaps Montreal, could be held; and believed that points west of Kingston could put up a spirited show of defence, but not much more.[11]

What the document also underlined is the extent to which the British government retained sovereign authority when it came to the defence of British North America. The colonial governments mattered, were consulted, and were depended upon to raise funds and recruit militiamen for the effort. While on paper the British seemed to be fully committed to the defence of the empire's North American territories, the whole exercise could be interpreted as little more than going through the motions. John A. Macdonald and other Canadian political leaders knew that time was limited to create a viable British North American federal state. With an evident threat from the south and the prospect of waning British backing in the years to come, the window for success was clearly a narrow one.

CONCERNS ABOUT THE defence of British North America helped cement the resolve of politicians to complete the Confederation process. While the highly visible Fenians never really posed a serious challenge to the northern provinces, major political leaders in the United States who adhered to the clarion cry of Manifest Destiny posed a much more significant annexationist threat during these years. Crucial among these was William Seward, who continued as secretary of state under President Andrew Johnson following the assassination of Abraham Lincoln.

Seward was a firm believer in the idea that the United States was destined to become the greatest economic power in the world and that its destiny included territorial expansion north to the Arctic. Seward was not completely consistent in his views on Canada. He did generally believe Canada would be annexed by the United States, but following a visit to Canada in 1857, he wrote a letter that was published in the *Albany Evening Journal*, in which he concluded that Canada was a vast country inhabited by "vigorous, hardy [and] energetic people." He forecast that Canada would separate from Britain and become an independent country that could pose a threat to the U.S. if the Americans allowed themselves to be weakened by the power of the slave states. [12]

Seward oversaw the purchase of Alaska in 1867, known as "Seward's Folly," and he generally hewed to the line that Canada should and would become part of the United States. Following the Civil War, he reasoned that if Britain handed Canada over to the United States, it would wipe away the bad feelings that had been generated among Americans by the construction of warships in Britain for the Confederacy and British recognition of the Confederacy as a belligerent.

Seward had opposed the U.S. war against Mexico, not because he opposed territorial expansion but because he thought the war was being fought to enlarge the empire of the Southern slave owners. Further, he believed that territorial acquisitions should occur peacefully and naturally.

As they worked to counter any threat from the south, British North American leaders, with the steady support of the British government, continued the drive for Confederation. This involved far more than a series of high-minded debates about the nature of government and how the proposed British North American federal state could avoid the errors of American federalism. The dark arts of political arm-twisting were required to keep New Brunswick, and to a lesser extent Nova Scotia, on board for the project.

On March 4, 1865, the project of the British North American union encountered a serious setback with the defeat of pro-Confederation forces led by Premier Samuel Tilley in a New

Brunswick general election. The victor, who headed the province's opposition to Confederation, was Albert Smith, a descendant of United Empire Loyalists. Born in Shediac, New Brunswick, Smith had developed a reputation as an independent political figure, able to cross swords effectively against his adversaries. In 1861, when Tilley became premier, Smith had been his chief lieutenant, holding the position of attorney general. What caused Smith to fall out with Tilley was the issue of competing railway projects. Tilley and his associates backed the proposed Intercolonial Railway that would link Canada and New Brunswick and would run entirely on British North American soil — the same rail line that was endorsed at the Quebec Conference with a promise that its construction would be financed out of the public purse.

The alternative scheme, supported by Smith, was the Western Extension Railway, part of the European and North American Railway, which was to run from Saint John to the U.S. border. With their historic ties to the "Boston States" (New England), despite the Loyalist legacy, many New Brunswickers were drawn to the idea of closer commercial ties to New England, and they looked askance at Confederation with distant Canada.

Even before Tilley called the general election, Smith had begun his campaign against Confederation. In late November 1864, he issued "A Letter to the Electors of the County of Westmorland," in which he lambasted the Maritime delegates to the Charlottetown Conference who had allowed the Canadians to woo them away from the concept of Maritime Union. He said those delegates had acted unconstitutionally, since they had had no mandate to pursue a federal union that would tie the Maritimes to Canada. He claimed that Confederation would subordinate New Brunswick's interests to those of Canada, would involve prohibitive taxes, and would require the people of New Brunswick to contribute to the building of extravagant railways and canals.

When the election was called, Albert Smith took a highly effective stump speech on tour in New Brunswick to batter Tilley and Confederation. He charged that Confederation had been conjured up in the "oily brains of Canadian politicians" to suit Canadian interests. He challenged his audiences to consider two provinces, "one [Canada] suffering from anarchy and disquiet… [the other] New Brunswick… enjoying all the blessings of this life." [13]

Smith won the general election and became premier of the province. But within a year he encountered problems that cost him his office. By the time he came to power, the United States had announced that it was abrogating the Reciprocity Treaty. This meant that Smith's plan for a rail link with New England had had its commercial justification torn out from under it. Even more important was Smith's feud with the lieutenant-governor of New Brunswick, the haughty, aristocratic Arthur Hamilton Gordon, a Briton who had a generally contemptuous attitude toward colonial politicians. The problem for Smith was that while he opposed Confederation, Gordon backed it, as did the British government, and Gordon was determined to use his viceregal office to shoehorn New Brunswick back into support for the British North American union.

Smith journeyed to London to try to shore up his position there. In England, he pressed for efforts to negotiate a new reciprocity agreement with the United States, and he expressed support for a rail link between New Brunswick and Nova Scotia. In London, Colonial Secretary Edward Cardwell told Smith in no uncertain terms that he supported Confederation. [14]

Smith felt the tide of opinion in New Brunswick turning in favour of Confederation, and he was under constant pressure to shift his position in that direction. As a consequence, in March 1866 he decided to include in his government's Speech from the Throne a vague statement in support of some form of British North American union. [15]

On April 6, 1866, New Brunswick's upper house, the appointed Legislative Council — a large majority of which supported Confederation — passed two resolutions that declared support for Confederation based on the Quebec Resolutions and that backed any steps taken to push the project along. [16] The resolutions were intended as a formal address to the Queen. Lieutenant-Governor Gordon used the resolutions as his chance to push Smith out of office. At a meeting with the premier at Government House in Fredericton on April 7, Gordon told Smith that when the pro-Confederation motions were presented to him, he would likely have to express his approval. Later that day, when a committee of the Legislative Council presented the resolutions to him, Gordon decided to support them by making a broad statement backing the British North American union. He transmitted the message to Smith, who returned to Government House to strongly condemn what the lieutenant-governor had just done. Faced with this deadlock with the Legislative Council and with Gordon, Smith and the members of his cabinet handed in their resignations three days later.

This high-handed treatment of an elected premier by the Queen's representative did not pass without comment. The Saint John *Evening Globe* expressed the view that Gordon had "taken the business of the country into his own hands." The paper opined that it must now be decided "whether the Lieutenant-Governor or the House of Assembly is to control the government of New Brunswick." [17]

Called back to office following procedures that were hardly constitutional, Samuel Tilley formed a new government and subsequently led it through a successful election campaign in May and June 1866.

The passing of the political crisis in New Brunswick helped clear away a similar, if less serious, expression of political doubts about British North American union in Nova Scotia.

WITH THE SEVENTY-TWO resolutions passed by the Canadian legislature, and ministries in place in Nova Scotia and New Brunswick that were in support of Confederation, the next step was to take the project to London. The scheme, at least initially, had lost two provinces along the way: Prince Edward Island, which did not join the Confederation until 1873, and Newfoundland, which became a Canadian province in 1949. In London, British North American political leaders were to work with members of the British government to prepare the final text of the British North America Act, the act of the British Parliament that would serve as the constitution of the new Dominion of Canada.

On December 4, 1866, the members of the Canadian and Maritime delegations met in London to begin the final drive to complete Confederation. Tupper and Tilley remained the most important members of the Nova Scotia and New Brunswick delegations. In the Canadian delegation, Macdonald and Cartier were present as leaders of the government, and Galt, who had left the ministry, had been invited to participate. George Brown was absent. He had left the government the previous December and had turned down an invitation to participate in London.

The first decision made in London was to elect John A. Macdonald chairman. Since the beginning of this great undertaking, Macdonald had made himself an indispensable leader, the first among equals. His unanimous selection as chairman was entirely predictable. The London Conference made no fundamental changes to the Quebec Resolutions. Amendments were proposed and carried, but the overall design remained intact. Members of the British government imposed one substantive, if seemingly symbolic, change. Some of the delegates from British North America had wanted the new country to be called the "Kingdom of Canada." The British government, however, took the view that the word "kingdom" would offend the republican Americans. Instead, the word "dominion" was chosen.

On March 8, 1867, the British Parliament passed the British North America Act. The delegates could return home, ready to play their roles when the act came into effect on July 1.

The Confederation project established governments based on the Westminster parliamentary model at both the federal and provincial levels. The head of the federal government would be a prime minister, in theory appointed by the governor general, the head of state acting for the monarch. In practice, the prime minister was the leader of the party enjoying the confidence of the majority of members of the House of Commons. In the event of a parliament in which no single party enjoyed a majority — this did not occur until 1921 — the leader

of the party in first place, or possibly in second place, would negotiate with other party leaders to try to form a government that could
win the confidence of the House.

This structure, which differed so significantly from the U.S. and
Confederate governmental systems, had a palpable effect on the substance of politics. Governments changed quickly following elections.
While not worth pursuing at any length, it is not outside the realm
of possibility that if the United States had operated under a parliamentary system at the time of its crucial election in 1860, the political
outcome could have been very different. Likely a coalition government, or a government in which one party negotiated the backing of
others to gain the support of a majority, would have been sworn in
by the end of November 1860. Whether that government could have
negotiated a deal to stave off the secession of Southern states is, of
course, unknowable. As it was, the four months between the election of Abraham Lincoln as president and his inauguration provided
enough time for seven Southern states to secede and to come together
to form the Confederate States of America.

The federal government obtained the power to raise revenues
through both direct and indirect taxes. In addition, and of immense
importance for the future, the federal government was equipped
with the so-called "spending power," allowing it to spend on whatever it liked, and that extended to areas of provincial jurisdiction. This
allowed Ottawa to set up shared cost programs with the provinces and
to use its financial might to entice, or pressure, provinces into fed-
erally designed projects in health care or highways. That was much
more a matter for the twentieth century than the nineteenth, however.

At the time of Confederation, what really counted, in addition to
the federal taxing power, was control over banking and jurisdiction
over railways that crossed interprovincial or international boundaries. In Canada, the 1860s nation building project was crucially linked
to railways. With regions separated by great distances, the country
would exist in theory only unless rail lines brought it together. The
opponents of Confederation drove home their point that the managers

of the railways were the true power behind the Coalition government and that the Confederation scheme was railway-driven. Alternatively, one could argue that no extensive country could be created unless the railways were built. It was vital to the creation of the dominion that the country's constitution, the British North America Act, included a clause that committed the federal government to financing and building the Intercolonial Railway. A not inconsiderable reason for the creation of a powerful federal government was that it was needed to encourage investors in Britain and the United States to invest in Canadian railways, secure in the knowledge that a solvent state stood behind those projects. Once the four provinces set out to make the leap to embrace the West and the North, the close ties between railways and Ottawa would determine whether Confederation would succeed or fail.

Compared to Ottawa's powers, those vested in the provinces seemed secondary. Twenty-first-century observers will be surprised by the list of supposedly less important powers. The three key areas of jurisdiction were: education, roads, and health care. By the middle of the twentieth century, these fields had migrated to the very centre of government activity and spending.

DESPITE THE CONTINUING belief in important American circles that the United States was destined to expand northward, on July 1, 1867, the British North America Act came into effect and with it a new nation state on the North American continent. The people in its four provinces greeted the Dominion of Canada in a variety of ways. In New Brunswick, the province that had been shoehorned into the federation, people were rather taciturn. At best, they were willing to go along with the new arrangements to see how they would work out. In Nova Scotia, with its longer history and its proud seafaring tradition, numerous people were negatively disposed to the idea of the dominion. Nova Scotians felt closer to Britain and the Caribbean, as a consequence of the triangular trade that linked them, than to distant

Canada. With the Royal Navy securing them against any risk of attack from the United States, the people of Nova Scotia saw themselves as a people in their own right, very much a British people but with their own firm identity. In some Halifax windows, residents hung black curtains on July 1 to mark their displeasure with the new constitutional arrangements. On the other side of the Northumberland Strait, Prince Edward Islanders clung to their own ways, happy enough, at least for the time being, to be outside the new Dominion.

In Quebec, the former Canada East, French Canadians celebrated possession of their own province, while they were more wary about the larger Canada to which they now belonged. A minority people on the continent, in the empire, and in the dominion, a people conquered a century earlier and torn from France, the French Canadians were determined to sustain their language, culture, and institutions. In the phrase of their first great historian, François-Xavier Garneau, the French Canadians had the capacity, whatever the challenge, to survive. According to Garneau, they were gifted with a tenacious capacity for "*la survivance.*"

In Ontario, the most populous province, there was considerable enthusiasm for the Dominion of Canada. Upper Canadians thought of themselves as a British people who resided in the heart of the continent. The Ontario of 1867 looked back on the waves of immigration over the past century that had shaped it. The Loyalists, who came north beginning in 1783, following the British defeat in the American Revolutionary War, had brought an American culture and sensibility to Upper Canada, but it was an American sensibility of a very particular kind: the Loyalists were deeply embittered toward the American Republic and determined in their new home to remain connected to the Mother Country. Next came the so-called "late Loyalists," those who arrived years after the original wave of Loyalists. These Americans came north in search of land, and as such their political loyalties were not strongly developed toward either the United States or Great Britain. The War of 1812, with its repeated U.S. military invasions and periods of American occupation of western regions, honed an identity that drew together the Loyalists, late Loyalists, and immigrants from Britain together into a powerful connection with the empire and rejection of the United States. During the three and a half decades following the war, large waves of immigrants from the British Isles brought English, Scottish, Welsh, and then a flood of Irish into Upper Canada in the late 1840s and early 1850s. On July 1, 1867, Torontonians celebrated their new country with fireworks.

Chapter 17

Red River Rebellion

T HE LAUNCH OF the new Dominion by no means ensured its long-term viability. The great question that hung over the new state was whether it could survive, or would be swallowed up by an expansionist United States. The challenge took two forms. First, could Canada acquire and successfully absorb the vast territories that had been controlled by the Hudson's Bay Company in the North-West? And could the new dominion manage to remain viable as the United States and Britain attempted to settle the bitter differences between them that had arisen during the Civil War? Would their settlement be reached at Canada's expense?

With the Liberal William Ewart Gladstone serving as prime minister of Britain and known to be anxious to resolve outstanding issues with the United States, President Ulysses S. Grant and his secretary of state, Hamilton Fish, seized the opportunity to put to rest America's Civil War grievances by striking an advantageous deal.

In early 1871, the British and American governments agreed to appoint a joint commission to canvass and resolve the issues. Hamilton Fish served on the commission, along with five other appointees. On the British side were Lord de Grey and Sir Stafford Northcote, both members of the Gladstone cabinet; three other appointees from Britain; and Sir John A. Macdonald (he had been knighted after Confederation).

This appointment placed Macdonald in an extremely awkward position as the leader of the Canadian government. One of six British commissioners, he could be outvoted on matters of great importance to Canada by commissioners whose overriding objective was to reach a deal with Washington. In Canada, he would be held responsible for whatever came out of the commission. This was not an enviable state of affairs for a politician who would be facing the electorate in a general election in 1872.[1]

The commissioners met in Washington, D.C., Macdonald arriving by train. No one from the U.S. government came to greet him. The commissioners concluded a treaty on May 8, 1871, that was speedily ratified by the British and American governments. While the main elements of the Treaty of Washington dealt with the settlement of the American complaint against Britain for the construction of the Confederate warship *Alabama* in a British shipyard, it also contained a provision that was decidedly negative from the point of view of John A. Macdonald and the Canadian government: American fishermen were granted rights to fish in Canadian waters.

When the details of the treaty were made public in Canada, Macdonald was lambasted by his political opponents, as well as by Maritimers, for whom the fishery was a vital interest. The British government softened the blow for the Macdonald government when it agreed to guarantee a loan of £2.5 million for the construction of the Pacific Railway when the Canadian parliament ratified the Treaty of Washington.[2] Considering how much worse things could have gone for Macdonald in Washington, he was lucky to escape with his infant country intact. One important consequence of the treaty and of Macdonald's role in the negotiations is that its ratification amounted to a de facto recognition of the new dominion by the United States government.

Then came the reach for the vast lands of the Hudson's Bay Company. The acquisition of this territory would be even more important to Canada than the Louisiana Purchase had been to the United States. With Rupert's Land, the dominion would become a continental entity with enormous potential for the future.

The Canadians who planned Confederation and led the country through its first years as a federal state knew that unless Canada asserted its effective claim to the British territory in the West, the Americans soon would. The initial plan was that the land was to be acquired on December 1, 1869, after being passed to the British Crown by the Hudson's Bay Company and then from the British government to Canada. The Macdonald government treated the matter as a real estate transfer involving London and Ottawa, taking next to no account of the people living in the territory.

Laying claim to a vast territory was one thing. Demonstrating the ability to control it was quite another. History is rife with episodes in which great powers have promoted unrest on such territories or have seized the moment when unrest arises to occupy lands that they covet. With no railway connecting Canada to the prairies, and no substantial police or military force to control the territory and to make the claim to sovereignty, the dominion risked a land grab from the south. While the United States had largely demobilized the great armies that had won the Civil War by the end of the 1860s, the military capacity of those forces could easily be re-established. Macdonald and the members of his government were keenly aware of that potent fact.

Meanwhile, influential Americans watched and waited for an opportunity to seize this vital portion of the continent on behalf of the United States. This was natural enough: when the people of the Red River territory in the 1860s focused on the outside world, they looked south to the rail lines that ran through Saint Paul, the capital of Minnesota.

Saint Paul merchants dreamed of their city becoming the entrepôt of commercial markets in the north. And railway owners saw the potential for their rail lines to be extended into the British territories. U.S. Senator Alexander Ramsey, a former governor of Minnesota, continually drew the attention of the United States government to the cause of annexation. [3]

Beginning in the late 1850s, James Wickes Taylor, a railway lobbyist, U.S. Treasury representative, undercover agent of the United

States government, and at times a U.S. consul, promoted the idea of annexation of the Red River territory and the whole of the vast British North-West for a quarter of a century. [4]

In 1866, Taylor, who saw no contradiction between his roles as a promoter of railways and his work for the U.S. government, helped draft a congressional bill that advocated "the admission of the States of Nova Scotia, New Brunswick, Canada East, Canada West" to the Union along with the territories of Selkirk, Saskatchewan, and Columbia (present-day Western Canada). In a letter to the assistant secretary of the United States Treasury the following year, Taylor continued to promote the bill, which had not been put to a vote in Congress: "I firmly believe, if the bill referred to was placed among the Laws of the United States, as a standing proposition for the consideration of Great Britain and the Provinces, that the state of public sentiment over the border...would soon be irresistible. We have only to deposit an 'open basket'...under the tree, and the ripe fruit will speedily fall." [5]

In the months following Confederation, the Macdonald government took the first concrete steps to acquire the territory from the Hudson's Bay Company. The parliament of the new dominion met for the first time in November 1867. In the House of Commons, on December 4, William McDougall, the minister of public works, expressed the view that the time had come to add the North-West to Canada so that "the whole expanse from the Atlantic to the Pacific would be peopled with a race the same as ourselves." [6] When Sir John A. Macdonald addressed the House a couple of days later, a Nova Scotia member of Parliament asked whether the people who lived in the North-West had been consulted. Macdonald responded by saying that they were "incapable of the management of their own affairs." Instead, he said, it would be necessary to consult with the Hudson's Bay Company and "arrange with the Imperial Government...for powers enabling the Parliament of the Dominion to provide a constitution which might be amended as necessary hereafter, to adapt it to the growing requirements of the new country." [7]

While the Macdonald government wrestled with other matters in the first months of 1868, it was not until the autumn of that year that William McDougall and George-Étienne Cartier were sent to London to begin talks with the Hudson's Bay Company about the terms of the land transfer. Continuing negotiations through British intermediaries, the Canadian government reached terms acceptable to both parties in March 1869. Negotiators for Canada undertook to deposit £300,000 in guaranteed bonds in a London bank. Canada agreed to make tax concessions to the Hudson's Bay Company and to allow the company to retain 5 percent of all the land in the territory regarded as particularly suitable for farming. In return, the company would relinquish all its claims to the territory to the British government. For its part, the British government would then turn the territory over to the Dominion of Canada. [8]

To finalize its part of the arrangement, the Canadian Parliament had to ratify the terms of the transfer and to set out Canada's policy for administering the North-West. In June 1869, the prime minister introduced legislation for the acquisition of the territory. The bill established that Rupert's Land would be administered by a governor and council whose members would be appointed by Ottawa. But this arrangement would be temporary. During this initial period, the bill enabled the governor to establish "Laws, Institutions, and Ordinances" without any need to consult the inhabitants of the region. Macdonald explained to the members of the House that the "act would remain in force until the end of the next session." After this period, he asserted, "a more permanent government" would be created. He did not, however, explain what sort of entity the North-West would then become. Would it be a province or a territory, and would the inhabitants have a right to elect their governors? These essential questions he left unanswered. [9]

In his personal correspondence during this period, Macdonald was blunt about what he wanted to happen in the North-West before he would bestow any form of democratic regime on the region. In a letter to J. Y. Brown, an Ontario member of Parliament whose brother was already living in Red River, Macdonald wrote: "in another year the present residents will be altogether swamped by the influx of strangers who will go in with the idea of becoming industrious and peaceable settlers." [10]

The prime minister's letter made it clear that his government intended to open the North-West to migrants from Canada and to pay as little attention as possible to the residents of the territory. The government issued a "Draft Order in Council for Uniting...the North-Western Territory to the Dominion of Canada." On the matter of land tenure, Article 10 of the order stated: "All titles to land up to the 8th March 1869 conferred by the company are to be confirmed." The problem with this assurance to residents is that it failed to cover the large majority who had no such documented title to their land. For most of the Métis, the fact that they occupied the land was the only proof of possession they could offer.

The Canadian government dispatched John Stoughton Dennis, a militia lieutenant colonel, and a crew of surveyors to the territory around Fort Garry to make recommendations about where the expected new settlers could be established. Not surprisingly, the arrival of the surveyors alarmed the existing residents. On August 21, Dennis dispatched a report to Public Works Minister William McDougall, who was shortly to depart for the territory as Macdonald's governor-designate. In his report, Dennis warned that "a considerable degree of irritation exists among the native population in view of surveys and settlements being made without the Indian title having been first extinguished." He reported that the "question must be regarded as the very greatest importance," stating that the "French half breeds...have gone so far as to threaten violence should surveys be attempted to be made." [11]

As the Canadians prepared to take control of the territory, they did not realize that the Métis were readying themselves to defend their lands against any interlopers. As early as July 1869, the Métis in one parish, with the strong backing of their priest, Father N.-J. Ritchot, established patrols to be alert and ready should strangers arrive. With two captains, Baptiste Tourond and Jean-Baptiste Lépine, in charge of the patrols, the people of St. Norbert were not leaving their fate to the goodwill of distant authorities.

Tourond and Lépine were typical of the men who assumed leadership roles in the community. With French-Canadian fathers and native mothers, these men had large families and were likely to be in their forties. They were determined to prevent newcomers from establishing themselves on the lands along the Red and Assiniboine Rivers.

Native people have lived on the prairies for thousands of years. During the decades prior to Canada's acquisition of the prairies in 1869–70, a new people formed on this territory: the Métis Nation. The Métis were a people of mixed origins, both native and European. For the past four centuries, populations of mixed native and European origins have lived in Canada. In the seventeenth and eighteenth centuries in the Acadian communities along the Bay of Fundy there were frequent marriages between Acadians and Mi'kmaqs, and children of mixed ancestry often lived in Acadian settlements.

The people who are the focus of this chapter are the Métis of the prairies, those who emerged as a consequence of unions between native people and white fur traders. The Métis had a sense of their uniqueness and saw themselves as a nation with links to both their French-Canadian and their native ancestors, but with a way of life that made them distinct from their forebears. Catholicism and strong ties to the clergy were key elements of Métis identity. Their nationhood was deeply rooted in an intimate knowledge of the northern terrain they inhabited and in the annual ritual of the buffalo hunt.

The major centre of the Métis people was the settlement at the junction of the Assiniboine River and the Red River (present-day Winnipeg). Fur traders, working for both the Hudson's Bay Company, based in London, and the North West Company, with its headquarters in Montreal, often formed liaisons with native women. Men of European origin who worked for the Hudson's Bay Company were generally expected to leave the territory when they retired. Not all did. Some remained to live out their lives as members of the families they had formed in fur trade country. The North West Company did not expect their men to leave the territory upon retirement. That was their choice.

Two streams of Métis emerged: one French speaking, the descendants of francophone voyageurs and native women; the other English speaking, the descendants of English or Scottish settlers and native women. While the two groups were distinct, they shared many interests and often made common cause with each other. Over the decades, the French-speaking Métis became numerically and politically the dominant branch in the Red River Colony.

There, the Métis worked as fur traders and participated in the buffalo hunt, converting buffalo meat into pemmican. A native invention, pemmican (the word is Cree in origin) is a concentrated mixture of high-protein meats to which cranberries or saskatoon berries were sometimes added. For ceremonies such as weddings, pemmican could contain cherries, currants, or blueberries. In the Red River area, buffalo was the chief source of meat, while in other regions native peoples made pemmican from moose, elk, or deer. Pemmican was highly valued as a concentrated product that could be packaged to supply food to voyageurs who travelled long distances by canoe. Native peoples also consumed pemmican, as did white settlers.

Along the Red and Assiniboine Rivers, near the Forks, Métis built houses, using the rivers as their highways. Behind the houses were long, narrow farms in the French-Canadian style, where people produced food for their own consumption and some to be sold on the market. A major problem for the Métis, then and in later decades, was that even if they had lived on and farmed a property for decades, they did not have a title to the land.

In 1812, Thomas Douglas, the fifth Earl of Selkirk, obtained a vast tract of land, 120,000 square miles in extent. This included the Red River Colony and lands west, east, north, and south of it. (The original Selkirk tract included lands in present-day Saskatchewan, Manitoba, Ontario, and across the border in the United States.) To gain control of a territory the size of a small European state, Selkirk purchased a controlling interest in the Hudson's Bay Company, which in turn granted the land to him.

In this vast undertaking, Selkirk was motivated by potential profits as well as by romantic and humanitarian impulses. He acquired the land, which he called Assiniboia, as a site for the resettlement of Scottish farmers driven off their small plots by large landowners who were creating vast estates for sheep farming through the Highland and Lowland Clearances. In 1811, Selkirk sponsored the expedition of a small party of Scots to Assiniboia. After they spent the winter at York Factory, they pushed on to Red River, where they built Fort Douglas. Having completed the fort too late in the season to begin farming, the settlers turned to buffalo hunting to acquire food for the coming winter. In the spring of 1813, the Selkirk settlers began farming, but the results fell short of what had been hoped for.

In 1814, both to husband food that was in short supply and also as a way of striking a competitive blow at the North West Company, Miles Macdonell, the governor of the Red River Colony, issued the Pemmican Proclamation. For a short period of time, the proclamation banned the export of pemmican from the Red River Colony. Since this cut into the market and reduced the price of pemmican, producers of the product were incensed. This triggered what was called, with a degree of exaggeration, the Pemmican War. Workers for the North West Company who relied on pemmican supplied by the Métis were so enraged that they attacked and destroyed Fort Douglas and burned down the buildings that surrounded it.

While the fort was rebuilt, the arrival of the Selkirk project continued to stoke tensions. As was later to be the case with the Canadians, Selkirk and those who worked for him approached the region as though no one of importance was already there. Native and Métis rights were simply brushed aside. When he received news of tensions in the colony, Lord Selkirk replaced the existing governor with a new one, Robert Semple, an American businessman.

In 1816, tensions exploded in the Battle of Seven Oaks. The battle erupted after a band of Métis men, accompanied by French Canadians,

English speakers, and native tribesmen working for the North West Company, seized a supply of pemmican from the Hudson's Bay Company, believing it had been stolen from the Métis. While en route to sell the pemmican to the North West Company, the armed party encountered Governor Semple, accompanied by Hudson's Bay Company employees and settlers. The groups met at a point along the Red River called Seven Oaks by the English and La Grenouillère (Frog Plain) by the Métis.

It is likely that, following a verbal confrontation, a fusillade ensued. The Métis sharpshooters, led by Cuthbert Grant, outnumbered their opponents three to one. They killed twenty-one men, including Governor Semple. Only one of the Métis men was killed. [12]

A Royal Commissioner named W. B. Coleman was appointed to investigate. He exonerated the Métis for their role in the battle.

OVER THE NEXT half decade, a number of important developments changed the circumstances of the Red River Colony. Under the Treaty of 1818, signed by the United States and Britain, the boundary between the United States and British North America was extended from the northwest point of Lake of the Woods to the 49th parallel, and west along that parallel to the Stony Mountains (Rocky Mountains). This cut off the southernmost portion of the Selkirk territory, which was now part of the United States.

In 1820, Lord Selkirk died; the following year, the Hudson's Bay Company and the North West Company merged. [13] On the whole, the Selkirk Settlement had been a failure, drawing only a small number of migrants to the Red River Colony. While the colony remained the property of Selkirk's family, the Hudson's Bay Company took over its management. In 1836, the sixth Earl of Selkirk gave up ownership of the lands that had been bestowed on his father, and the territory came back under the formal control of the Hudson's Bay Company. [14]

Over the succeeding decades, the Métis community continued to develop under the broad aegis of the Hudson's Bay Company.

Canadian interest in the territory waxed and waned over time. It was always in the background, as the good farmland of Canada West was fully occupied and farmers sought new lands to cultivate. Some of them migrated west into Michigan. Politicians and newspapers in Canada West promoted the idea that territory of the North-West, Rupert's Land, could provide arable fields for Canadian farmers.

By the 1850s, the Métis population in the Red River Colony had doubled from its level twenty years earlier. Those who produced the much-needed pemmican were, for the most part, the descendants of those who had supplied the Hudson's Bay Company a generation previous. Along the banks of the Red and Assiniboine Rivers, many new houses had been built, and the extent of cultivation had expanded, along with a growth in the number of livestock being raised by farmers. The French-speaking Métis continued to work for the Hudson's Bay Company, not as full-time employees but in the role of suppliers of provisions. The English-speaking people of mixed ancestry grew alongside the Métis. They were, if anything, more closely tied to the Hudson's Bay Company. Some of them were hired into clerical management positions, such as that of apprentice-postmaster.[15]

In 1857, both the British government and the government of the Province of Canada sent expeditions to the territory to evaluate the potential for large-scale agricultural development. The British sent Captain John Palliser, who concluded that the drainage basins of the Red and Saskatchewan Rivers held enormous promise for farming. H. Y. Hind, a geologist and explorer, led the Canadian expedition, and he drew the same broad conclusion. Hind, however, focused much more on the present and past human presence in the region than Palliser did. Hind's observations on this subject did much to hone an intensely negative view of the Métis and native peoples who lived in the territory. He recorded that Lord Selkirk's effort to populate the colony with Scottish migrants had not been much of a success. As a consequence, the settlement had regressed by falling into the hands of people he called "half breeds." He concluded that the "diminution of European settlers" had caused the colony to sink ever "nearer to the savage wildness of Indian life."

He noted that while on first glance, the "neat whitewashed houses" along the Red and Assiniboine looked European, when examined more closely the structures and lands around them were kept in "slovenly," "careless" fashion. He drew the conclusion that the North-West would one day become prosperous when it was populated by "an energetic and civilized race, able to improve its vast capabilities and appreciate its marvelous beauties." [16]

To his negative characterization, Hind added the assertion that the Métis had no legitimate claim to the lands they occupied. He wrote that they had "no paper or document of any kind to show that they held possession." He warned in his report that if an incoming wave of settlers, which clearly he favoured, should have to "thrust on one side" the people who were now on the land, the Métis could resist and could prove to be "a very formidable enemy." [17]

Hind's report was a classic statement of the white settler attitude. In the view of those who drew on his report for guidance, the present occupiers had no real claim to the land and should be cleared aside as painlessly as possible to make way for occupation by people of European stock.

In 1869, when Canada was about to gain control of the North-West, there were about six thousand Métis in Assiniboia; the native English numbered around four thousand, and there were fewer than one thousand Canadians. [18] When McDougall, the would-be governor, arrived with his party in Red River, what he encountered was a Métis people with its own government and police force.

During the last week of September 1869, McDougall and his men left Ottawa for the North-West. The weakness of the Canadian government's position was underlined by the fact that McDougall had to travel most of the way by rail through the United States. There was no route across Canadian and British territory for him to take. Alerted that there could be some resistance in the territory, the party took several cases of rifles with them. The idea was for them to use the rifles to arm a local police force to be recruited from the existing population. [19]

McDougall and his party travelled by train through the U.S. to the end of the rail line at St. Cloud, Minnesota. From there, they continued their journey to the border by ox cart. As he was about to cross into Rupert's Land, McDougall's right to enter the territory was disputed in peremptory fashion. An organization calling itself the National Committee of the Métis of Red River had drafted a note on October 21, 1869, to be presented to McDougall when he reached the border.

"The National Committee of the Métis of Red River orders William McDougall not to enter the Territory of the North West without special permission of the above-mentioned committee," the note read. [20] On October 11, 1869, one of John Stoughton Dennis's crews had been carrying out a survey on a property in Father N.-J. Ritchot's parish when the farmer on the land, Édouard Marion, and sixteen of his neighbours ordered them to leave. Present were Baptiste Tourond and Louis Riel.

LOUIS RIEL WAS just shy of his twenty-fifth birthday when he made himself the voice of the Métis Nation. Unlike Jefferson Davis, Abraham Lincoln, and John A. Macdonald, who also gave expression to the nationalisms of their peoples, Louis Riel was staunchly Catholic. Moreover, his nationalism was that of a people of mixed race and arose as a defensive response to the Macdonald government's white settler project.

Like the other three leaders, Louis Riel benefited from being tutored in life by a strong mother who loved him deeply, believed in his destiny, and drew him close to the church from his first days.

Riel, a gifted child, came to the attention of the influential bishop of Saint Boniface, Monseigneur Alexandre-Antonin Taché. In June 1858, Louis, along with two other boys from Red River, travelled to Montreal prior to his fourteenth birthday to continue his studies. He attended the Sulpician Collège de Montréal. Over the next few years, the young seminarian developed from a shy and awkward boy into a first-class student whose work drew high praise from his teachers. In March 1865, Louis Riel abruptly ended his studies at the college, four months before the end of the academic year, the likely reason being the sudden end of a love affair. He remained in Montreal for the next year and then spent time in Chicago, and likely in Saint Paul, before returning to Red River in July 1868. [21] What Louis Riel would make of himself was as yet unclear.

But the man and the moment came together in the summer and autumn of 1869, when members of the Métis community at Red River grew increasingly alarmed at Canada's acquisition of territory. It was not long before the young man's leadership skills and clarity of thought propelled him to the fore.

ON ÉDOUARD MARION's land on October 29, speaking in English, Riel declared to Dennis that Canada "had no right to make surveys... without the express permission of the people of the Settlement." [22]

It was one thing for the Métis to order surveyors off one piece of land. What they needed was an ongoing governmental structure to defend their lands and families and to negotiate with the Canadians. To form this governing body, they drew on the experience of a long-standing organization: the one that oversaw the annual spring buffalo hunt. Hundreds of Métis families took part in the hunt. The hunters formed teams, and each team chose a captain. In turn, the captains picked a principal leader to preside over the council of captains. Through this structure, regulations were set out to govern the hunt. Moreover, the council of the hunt dealt with those accused of committing offences against the laws of the community. Though the Hudson's Bay Company did not recognize this structure, it was already a de facto Métis government.

Although the importance of the hunt had declined and that of farming had increased, the structure of the hunt gave the Métis a model to draw on in the present crisis. Groups of families selected their captains. These leaders met at St. Norbert, and on October 16 they declared themselves the National Committee of the Métis of Red River. They chose a president, John Bruce, and a secretary, Louis Riel. [23]

The committee soon concluded that the struggle with Canada could become an armed conflict and that the Métis needed to take a firm stand. That is what drove them to issue the note warning McDougall not to enter the territory without permission. The note had the additional effect of alerting the Canadian government that the Métis had set up their own governing structure. McDougall, in the meantime, was confident that he would be able to draw reinforcements from Canadians already in the settlement or from the federal government, which could send an armed force overland to the North-West. He concluded that he should proceed to cross the border on December 1 — the legal date of the transfer of the territory to Canada — and take up his position as governor.

The Métis National Committee quickly consolidated its hold on the territory. On November 2, its troops seized control of Fort Garry without bloodshed. Then the committee took the essential step of reaching out to the native English communities by inviting them to elect twelve representatives; Métis communities would elect an equal number. These representatives would meet on November 16 to "consider the present political state of the country, and to adopt such measures as may be deemed best for the future welfare of the same."[24]

The representatives of the two groups met on November 16, which was about the date when Prime Minister John A. Macdonald learned that his governor-designate had been kept out of the territory. His initial source of information was newspapers from the United States. A few days later, Macdonald received McDougall's first report, which interpreted events as meaning that members of the local population feared that they would be excluded from the governing council that was to be established and that "the half breeds would be all driven back from the River and their land given to others."

McDougall told the prime minister that the permanent solution to the problem was to "call for volunteers from Canada to *settle* the country with a good Rifle among the implements of husbandry in each case." For the time being, the would-be governor reported, "I am not frightened and don't believe the insurrection will last a week."

To this missive, Macdonald responded on November 20 by telling McDougall that Canada would not send a military force, but instead would dispatch two representatives, both French Canadians, to try to calm the tensions in the region: Father J.-B. Thibault, a Quebec priest who had served as a missionary in the North-West, and Colonel Charles de Salaberry, a militia officer. Their task, Macdonald wrote, would be to inform the Métis that all "stories as to the intentions of Canada to deprive them of their lands and to govern...without any reference to the residents" were false.

The prime minister also hoped to recruit leading Métis to his cause. In his letter to McDougall, he wrote: "It occurs to me that you should ascertain from Governor McTavish [the outgoing Hudson's Bay Company governor] to name the two leading half-breeds in the Territory, and inform them at once that you will take them into your council. This man Riel, who appears to be a moving spirit, is a clever fellow, and you should endeavour to retain him as an officer in your future police. If you do this promptly it will be a most convincing proof that you are not going to leave the half-breeds out of the Law." [25]

Macdonald, who had reached the political heights largely through the arts of persuasion and patience, ended his letter to McDougall with a warning against hot-headed behaviour: "The point you must never forget is that you are approaching a foreign country under the government of the Hudson's Bay Company...You cannot force your way in." [26]

The prime minister wrote a further missive to McDougall urging a calm approach, but it was sent by ordinary mail on November 27, which meant it would not reach the governor-designate for about ten days. Had Macdonald wanted it to affect McDougall's actions on the critical day, December 1, when Canada legally acquired the colony, he would have needed to send a telegram to Fort Abercrombie in the Dakota Territory, the northernmost point that could be reached by telegram on the Red River. From there, riders on horseback could have conveyed the contents of the telegram to McDougall.

In the absence of instructions from the prime minister, McDougall crossed the border into the territory in the early hours of December 1 and verbally proclaimed his power as governor to a dark stretch of prairie. Later that day, printed copies of the governor's proclamation were posted at many points in Red River. [27]

McDougall's arrival prompted Louis Riel, the Métis, and the native English to finalize the list of demands they would make before allowing Canada to take possession of the territory. Riel placed a fifteen-point document before the council. Among the demands were: an elected government with the power to legislate on issues "local to the Territory"; recognition of the French and English languages as having equal status; and security of land tenure for all those who occupied land and not just those whose land titles were registered. On the crucial issue of land tenure, the Métis and the native English were in agreement. Where they parted company was on how far the council should go in proclaiming itself to be the local government. The native English were not prepared to have the council take unto itself the role of a government, insisting that to do so would amount to an act of rebellion.

Disagreeing on this crucial point, the council ceased to sit on December 1. Riel charged that the native English, while agreeing with the Métis on the enumeration of their rights, were unwilling to do what was necessary to enforce them. He chided them: "Go, return peacefully to your farms! Stay in the arms of your wives. But watch us act. We are going ahead to work and obtain the guarantee of our rights and yours." [28]

Things moved quickly thereafter. With the Métis and the native English divided over how to act, Canadians in the territory, although distinctly in the minority, persuaded McDougall that he should attempt to recruit some of the native English to his standard, and if necessary should be willing to fight the Métis. When Riel learned that about fifty Canadians and their backers had barricaded themselves in a store in the village of Winnipeg, the Métis transported pieces of artillery to the store and threatened to open fire. Then they broke in and rounded up the party and marched them off to jail in Fort Garry.

When the Canadian surveyor, Colonel Dennis — it had been hoped by some of the Canadians that he could lead an armed force against Riel — heard about the jailing of his allies, he fled overland on foot through the snow to Minnesota. Having tried and failed to assert his role as governor, McDougall travelled back to Ottawa in late December. A few days later, Macdonald charged that McDougall had made "the greatest possible mess of everything." [29]

MACDONALD'S ATTEMPTS TO send new representatives to the territory to restore order quickly failed. Colonel de Salaberry and Father Thibault arrived in Red River, but Thibault was soon won over by the Métis position. Next to arrive from Canada was Donald A. Smith of the Hudson's Bay Company. The prime minister had charged him with the task of acting as a commissioner, but his real mission was to divide the opposition in Red River and to win over the native English and the Canadians to offset the power of the Métis.

Once Smith was in Red River, however, he set out to persuade the local population, including the Métis, that they could enter Confederation assured of the recognition of their rights as a distinct political community. On January 19, 1870, at a large public meeting in the courtyard of Fort Garry, Smith delivered a speech promising the people that they had no reason to fear a loss of their rights. Having been told that they could set out the terms on which their territory would be transferred to Canada, the Métis and the native English decided to elaborate the details of their position. Before doing so, Riel ended the meeting with Smith with a play on the derogatory term "half breeds": "We claim no half rights...but all the rights we are entitled to. Those rights will be set forth by our representatives, and what is more, Gentlemen, we will get them." [30]

The Métis and the native English proceeded immediately to elect forty delegates to a convention tasked with setting out the concerns of the people. Beyond that, the idea was to send a party of representatives to Ottawa to convey their position and to obtain from the Canadian government the recognition of their rights. The convention held its first meeting on January 26 and chose six people, three Métis and three native English, to prepare a list of demands.

Within three days, the six members came up with their text, which was very similar to Riel's earlier draft. Then the entire convention debated and adopted it. Finally, they turned over a copy of the demands to Smith at 11:00 p.m. on February 7, requesting that he respond two hours later with yes or no answers. [31]

When Smith appeared before the convention, he refused to give simple positive or negative responses. For the most part, he appeared accommodating on the major issues. On the matter of autonomy for the region, drafted so as to be very similar to provincial status, he said the demand would be "fully and liberally considered." On equal status for the French and English languages, he said this would be "unquestionably... provided for." On the crucial issue of land tenure, Smith was positive. He agreed that "property held by residents in peaceable possession will be secured." He saw no difficulty with Article 16 on the list of demands, which read: "That all properties, rights and privileges, as hitherto enjoyed by us, be respected and the recognition and arrangement of local customs, usages and privileges, be made under the control of the Local Legislature." On the demand for a broadly inclusive franchise, Smith would not commit himself, because he did know whether the absence of a property qualification and the inclusion of native people as voters would be agreed to by the government of Canada. [32]

The convention, the demands, and the virtual recognition by Smith of the government established at Red River represented a high point for the cause of the Métis and the native English. Despite their differences, they had managed to make common cause.

The prime minister was intent on ruling the territory from Ottawa and bringing the local people into degrees of self-government only when a large migration from Canada had swamped the Métis and the native English with white settlers. He was prepared to establish a council with two-thirds of its members drawn from the local population.

But this council was to be purely advisory, not the legislative body that Riel, the Métis, and the native English were demanding. Just as important, Macdonald was not prepared to agree to recognize the land rights of persons whose claim to the land rested solely on possession.

Macdonald drew the conclusion that only a military expedition from Canada to the territory could establish Canadian possession on terms acceptable to his government.

In mid-February 1870, with Riel's provisional government in charge at Red River and Ottawa planning to send a military force in the spring, a group called the Canadian Party launched a new attempt to seize Fort Garry. Once again, the coup failed. The most vociferous of the Canadians, Irish-born Thomas Scott, was jailed. Scott verbally hurled abuse at his jailers until his continual taunting drove tempers to the breaking point. President Louis Riel, the head of the provisional government, set up a special tribunal to try Scott for treason against the Riel government. On March 3, 1870, a majority of the members of the tribunal voted in favour of execution. The next day, Scott was led from his cell and placed before a firing squad. When the execution squad fired, Scott was struck. As he lay dying, he was dispatched by a member of the squad who stepped forward and administered the *coup de grâce*.[33]

There continues to be controversy over whether the tribunal and the firing squad intended to execute Scott or merely to carry out a mock execution and frighten him. According to one version of events, the firing squad loaded their guns with powder and wad but no bullets. When these men fired, loud noises were heard but Scott was not hit with bullets. As this version goes, an Irish nationalist by the name of William O'Donoghue was in the crowd watching the execution, and when the members of the firing squad pulled their triggers, O'Donoghue fired his revolver and struck Scott. Then François Guillemette walked up to the wounded man and shot him.[34]

Whatever the truth about Scott's execution, there is no doubt about the long shadow his death cast over Canada for years to come. In Protestant Ontario, Scott took on mythic status as a victim of Roman

Catholic criminals. From March 1870 on, the issue of the Métis and the merits of their cause could not be separated from the alleged crime against Scott, a Protestant.

A month after Scott's execution, on April 6, 1870, Prime Minister John A. Macdonald weighed in with his opinion in the House of Commons: "The intelligence is complete as to the fact of the man [Thomas Scott] having been shot by a party of men calling themselves a Court Martial.

"That the man was murdered there can be no doubt." [35]

THREE MAJOR EVENTS completed the tempestuous year 1870 in the North-West: the arrival in Ottawa of a delegation from the North-West to negotiate with the federal government; the creation of the province of Manitoba through the passage of the Manitoba Act; and the dispatch of a military force from central Canada to the North-West under the command of Colonel Garnet Wolseley.

On April 11, 1870, the three-man delegation representing the provisional government in the North-West arrived in Ottawa. Alfred H. Scott, a Winnipeg bartender; Judge John Black, the principal law officer of the Red River Colony; and Father N.-J. Ritchot met with the prime minister to make the case that the settlement should be admitted to Canada as its fifth province. The delegation further demanded that all those who had participated in the rising and the formation of the provisional government must be amnestied. The three men also strongly put the case for the protection of the lands occupied by the population of the North-West.

The upshot of the negotiations was the drafting of the Manitoba Act, which would create a new province and admit it into Confederation. Receiving royal assent on May 12, 1870, the Manitoba Act established a territorially small province, in the shape of a postage stamp, that surrounded Fort Garry, present-day Winnipeg. In one crucial respect, Manitoba was not to be the constitutional equal of the other provinces — the lands and resources of the new province were to be owned by the federal government rather than the province, a situation that would not change until 1930, with an amendment to the British North America Act that transferred ownership to the provinces of Manitoba, Saskatchewan, and Alberta. The French and English languages enjoyed equal status under the Manitoba Act, but there was no provision that ensured public schools in the French language.

Having agreed to establish the new province, Macdonald was loath to leave de facto power in the hands of Riel's provisional government. In the spring of 1870, Colonel Garnet Wolseley led a British military expedition to the North-West. Having been denied passage across American territory by the U.S. government, the force had to travel across the very rugged territory of present-day northern Ontario. Making their way by ship on the Great Lakes and across the terrain of the Canadian Shield, the expedition arrived at Fort Garry in late August. Wolseley immediately assaulted the Fort, only to discover that Riel and his men had abandoned it.

The British government had been reluctant to send British troops into the North-West; it feared angering the United States government if the expedition was seen to conquer the Métis and the native peoples of the region. That is why the British insisted that it would not send the expedition until Macdonald had come to terms with the Riel government. The Manitoba Act and the Wolseley mission were intimately connected.

The creation of the Province of Manitoba did not erase the Métis issue or the controversy surrounding Louis Riel. Instead, polemics about Riel and the execution of Thomas Scott engendered a deep divide between English and French Canada. Politicians, newspapers, opinion makers, and the general public in Ontario and Quebec were on opposite sides of what can be called the "Riel Question." In Ontario, anti-Riel sentiment was kept at a fever pitch, driven by personalities who had been closely tied to the Canadian Party at Red River, such as the poet Charles Mair and other members of the "Canada First" movement. Meanwhile, in Quebec, the newspapers, major Catholic Church figures, and the general public strongly backed Riel and called for a general amnesty for those who had been involved in the Red River Rebellion, including Riel.

This was an era in which Canadian politics often descended into recriminations between Protestant Orangemen in Ontario and the Roman Catholic Church in Quebec, especially its ultramontane wing. In the aftermath of the Red River Rebellion and the execution of Scott, Riel became a symbol not only of the Métis but also of French Canada. His cause became the cause of French Canada and the Catholic Church, the cause of ensuring a place for French Canadians in the West. During these years, John A. Macdonald's public posture toward the Métis and Louis Riel shifted according to the tone of the political debate. Macdonald was not alone in trimming his political sails to suit the times. When Liberal Alexander Mackenzie replaced Macdonald as prime minister in 1873 as a consequence of the Pacific Scandal, he also found the amnesty issue highly difficult to navigate.

In 1873, Wilfrid Laurier, who later won solid support from French Canadians for the Liberal Party, argued the case for amnesty for Louis Riel in the House of Commons. In his speech, the young member of Parliament for Quebec East advanced two reasons for an amnesty. The first was that during the Red River Rebellion of 1869–70, "the Canadian government received the delegates of Mr. Riel's government and treated with him as one power treats with another power."

His second reason focused on the execution of Thomas Scott: "All the acts with which Mr. Riel is charged are purely political acts. It was said here yesterday that the execution of Scott was a crime; granted, but it was a political act... Mr. Riel, in signing the warrant for Scott's execution, did nothing but give effect to the sentence of a court.

"However illegal may have been that court," Laurier reasoned, "however iniquitous may have been the sentence rendered by that court, the fact alone that it was rendered and that that court existed *de facto* was sufficient to impart an exclusively political character to the execution.

"His [Riel's] whole crime and the crime of his friends was that they wanted to be treated as British subjects and not to be bartered away like common cattle." [36]

But by 1875, Riel was living in exile with his wife and two small children in Montana, after three times being elected to the Canadian House of Commons from the Manitoba riding of Provencher. Threatened with the possibility of arrest or even assassination, Riel did travel to Parliament on one occasion to sign in as a member of the House of Commons. He then immediately departed. Because the threats continued, Riel chose exile, a decision that was agreeable to major Canadian political leaders, who were content not to have to deal with the emotions and political schisms generated by his presence.

FIFTEEN YEARS AFTER the Red River Rebellion, a second rebellion erupted in the Canadian North-West. And again Louis Riel was its most important leader.

In the summer of 1884, Gabriel Dumont, who would become the Métis military leader the following year, travelled with three companions to Montana to beseech Riel to come once more to the aid of the Métis and the native peoples of the North-West.

In 1870, when the Macdonald government had agreed to create the province of Manitoba, it had undertaken to ensure a fair land settlement for the peoples of the Red River Territory. While some lands had later been distributed under the auspices of the federal government, the Métis did not receive anything like a reasonable share of desirable land grants that included river frontage. Over the years that followed, thousands of Métis had left Manitoba to migrate farther west to territory along the South Saskatchewan River, centred on the settlement at Batoche. By the mid-1880s, the days of the buffalo hunt were over and the Métis of the region had mostly taken up farming.

During the same years, many of the native peoples of the region had been settled on reserves under the watchful eye of the North West Mounted Police. First attempts to take up farming on these lands had had mixed results, and native peoples were often desperately short of food.

Riel decided to return from exile to Canada. He travelled to the Saskatchewan country with Dumont and the others, and while he did not take a formal position in the governing structure established by the Métis, he succeeded in making himself both the political and spiritual inspiration of this troubled people. Under his charismatic leadership, the Métis of Saskatchewan set up a governing council. Riel named it the Exovedate, a theological term which roughly meant "those who have left the flock." [37] For his followers, including Dumont, the name was daunting and not particularly useful. They called their new government "*le petit provisoire.*" [38]

The 1885 rebellion was eventually put down by Canadian militia forces that made use of the nearly completed Canadian Pacific Railway line to reach the area of the uprising in Batoche. Louis Riel was taken prisoner and was charged with high treason.

On July 6, 1885, John A. Macdonald delivered a long, self-justifying address in the House of Commons, describing Riel as "that unfortunate man." Defending the actions of the Canadian government from 1869 to the rebellion of 1885, Macdonald contrasted what he regarded as the relatively peaceful relationship of the Dominion of Canada with native peoples to the much more bloody record south of the border, referring to the massacre of General Custer's forces at Little Bighorn in 1876. He attributed the recent uprising of the Métis at Batoche to, among other things, white land speculators who had their own reasons for stirring up the troubles. [39]

At Riel's trial, the prosecutors depicted the Métis leader as self-consciously and rationally provoking a people to acts of rebellion against the Crown. The defence lawyers, who were from Montreal, attempted to portray him as insane, as evidenced by his visions of himself as a man with a divine mission at the centre of a New World religion.

When the Crown and the defence had presented their cases, Louis Riel rose to address the court. Whatever might be the consequence, his goal was to remove the stain of insanity from his character, his actions, and his whole career.

"It is true, gentlemen," he exclaimed, "I believed for years I had a mission, and when I speak of a mission you will understand me not as trying to play the role of insane...so as to have a verdict of acquittal upon that ground.

"I know that through the grace of God I am the founder of Manitoba.

"I worked to better the condition of the people of the Saskatchewan at the risk of my life, to better the condition of the people of the North-West...If you say I was right, you can conscientiously acquit me, as I hope through the help of God you will. [40]

"If you take the plea of the defence [Riel's own lawyers]," he continued, "that I am not responsible for my acts, acquit me completely since I have been quarreling with an insane and irresponsible Government. If you pronounce in favour of the Crown, which contends that I am responsible, acquit me all the same. You are perfectly justified in declaring that having my reason and sound mind, I have acted reasonably and in self-defence, while the Government, my accuser, being irresponsible, and completely insane, cannot but have acted wrong, and if high treason there is it must be on its side and not on my part." [41]

Riel's powerful address to the jury undercut the defence of insanity, as indeed it was intended to do. When the jury foreman later reported a verdict of guilty to the court, he had tears in his eyes and added, "Your Honour, I have been asked by my brother jurors to recommend the prisoner to the mercy of the Crown."

Riel then addressed the court again, and when he concluded, Judge Hugh Richardson coldly and without emotion sentenced him to death by hanging. [42]

Following two appeals, his conviction was upheld, and Riel was executed on November 16, 1885, in Regina. Protestant English-speaking Ontario cheered the hanging as justice done at last. Catholic French-speaking Quebec protested the execution — tens of thousands of people assembled at the Champ-de-Mars in Montreal to voice their outrage. Present at the demonstration was Wilfrid Laurier. Riel, the Métis leader, had become a francophone martyr. Macdonald was wrong when he predicted that Quebec's anger about the hanging of Riel would soon evaporate. In a notorious outburst prior to the execution, Macdonald had shouted: "He shall hang though every dog in Quebec bark in his favour." [43]

THE EXECUTION OF Riel shook John A. Macdonald's Conservative Party to its core. One of Macdonald's great political achievements had been to maintain a political party and successive governments that had both Protestant and Catholic representation. At a time when the Protestant Orange Order was on the rise in Ontario and a wave of conservative Catholicism had swept Quebec, this was no mean achievement. The hanging of Riel ruptured Macdonald's party, and although he was to lead the Conservatives to victory in two more elections, in 1887 and 1891, the era in which his party was "the natural governing party" was drawing to a close. In 1896, when Wilfrid Laurier led the Liberals to power in a general election, he became the country's first French-Canadian prime minister. Riel's death was a seminal event in transforming Quebec into a Liberal fiefdom for many decades to come.

Sir John A. Macdonald did succeed in bringing the North-West into Canada. But his prejudices against the Métis and the native peoples of the territory made the acquisition of the North-West much more fraught than it would have been had he been willing to treat the peoples of the region as he would have treated white settlers. Had the majority of the population at Red River been composed of white settlers, the government of John A. Macdonald would have ensured the property rights of the people of the settlement the way they did in 1873, when Ottawa bought out the absentee British landlords of Prince Edward Island and transformed the farmers of the island from tenants to owners.

Not so for the people whose leader was Louis Riel. Macdonald's approach was to control that population until the migration of white settlers, mainly from Ontario, created a new majority. His strategy was the same in 1885, when the rebellion on the banks of the Saskatchewan River erupted. This time, he relied on the Canadian Pacific Railway to send troops and later to transport migrants who would reduce the Métis and the native peoples of the region to defencelessness.

And while Macdonald presided over the launch of the original Confederation in masterly fashion, he bungled the acquisition of the West to such an extent that he nearly allowed this essential territory to be lost from Canada.

As was the case with most mid-nineteenth-century North American settler politicians, Macdonald conceived of the enormous territory that was being transferred to Canada as a tabula rasa with which the federal government could do as it pleased. While he was aware of the native peoples and the Métis who lived in the territory, he regarded them at most as obstacles to be surmounted. He was fully convinced of the superiority of European civilization, particularly its British manifestation. Sweeping aside indigenous peoples to make way for settlers represented the march of nineteenth-century progress. Where indigenous peoples were concerned, Macdonald had no creative ideas. He was imbued with the commonplace settler mentality of the age: that some peoples were superior to others and ought to prevail.

Epilogue

Legacies of Three Leaders

"'Tis been said that I should apply to the United States for a pardon, but repentance must precede the right of pardon, and I have not repented. Remembering as I must all which has been suffered, all which has been lost, disappointed hopes and crushed aspirations, yet I deliberately say, if it were to do over again, I would again do just as I did in 1861." — Jefferson Davis, speech before Mississippi legislature, Jackson, Mississippi, March 10, 1884.[1]

"With malice toward none, with charity for all, with firmness in the right as God gives us to see the right, let us strive on to finish the work we are in, to bind up the nation's wounds, to care for him who shall have borne the battle and for his widow and his orphan, to do all which may achieve and cherish a just and lasting peace among ourselves and with all nations." — Abraham Lincoln, second Inaugural Address, Washington D.C., March 4, 1865.[2]

"As for myself my course is clear. A British subject I was born — a British subject I will die. With my utmost effort, with my latest breath, will I oppose the 'veiled treason' which attempts by sordid means and mercenary proffers to lure our people from their allegiance." — John A. Macdonald, in opposition to free trade with the United States, at the beginning of his final federal election campaign, February 3, 1891.[3]

JEFFERSON DAVIS, ABRAHAM LINCOLN, and John A. Macdonald bequeathed legacies that left deep imprints on the societies and states of the North American continent. Indeed, the mid-nineteenth-century struggles for shares of the continent had immense implications for the wider global order that reverberate to the present day.

Two of the national projects were successful: that of the North and that of Canada.

The Southern nation state was destroyed on the field of battle.

The Civil War was followed by Reconstruction, an era that lasted up to a decade, during which the states that had seceded were subject at times to military occupation prior to their readmission as active states in the Union.

Then came a counter-revolution in the South. As the occupying military forces were withdrawn, white Southerners — spurred on by secret societies, the most famous of which was the Ku Klux Klan — drove the newly freed back to the political margins. All-white regimes, under the banner of the Democratic Party, were entrenched across the region. Many of the freedmen worked the land they had previously toiled as slaves. As tenants or smallholders, they bought supplies from landowning merchant magnates to whom they pledged their crops, an arrangement that drove them deeper into debt. Through this system and the barring of most occupations to them, African Americans in the South were reduced to a state of peonage, little better than slavery. This condition endured for nearly a century. During the long age of segregation and lynch law, thousands of blacks became convict labourers for large corporations, including giants such as U.S. Steel. Across the South, formal slavery was succeeded by racial terrorism.

While the South lost the war, to a quite remarkable extent it won the peace. The Southern project enjoyed a second life in the century following Reconstruction, a century during which African Americans in the former Confederacy lived in a demi-world of subjugation and segregation, in which their capacity to travel was largely denied. They also lacked the right to vote and other democratic rights.

The slave-owning Southern gentry lost enormously as a consequence of the war, but some of the old families clung to their power and were joined by a new class of landowners, merchants, and industrialists. The formal abolition of slavery wiped out a huge proportion of the slave owners' capital base. On the eve of the war, the four million slaves in the South and the border states constituted a vast stock of capital, worth several billion dollars at the time. Slaves could be sold in the marketplace just like other capital goods, such as machinery and factories, which gave major slave owners the status of leading capitalists. In contemporary terms, while comparisons are far from precise, the loss of the slaves was equivalent to the destruction of a trillion dollars' worth of capital. Even today, derelict antebellum mansions are skeletal reminders of how much the Southern gentry lost. What the members of the gentry and the new class of landowners who followed them did not lose was ownership of their land, although its value dropped to a fraction of its former worth.

ONE OF THE underpinnings of the re-subjugation of blacks in the South was the development of the cult of the "Lost Cause" among white Southerners. Having been decisively defeated in the war, former Confederates set out to ensure that their interpretation of the conflict would predominate not only in the South but in the North as well. In this, they were hugely successful. They fabricated a vision of the South that clouded the ability of future historians and future generations of the wider public to comprehend the actual South of the Civil War years and its nation state project.

The Lost Cause ideology — it bore the hallmarks of a religion, with its sacred and sanctified heroes, its evil foes, and its despised traitors to the cause — was carefully nurtured by former Confederate officers and soldiers, and authors who shared their outlook. According to the tenets of the Lost Cause myth/religion, the South had waged a valorous and just war in its quest to secede from the United States and establish an independent sovereign state. The Confederates thus fought for liberty as the true heirs to the American Revolution. Purveyors of the Lost Cause myth denied that the Confederates had launched their war for independence principally to sustain the system of slavery and therefore to continue to hold other men in bondage. Some argued that the South was moving toward its own elimination of slavery. Others maintained that slavery had been far milder and more humane than Northern abolitionists had claimed.

Edward A. Pollard, who had been the editor of the *Richmond Examiner* during the war, was an early and influential source of the Lost Cause. In 1867, he published *The Lost Cause: The Standard Southern History of the War of the Confederates*. The previous year, in a book titled *Southern History of the War*, Pollard rationalized the slavery question with this assertion: "The occasion of that conflict [the Civil War] was what the Yankees called — by one of their convenient libels in political nomenclature — slavery; but what was in fact nothing more than a system of Negro servitude in the South...one of the mildest and most beneficent systems of servitude in the world." [4]

Lost Cause proponents defended the Confederate outlook on race, and some argued that the North had long profited from the slave trade and that the Northern system of relations between capital and labour was itself a form of slavery.

In the works of Lost Cause apostles, Robert E. Lee and Jefferson Davis ascended to the status of Christ figures who embodied the virtues of Southern manhood and who had devoted and sacrificed themselves to the cause. Robert E. Lee enjoyed this status from the moment the war ended. For Jefferson Davis, the rise to sainthood followed the two years he spent in a federal prison.

Stonewall Jackson, ferocious and cunning in battle — a staunchly fundamentalist Christian — became a Moses of the Lost Cause. The Judas Iscariot of the faith was General James Longstreet, whose post-war writings critical of Robert E. Lee's generalship were seen as traitorous.

As is often the case with religious doctrines, artifacts that achieved the status of sacred relics were worshipped by the Lost Cause faithful. Chief among these were the Confederate flag, the grey uniform of CSA soldiers, and the song "Dixie," the hymn of the movement. As is typically the case with romantic conservative movements, the Lost Cause harkened back to a perceived "golden age" that embodied the values and the vision of the movement. The golden age of the Lost Cause included both the antebellum South and the era of the war itself.

LaSalle Corbell Pickett, the widow of General George Pickett — his name is forever associated with the disaster of Pickett's charge at Gettysburg in 1863 — became a highly successful writer adept at portraying the vanished world of the South before the war. When her husband died suddenly in 1875 (she would outlive him by fifty years), leaving her a single mother and short of money, she took up the pen to make her way in the world. She quickly discovered, as did other authors, that there was a large appetite in the South, as well as among an increasing number of Northerners, for her kind of storytelling.

Her lost South was a happy, kindly place, free of conflict. Men were sophisticated, cultured, and polite to the point of fussiness. Women were dashing, beautiful, and faithful. Slaves were childlike, innocent, and friendly, and they depended heavily on the paternalism of their masters. She told tales of male slaves who were so attached to their masters that in some cases they even insisted on accompanying them onto the field of battle. Such people, she informed her readers, were happy in their appointed place, did not welcome emancipation when it came, and did not understand what it meant to vote. The antebellum South was so blessed that the water there tasted as sweet as wine.

Such authors — her role as the widow of the famed General Pickett helped, of course — played starring roles at reunions of the United Confederate Veterans and at battlefield commemorations, where they made speeches and signed autographs. The connection of these figures with the South gave them an important cultural — and, in the case of the men — political role.

Lost Cause proponents put the blame for the war on the North. They argued that since the Southern states had entered the Union voluntarily, they retained a right to secede. They insisted that secession and the war were generated by issues such as states' rights, tariffs, and the widening divide in values between South and North, rather than by slavery.

Lost Cause promoters made Herculean efforts to show that Robert E. Lee was an inspired military genius, while Ulysses S. Grant was a mere brute whose only strategy was to dispatch ever more men to be slaughtered. After the war, Confederate diehards insisted that Lee's Army of Northern Virginia was never really defeated on the battlefield and only succumbed to the North's vast superiority in weaponry and in manpower. The Lost Cause authors won this argument more completely than they could ever have hoped.

While Lee's trajectory from rebel general to full-fledged American hero is astonishing, it is not entirely unique. The English-speaking world lavished praise on German general Erwin Rommel after the Second World War. This is partly because he was the general the Americans, British, and Canadians fought in North Africa, and they were not as familiar with more important German generals who served on the much more consequential Eastern Front.

Lee's rise to the status of legendary American icon, which persists to this day, was more than mere nostalgia. It was central to the rehabilitation of Confederate leaders and soldiers as Americans, not treasonous rebels. Far more consequential, it rehabilitated white Southerners and aided them in speeding the close of the Reconstruction era.

One of the most influential of the Lost Cause writer-propagandists was former Confederate General Jubal Anderson Early, who had served in the Army of Northern Virginia and spent several years in self-imposed exile in Canada following the war. He understood that while the South had lost on the field of battle, it could win the crucial coming battle for hearts and minds. He strove to propagate the case for Lee's greatness while characterizing Grant as a butcher.

Early stressed the North's vast superiority in manpower, which made Lee's stunning feats on a number of battlefields all the more remarkable. Early attributed Lee's defeats — most notably Gettysburg and the fall of Richmond in April 1865 — to the shortcomings of other Confederate commanders and to developments in other theatres of war. At Gettysburg, Early pointed to Lee's lieutenants, especially General James Longstreet, as responsible for the defeat. The fall of Richmond and the subsequent surrender of Lee's army at Appomattox, he explained, were the "consequences of events in the West and Southwest, and not directly of the operations in Virginia."[5]

Early went to great lengths marshalling figures to show just how large the Union's manpower advantage over the Confederacy was. When Northern proponents presented the case that the Union's manpower in key battles was not as great as pro-Confederates had claimed, Early was quick to challenge them, in one case insisting that published works were part of "a persistent and systematic effort to falsify the truth." [6]

As for Grant, despite his victories in the west at Vicksburg and Chattanooga, where he had shown great perseverance and ability to manoeuvre, Early brushed him aside, saying he "had none of the requisites of a great captain, but merely possessed the most ordinary brute courage, and the control of unlimited numbers and means." [7]

Further, the Lost Cause denied that African Americans were overwhelmingly opposed to slavery. This claim was made despite the fact that when they had the chance, tens of thousands of slaves escaped behind Union lines, and that close to two hundred thousand former slaves joined the Union army and in some notorious cases, such as the massacre at Fort Pillow, Tennessee, in April 1864, were slaughtered by Confederate soldiers after they surrendered. The Lost Cause denied agency to the slaves, to the blacks who fought for the Union, and to the freedmen whose tragic history followed the war.

The appetite of many Northerners for the Lost Cause mythology grew out of a similar denial of agency to African Americans. With the withdrawal of the last Union troops from the South in 1877, Northerners and their political leaders gave up their half-hearted efforts to reform the South and to protect the newly gained rights of the freedmen that had been enshrined in the Fourteenth and Fifteenth Amendments to the U.S. Constitution. The racism of Northerners and that of Southerners allowed the Southern states to effectively ignore the amendments.

The age of segregation for blacks in the South, sustained in part by the Lost Cause outlook, lasted until the 1950s and 1960s, when the U.S. Supreme Court ruled segregation in the schools unconstitutional. Under the pressure of the Civil Rights movement, the administration of Lyndon Johnson pushed bills through Congress that ensured the vote for blacks; ended segregation in housing, transportation, and employment; and established affirmative action to encourage the economic advancement of black Americans.

While Jefferson Davis's project, the Confederate States of America, was a casualty of the war, Confederate progeny, in the form of the re-subjugation of black Americans, the spawning of the gun culture, support for capital punishment, and opposition to the welfare state and trade unions, remained key elements of the American social order. All but the first of these is still potent in the twenty-first century.

AFTER A PERILOUSLY difficult beginning, Lincoln's project was a brilliant success on the field of battle and in the salvation of the Union. Northern victory in the Civil War suppressed the secession of the Southern states, thereby removing the threat of an expansionist slave state to the south. In the decades following the Civil War, the United States consolidated a continental country. Lincoln's project had enormous consequences not only for the United States but for the world.

A significant element of the Lincoln legacy had to do with race, and that element of the legacy is inseparably linked to the Lost Cause of the South. In the post-war decades, Lost Cause proponents effectively played to Northern attitudes toward blacks. While the war itself divided Southern whites from Northern whites, allowing blacks to emerge for a time into the light of freedom, by the late 1870s Southern and Northern whites had effectively come to terms.

The fact that a majority of Northerners was won over to the abolition of slavery did not mean that they were free from racism. Far from it. Several Midwestern states had Negro exclusion laws on the books that predated the war. In 1862, roughly 40 percent of pro-Republicans in Illinois joined with Democrats in a referendum whose result was to reaffirm the state's exclusion law.

Senator Lyman Trumbull of Illinois concluded: "There is a very great aversion in the West — I know it to be so in my state — against having free Negroes come among us. Our people want nothing to do with the Negro." [8] Opposition to the slaveocracy of the South and the threat it posed to the American Republic proved to be compatible with a fiercely negative view of the prospect of the migration of former slaves to the North.

During the war, an option that drew significant support in the North, at times from Lincoln himself, was to promote the creation of colonies outside the United States to which blacks would be sent. The Lincoln administration's approach to slavery changed over the course of the conflict. It pushed forward the case for emancipation as a necessary measure to win the war, while being ever cognizant of the need to avoid adopting measures that would provoke anti-black sentiment in the North.

On the great question of emancipation, therefore, we must conclude that Lincoln's legacy was a huge step forward followed by a tragic reversal.

Lincoln's more certain and enormous legacy was the saving of the Union. It was, as he proclaimed repeatedly during the war, his overriding goal. For him, the Union was the cause that subsumed all others. It was also the cause that was embraced by his mass political base of white Northerners. The Union cause meant much more than preserving a single U.S. federal state. It was also about saving the American system of government, a system that was "of the people, by the people, for the people," in Lincoln's phrase. Lincoln's "new birth of freedom," as envisaged at Gettysburg, could be secured only through the military defeat of the slaveocracy.

The victory of the North ensured that the United States would rule a continental territory, the proving ground for the rise of American industrial capitalism to global dominance. Americans waged the Civil War at the dawn of a new industrial age. Railroads, which had spread in a web east of the Mississippi, had transformed travel and the shipment of raw materials and finished products. On the eve of the war, politicians and rail company magnates were furiously debating the viability of competing proposals for rail lines to the west coast. Railroads were knitting the United States together, replacing local with regional and national markets. Larger markets spurred the shift, already underway, to mass production, initially in water-powered mills.

The first oil wells in Canada and the United States were drilled just prior to the outbreak of the war. This new industry, which would play an immense role in the rise of the United States to global power, was a mere curiosity during the Civil War, its impact to be felt only in the future.

Indeed, the Civil War was the world's first great conflict in which railroads were crucially important. It was also the last major war fought before the revolution in weaponry that was a product of the new industrialism. Overwhelmingly, soldiers were armed with muskets. The revolutionary Minié rifle, invented in 1849, was used on a limited scale to devastating effect. Had the North acquired the weapon on a truly large scale, it would almost certainly have won the war more quickly. The machine gun and its predecessor, the Gatling gun, had not yet been developed. These high-powered automatic weapons were decisive, along with much more powerful artillery, in creating the conditions for the mechanized trench warfare of the First World War. Only in the Battle of Petersburg, in the final stages of the Civil War, was there a foretaste of the nightmare of trench warfare.

As a war of movement, the Civil War harkened back to the past, with men fighting in tightly packed formations similar to those seen in the War of 1812. And cavalry still mattered: it was essential to reconnaissance and in pitched encounters.

While Lincoln fought for a Union in which the common man could thrive, the tycoons of the new industrialism dominated the American society that emerged in the late nineteenth century. Thomas Jefferson's dream of an Arcadian America of yeoman farmers was already anachronistic in 1860. In the post-Lincoln decades, Pittsburgh, Chicago, and America's other great cities morphed into hives of industrial activity in dangerous factories and stockyards, or in the case of New York, textile sweatshops run in wretched apartments that housed the families that worked in them.

Following the Civil War, capitalists created their own corporate empires in oil, steel, finance, and later the electronics, chemical, and automotive industries. The tycoons generated wealth and power for themselves beyond what the slave owners had ever possessed. As it turned out, Lincoln's vision of an America fit for the common man soon disintegrated in the face of a tougher, meaner capitalism. By the end of the nineteenth century, the American productive apparatus and national market were the greatest in the world. While the leaders of Europe still considered their continent the centre of the world, they were peering uneasily at the new giant across the Atlantic. Lincoln's most enduring legacy was to position the American state as a world power that would dwarf the other great powers in the twentieth century.

Far from "government of the people, by the people, and for the people," during the post-Lincoln decades, corrupt politicians, some of them running political machines that effectively ruled big-city governments, worked hand in glove with the tycoons to promote their favourites, while the mass of the population toiled for meagre pay. This was the age of crony capitalism, when workers were exploited, farmers were gouged by banks and railroads, and Southern blacks lived shantytowns, where they worked for bosses who kept them in poverty and perpetual debt.

In response to the rise of the trusts, workers organized unions, farmers created populist political movements, muckraking writers exposed the shady dealings of the tycoons and the unsanitary methods used in the meat-packing industry. Reform politicians proposed measures to control the trusts, and if necessary, break them up.

In the late twentieth and early twenty-first centuries, Lincoln's overriding political goal, which was to save the Union, has often been recast by writers and filmmakers in universalist terms, to render it appealing to people everywhere. A myth has grown around Lincoln that, in some respects, is similar to the myth of the Lost Cause. The Lincoln myth portrays his outlook as a vision of freedom for all peoples. What makes it appropriate to term this a "myth" is not that it does not contain important elements of truth, but that as with the Lost Cause myth, it distorts the reality of the Lincoln project and its consequences.

The myth of Lincoln as the universal emancipator takes him out
of his historical time and place. Removing the man and the politician
from the specifics of his historical moment does a disservice to the
real Abraham Lincoln. Brilliant though *Lincoln at Gettysburg* is, Garry
Wills contributes to the myth when he insists that at Gettysburg,
Lincoln "had revolutionized the Revolution, giving people a new past
to live with that would change their future indefinitely." [9] While Wills
certainly recognizes that Lincoln's first priority on taking office was
to preserve the Union and that his positions on African Americans
and on slavery evolved, his conclusion is too abstract, too ahistorical.

Lincoln emerged at that moment in American history when the
slave owners still had the power to safeguard their system by establishing a state of their own. It was also the moment when the North
and the Midwest had already outstripped the South in population and
economic might, but before the second industrial revolution launched
the rise of the great tycoons. If he had appeared a couple of decades
earlier, Lincoln might have played the role of a Daniel Webster, pro-
mulgating an American vision to counter the raw sectionalism of the
South. If fate had had him appear a couple of decades later, he would
have been compelled to choose between the interests of the ascendant
capitalist and exploited labour.

It was Lincoln's fate to represent Northern interests before the war
of the classes and just at the moment when the election of a president
committed to opposing the spread of slavery was enough to trigger the
secession of the South. It was this mixture of elements, so particular
to the time, that permitted Lincoln to speak with a voice so seemingly
universalist on the themes of Union and emancipation.

Lincoln's vision was appropriately particular to his time; it would
have been out of place at any other time.

JOHN A. MACDONALD's legacy, much more than those of Davis and
Lincoln, is still taking shape. To an extent that is certainly not true
for the South or the North, the Canadian project continues to achieve

definition. It will be neither a Lost Cause nor a global superpower, but rather a transcontinental project comprising English- and French-speaking nations, and immigrants from around the world, settled on the traditional territories of hundreds of native peoples. Will it remain a single country over the course of the twenty-first century, or will it break into its component parts or be swallowed in a wider union with the United States?

Macdonald was a party leader, a coalition partner, a consummate deal maker, a Canadian visionary, and an adept participant in the complex ritual of imperial politics. To a far greater degree than Jefferson Davis and Abraham Lincoln, he had to manoeuvre in a setting where his power was far from total. Macdonald practised politics in a parliamentary system in which he not only had to seek agreement with cabinet colleagues but also had to sustain the support of the legislature, and later the Parliament. Macdonald was a colonial politician whose power was always limited by the long reach of Westminster. Not only did the British government directly control Canadian foreign and defence policies; it also chose governors general before and after Confederation. While these royal representatives had to operate within the bounds of responsible government, their influence on politicians and governments was much greater than is the case for governors general today. Moreover, leading Canadian politicians always had to be acutely aware of the English-French duality within the Canadian state. Macdonald could never adopt a position on a major question without carefully considering how it would play in French Canada and directly among his francophone colleagues.

These constraints meant that Macdonald always had to ground his politics in the possibilities of the present. He could dream of the creation of a great British American country that would one day span the continent. But that dream could be directly pursued only when favourable political conditions presented themselves. Prior to the American Civil War, Macdonald was much more inclined to try to make the old Canadian system work than to create a wholly new one.

But once the Civil War transformed continental realities,

Macdonald seized the opportunity handed to him in 1864 by George Brown, his political nemesis. Macdonald was so proficient as a deal maker, as a chairman who could coax mutually antagonistic leaders to work together, that this ability has often been considered to be his overriding skill. While Macdonald was much more than a deal maker, his capacity to bring disparate parties to agreement was critical to the Confederation project during the vital period from 1864 to 1867.

Beyond that, Macdonald was a visionary, whose conservative philosophical outlook was the basis for his enormous contribution to nation building in Canada from the mid-1850s to his death in 1891. Just what was the essence of Macdonald's conservatism? His vision had a Burkean cast (in the mould of British philosopher Edmund Burke) that was softened and even disguised by his jocular style. But the hard centre was there, except for the not-infrequent occasions when his ventures into crony capitalism led him into the shoals. His conservatism was rooted in conceptions of the state and of democratic politics that were distinctly un-American. Throughout his political career, Macdonald adhered to the notion that Canada required a strong state, and not just for defence and the punishment of criminals. If Canada were to evolve into a transcontinental country, the government would have to play a central role in shaping its economic strategy. His economic philosophy was at odds with the laissez-faire ideology of American politicians. When governments were most hands-off south of the border, Macdonald promoted active government.

Macdonald never had a clear and principled conception of the ethical boundaries that should separate the state from business, and both of these from political parties. This failing on his part was far from unusual during the late Victorian era. The most grievous case of blatant crony capitalism during Macdonald's long career was the so-called Pacific Scandal.

Macdonald regularly sided with costly railway projects. Most importantly, as prime minister, he agreed to commit Canada to the construction of a Pacific railway within ten years of British Columbia becoming a province in 1871. There were two severe problems with

Macdonald's far-sighted vision. The first was that with a population of only 3.5 million people, the dominion would be hard pressed to finance the railway on its own. To make a go of the railway, investors in both the United States and Britain would need to be attracted to the project. The second problem, tied closely to the first, was that Macdonald's government was committed to the proposition that the railway must follow an all-Canadian route through the forbidding terrain of the Canadian Shield, a land of Precambrian rock, lakes, rivers, and pines. Later in the century, when mineral deposits — nickel chief among them — were discovered in the Shield, the attitude to this territory altered profoundly.

Two business groups competed for the contract to build the railway. Sir Hugh Allan's Canada Pacific Railway Company was closely, if secretly, tied to John A. Macdonald, as well as to American railway financiers, principally George W. McMullen and Jay Cooke. These Americans, in turn, were heavily involved with the Northern Pacific Railroad venture in the United States, which was a major potential competitor against the proposed Canadian project.

During the 1872 federal election campaign, the Macdonald government had received as much as $360,000 from Sir Hugh Allan. In addition, Allan had been receiving funds from the American railway financiers, although Macdonald insisted that he was unaware of this. The scandal broke on April 2, 1873, when Liberal MP Lucius Seth Huntington rose in the House of Commons to drop the bombshell. He declared that he had the evidence that Sir Hugh Allan and his corporate partners had received the Pacific Railway contract from the government in return for political donations to the Conservatives. It was Huntington who came up with the $360,000 figure.

The Liberals charged that this was a case of bribery, that the exceptionally important Pacific Railway contract had been bought from the government, and that the prime minister was deeply involved. Liberal newspapers, and especially George Brown's *Globe,* trumpeted the allegations against Macdonald. The prime minister denied the charges, but when receipts for money paid to him and his colleagues by Allan became public, and when a telegram from Allan to Macdonald fell into the hands of the Liberals, the prime minister's position became untenable.

Following the general election of 1872, Macdonald's control of the House of Commons was less than secure. Too many of the members on whose votes he counted on in Parliament were "loose fish," MPs not tied securely to the Conservative Party. When evidence emerged that Macdonald had been engaged in a completely inappropriate relationship with Allan, his ability to hold on to the confidence of the House disintegrated. He resigned as prime minister on November 5, 1873, and also offered to step down as leader of the Conservative Party. The party caucus refused to accept his resignation from the latter post, which opened the way for his rehabilitation after years in the political wilderness.

In the general election of 1874, the Liberal Party, under the leadership of Alexander Mackenzie, won power, consigning Macdonald's Conservatives to the Official Opposition. The Mackenzie government had the misfortune of holding power during a global economic downturn. In sharp contrast to the Civil War years, when Canada enjoyed booming exports to the United States, the mid-1870s was a time of economic misery. Immigration slowed, and an ever larger number of Canadians left for the United States. From Ontario, many moved west across the border into Michigan to acquire farmland. From Quebec, tens of thousands of French Canadians migrated south to take jobs in industry in the New England states. During this time, the Liberal government attempted to negotiate a free trade agreement with the United States along the lines of the Reciprocity Treaty that had been abrogated by Washington in 1866. George Brown headed up the Canadian trade delegation to Washington but came home empty-handed. American industry was solidly in favour of high tariffs, and the administration showed no interest in reciprocity with Canada.

While in the Opposition, Macdonald conceived an alternative way forward for Canada: the National Policy. His Conservatives were returned to power in the general elections of 1878, and in 1879, they introduced a steeply increased tariff on goods imported to Canada. The tariff was frankly protectionist; its goal was to direct domestic purchases away from imports so that a larger portion of goods produced in Canada would be reserved for the national market. The policy was intended to promote manufacturing and job creation. In the spring of 1881, Macdonald addressed a large audience of workingmen in Toronto on how the benefits of the National Policy would be realized over time: "At the end of five years the manufacturers will have generated so much capital, while the workingmen, the skilled and unskilled labour that surround those varied industries, will have become so powerful, the capitalists will be linked together in associations, and workingmen will be bound together in trades unions, and they will fight the battle together. [loud cheers] Capital and labour will go hand in hand, and they will put down all attempts to make this country what it was before, a mere agricultural country, from which all skilled labour went to the United States to find employment, and that skilled labour will remain in the country. [Hear, hear]"[10]

For decades to come, the National Policy tariff was to serve as a pillar of Canadian economic strategy. It also buttressed Canada's transportation policy. Macdonald was determined to complete the transcontinental railway as quickly as possible. His government poured $20 million into the project, granted the CPR twenty million acres of land along the railway's right of way, and freed the company from paying property taxes on those lands. On top of all this, the company was guaranteed a twenty-year monopoly on rail traffic in the West. As Macdonald told the House of Commons in January 1881: "We desire, the country desires, that the road, when built, should be a Canadian road; the main channel for Canadian traffic for the carriage of the treasures of the west to the seaboard through Canada. So far as we can, we shall not allow it to be built for the benefit of the United States lines."[11]

The rail line linking Montreal to Vancouver was completed in November 1885, the same month that Louis Riel was hanged in Regina. The two events were not unrelated. Macdonald's approach to the prairies had been to treat the region as a colony of Canada.

The National Policy tariff and the construction of the railway were to open the prairies to immigration and agriculture for export. Macdonald's western policies were to prove an immense economic success in the decades following his death in 1891. The Canada he passed on to his political successors, especially Liberal Prime Minister Wilfrid Laurier, was no longer a land of disconnected territories. It had become a country whose regions were linked by the railway and drawn together economically by the tariff and eventually by the great wheat export boom that began in the mid-1890s. The policy especially favoured the railways, the banks, and the major manufacturers, and was deeply resented by western farmers, who had to sell their products on the global market while they purchased their manufactures from central Canadian industry. Despite the social and political inequities on which the policy rested, a country was established — a country that proved capable of adaptation and survival over the decades to come.

Appendix

Nation State Projects in Nineteenth-Century North America and Europe

T HE MID-NINETEENTH CENTURY was an age of nationalism and the creation of nation states on both sides of the Atlantic.

Nationalism burgeoned among many peoples in the wider European world, including North America in mid-century. This was a distinct phase in the emergence of modern capitalism, when members of local capitalist classes asserted their leadership and aspired to establish states tailor-made to serve their interests. The economic, political, and intellectual elites of many peoples — among them Germans, Italians, Poles, Hungarians, Czechs, Slovaks, Serbs, and the Irish — attempted to erect their own sovereign nation states, with these attempts failing more often than they succeeded. One of those failures was the Confederate States of America.

Similar struggles to forge nation states erupted in mid-nineteenth-century Europe. The character of mid-nineteenth-century nationalism was quite distinct from that of the nationalism of the era of the American and French Revolutions. Over the millennia — the idea of nationalism can be traced back in ancient times to the Greeks and the Jews — nationalism has assumed different forms as it gives expression to the aspirations of peoples in very different socio-economic and historical settings. In the early modern era, as the Protestant Reformation challenged Catholicism, as states used gunpowder to suppress the power of armed nobles and their fortresses, and as authors and governors deployed the printing press to flood Europe and the North American colonies with works in a myriad of languages, the way was prepared for modern nationalism and the modern nation state.

Modern nationalism in its initial form emerged cloaked in the ideas of the Enlightenment. In the eighteenth century, as the rising forces of capitalism struggled against the Old Regime, most potently in France, universalist notions combated particularism. Enlightenment thinkers promoted rationalism against obscurantism and the rights of man against the inherited privileges of monarchy and aristocracy. These ideas flowered in France during the first stages of the Revolution of 1789. The French Revolution generated a new form of patriotism that encompassed a whole people and not just its privileged elites. As American sociologist Rogers Brubaker has written: "Modern national citizenship was an invention of the French Revolution.... The Revolution...invented both the nation-state and the modern institution and ideology of national citizenship."[1]

Paradoxically, this meant that universalist concepts, the rights of man and democracy, took the stage alongside the particularism of patriotism. By definition, patriotism and nationalism emerge in specific societies or countries, and these societies have boundaries that mark them off from those outside those boundaries. At the end of the eighteenth century, nationalism and democracy in revolutionary America and France, far from seeming contradictory, appeared to reinforce each other.

In August 1789, the French Constituent Assembly adopted the Declaration of the Rights of Man and of the Citizen, which proclaimed that: "The principle of sovereignty resides essentially in the Nation; no body of men, no individual, can exercise authority that does not emanate expressly from it."[2] Although this notion does not appear particularly controversial today, in 1789 it was revolutionary in its implications. It was an idea with the potential to overturn the existing system of European powers and to call into question the very legitimacy of almost all European states.

Prior to the French Revolution, the boundaries of European states were legitimized by treaties signed at the conclusion of wars, which transferred territories from defeated states to victorious ones. In addition, dynastic alliances through marriage often resulted in particular territories being passed from one monarchical regime to another. The proclamation regarding sovereignty in the Declaration of the Rights of Man and of the Citizen cast this system into question. Henceforth, according to the Declaration, sovereignty would reside in nations. Nations were to rule themselves as a matter of right. Therefore, it was essential to decide what constituted a nation.

This was no mere abstract question. Deciding which human populations on which pieces of territory were, in fact, nations, would embroil Europe, North America, and ultimately the whole world in struggles and wars in which millions of lives were spent. Did the national projects of the South, the North, and Canada in the 1860s emerge out of real nations as that notion had come to be understood in the mid-nineteenth century?

The matter of what constitutes a nation is more complex than it initially seems. Many people, when asked to define a nation, begin by saying that a nation is characterized by the existence of a sovereign state that is distinct from other sovereign states. According to this definition, a nation and a country are coterminous. But that definition creates implacable problems.

Consider the case of Poland. Few people would dispute that the Poles constitute a nation. During much of the period from the late eighteenth century until the end of the First World War, Poland was divided among three empires: the Prussian (later German), the Austrian (later Austro-Hungarian), and the Russian. Is it reasonable to conclude, therefore, that during this lengthy historical epoch, the Polish people, despite their common language, customs, religion, and traditions, did not constitute a nation?

If the answer to this question is that the Poles made up a nation even when the territory on which they lived was divided among three empires, then we require a more far-reaching definition of a nation.

Quite apart from whether a nation has its own sovereign state, we can assert that nations tend to have certain common characteristics. Among those characteristics can be: a common language; a common religion; a territory on which the people in question live; shared history, traditions, and aspirations; and a shared economy. Not all nations have all of these attributes. For instance, while Germans share a common language, for centuries they have been divided when it comes to religion, for the most part between Catholics and Protestants, and more recently by the presence of a large Muslim population. Or take the case of Austria. While most Austrians are Roman Catholics, they share the German language with neighbouring Germany. Does this shared language negate Austria's claim to being a distinct nation? During the nineteenth century drive for German unification, there were those who wanted to include Austria in the national project and those who wanted to exclude it — does that call Austrian nationhood into question?

Despite the list of characteristics nations often have, what constitutes a nation may come down to the political will of a particular people on a particular territory as they assert their nationhood and establish their own effective sovereign state. This matter of political will is crucial.

In sorting out this matter of nations, nationalism, and patriotism, while it makes sense to group the nationalisms of revolutionary America and France together in the late eighteenth century, it is also relevant to briefly examine the nature of British patriotism, which burgeoned during this era as well. British patriotism was an odd, hybrid creature that evolved within the framework of an empire in a society and political system in which aristocracy and monarchy were prominent. It displayed its own peculiar mixture of particularist qualities and universalist claims. The British boasted that their imperial role was to shine the light of civilization on backward peoples. The patriotism of the British Empire was self-centred, and yet it arrogantly claimed that Britain unselfishly pursued wider human goals.

Reputedly, it was in the 1730s, at the Dove — a pub that has existed on the Thames for centuries — in the London borough of Hammersmith, that the Scottish poet James Thomson wrote the poem "Rule, Britannia." Likely inspired by the sweep of the river, Thomson combined key elements of British patriotism in what would become the lyrics to a popular national air. He fused the identities of the English, Scottish, Irish, and Welsh under the all-embracing term "Britannia." Britannia's mission was to rule the waves, pursue commerce, and to ensure that Britons never would be slaves.

One verse in Thomson's original version sums this up:

To thee belongs the rural reign;
Thy cities shall with commerce shine;
All thine shall be the subject main,
And every shore it circles thine.

Rule, Britannia! rule the waves:
Britons never will be slaves.

Although they were the bitterest foes of revolutionary France and the thought of the Enlightenment, the members of the British elites appropriated many of the broad principles of the Enlightenment, precisely so they could combat them. Over the course of history, it has not been unusual for deadly enemies to take over many of the ideas and approaches of their opponents to negate them more effectively.

These early nationalisms were quite different in character from later nationalisms that sprang up in many other societies in the mid-nineteenth century — for instance, those of the Germans and the Italians. One reason for this was that the world was not then crowded with competing nationalisms and national projects. On the as yet uncluttered highway of nationalism, the idea that nations bent on self-determination could coexist with one another appeared not unreasonable. Later, when the highway was jammed with national projects whose claims often dangerously overlapped, the idea of nationalism came to be seen as less benign.

The nationalist movements that arose later in the nineteenth century were fuelled intellectually by a spirit of romanticism that was quite at odds with the universal values of the Enlightenment. In Europe, these later movements drew upon the works of writers and thinkers who traced the origins of particular peoples to their early beginnings. Instead of focusing on rationality, liberty, and democracy, these nationalisms were rooted in ethnicity, language, and often the idealization of a lost golden age. The later nationalisms were openly antagonistic to the Enlightenment and to the legacy of the French Revolution. Mid-nineteenth-century nationalists viewed the French ideas as a universalist fetter that must be cast off so that peoples such as the Germans, Italians, Hungarians, and Slavs could realize their own particular national destinies.

While at the end of the eighteenth century early German patriots had drawn enthusiastically on French Enlightenment thought, their successors had come to see French ideas and writings as soft, inauthentic, and decadent. They hungered for what they regarded as the purity of ideas expressed in the German language, a language they saw as unencumbered by the hybrid origins of French and English. Such German nationalists believed that throwing off the yoke of French culture was essential to the elaboration and realization of the German national project, whose end goal was a unified and sovereign German state. A crucial transitional figure in the shift from Enlightenment to romanticism was Johann Gottfried von Herder, an eighteenth-century German philosopher and poet. Though he was too deeply imbued with Enlightenment universalism to cast it off entirely, he turned to the origins of each individual nation, which he unearthed in its myths and its own unique language, as the source of its authenticity. In elaborating his Volk (folk) theory, he wrote: "There is only one class in the state, the Volk (not the rabble), and the king belongs to this class as well as the peasant."

In a poem titled "To the Germans," Herder condemned the German tendency to regard France and the French language as the source of the highest culture:

Look at other nationalities,
Do they wander about
So that nowhere in the whole world they are strangers
Except to themselves?
They regard foreign countries with proud disdain.
And you German alone, returning from abroad,
Wouldst greet your mother in French?
O spew it out, before your door
Spew out the ugly slime of the Seine
Speak German, O you German![3]

At the end of the 1840s, Americans generally believed that their own country was immune to the kinds of revolutions and counter-revolutions that had resulted in the loss of tens of thousands of lives in Europe. What was imperfectly recognized, however, was that the United States contained within its boundaries two national projects, both highly developed and increasingly antagonistic toward one another. There was the free states project in the North and the slave states project in the South.

The two projects could be traced back to the era of the American Revolution. In the creation of the United States of America, Massachusetts and Virginia, the most characteristic of the Northern and Southern states, played seminal roles.

North of the border, Canadians and those who governed them were also well aware of the 1848 revolutions in Europe. In March 1848, Canada's governor, Lord Elgin, called on the Reformers, Louis-Hippolyte LaFontaine and Robert Baldwin, to form a government, since they were the leaders of the majority of members in the legislature. Responsible government — the selection of ministers of the Crown from those who enjoyed the support of the elected legislature — thus came to Canada not as a consequence of revolution but as a decision of the British government. But the policy was adopted in turbulent times. A missive from the Colonial Office to Elgin noted that it was a good thing that a Canadian government with the support of the legislature had been formed just before the news of the Revolution in France in February 1848 had become known in Canada. Elgin replied: "They are not wanting here, persons who might under different circumstances have attempted by seditious harangues, if not by overt acts, to turn the examples of France and the sympathies of the United States to account."[4]

The British government's decision to bestow responsible government on its settler colonies was not made as an act of political charity. It was made in response to the vast socio-economic changes that were transforming Europe and North America. In the advanced regions of Europe, as well as in the U.S. North, a new industrial revolution had commenced. The first industrial revolution, during which Britain's cotton manufacturing was king, was beginning to be superseded. In the second industrial revolution, steel, chemicals, oil, and the beginnings of the electrical age were already transforming economies and states. Closely associated with steel, rail transport, and the telegraph was a revolution in military power that opened the way for mass armies that could be swiftly deployed and supplied. In Europe and in the U.S. North, industrialists and the bankers who financed them demanded state support to stake out secure markets and to protect them from foreign competition. These challengers to British industrial supremacy called for tariffs to shelter their home markets and internal improvements, principally the construction of railways, to bring raw materials and markets within easy reach.

In the western hemisphere, the United States had already proclaimed a unique status for itself, enunciated in the Monroe Doctrine of 1823, which warned against new powers butting into the affairs of the hemisphere. But as Americans pushed westward, acquiring vast new territories, the settled order within their state was subjected to severe and growing stresses.

In Europe, there were a number of models for the creation of nation states; no single model could be regarded as the classic. That has not been the case in North America, however. The United States has been seen, both by historians and in the popular imagination, as the classic model.

Just what are the elements of the American model? The American model holds that English-speaking colonists migrated to the New World during the early modern age in a quest for religious and political liberty. These colonies are conceived as post-aristocratic, born broadly speaking in a setting of market economics, and that includes the slave-owning colonies. They are thought, as well, to be naturally inclined in their politics toward the concept of a limited state; that is to say, they are inherently drawn to the political philosophy of John Locke. They instinctively lean toward the notion of a contract between governors and the governed. Once these colonies have been firmly established and have developed their own identities, commercial and agricultural economies, and political leaders, they enter into an inexorable conflict with the imperial power to which they are attached. The economies and the politics of the colonies are limited by imperial fetters that grow increasingly nettlesome. Through a process that is more or less revolutionary — and if necessary, by resorting to armed force — the colonies throw off the imperial yoke to become an independent state or states.

In fact, only the United States fits this supposed classical model. Through their struggles to cast off imperial rule from Europe, a number of Latin American countries have evolved along paths that feature some elements of the model. One essential reason why no other country ever followed the American model fully is because the United States got there first. From the beginning of its life as a nation state in the late eighteenth century, the United States was an incipient imperial power. Its claim through the Monroe Doctrine in the 1820s to a role as a regional hegemonic power in the western hemisphere closed off the classic American nation state route to other potential powers.

From its earliest days, American nationalism was cloaked in

universalist garb. It was the claim of American leaders, some might say their conceit, that Americans were undertaking an experiment in which all of mankind had an interest, indeed a stake. In a letter to Dr. Joseph Priestley, written on June 19, 1802, President Thomas Jefferson proclaimed: "We feel that we are acting under obligations not confined to the limits of our own society. It is impossible not to be sensible that we are acting for all mankind; that circumstances denied to others, but indulged to us, have imposed on us the duty of proving what is the degree of freedom and self-government in which a society may venture to leave its individual members."[5]

Jefferson's claim notwithstanding, by the mid-nineteenth century, the explosive rise of the population and economic might of the U.S. North and Midwest generated pronounced political unease in the U.S. South and to an increasing extent in the British North American provinces.

Indeed, it was the emergence of the U.S. North as a veritable new power in the Atlantic world that triggered the struggle among three would-be nation states to stake their claims to portions of the North American continent. The Confederate States of America and the Dominion of Canada were both established in response to the take-off of the North.

The most dynamic of the three national projects was that of Lincoln's North. It was the foundation on which a new power was to be constructed, a power that would one day dominate the world. While Lincoln did perceive the global importance of the struggle unfolding in the United States, he could have no way of knowing how the revolutionary capitalism of the North would transform class relations in America or how the American Republic would morph into the hub of a global empire.

Although the South was a capitalist state relying on slave labour, the character of its nationalism bore a marked resemblance to the nationalisms that emerged in a myriad of European states in the mid-nineteenth century. The ideologists of the South gave voice to a wide-ranging, romantic conception of their national identity.

Ethnicity, race, theology, history, and the land itself were all elements of the Southern outlook.

Southern ideologists made the claim that white Southerners were distinct from white Northerners; that while white Southerners were descended from aristocratic Normans, white Northerners were a mongrel people, a mixture of Anglo Saxons and European immigrants. They also made the claim that slavery was, and always had been, the foundation of civilization, and essential to democracy.

Southern justifications of slavery had two origins: theology and the more modern biological-evolutionary theories of racial differences that were coming into fashion in the mid-nineteenth century. Giving voice to the former, for instance, in November 1860 shortly after Lincoln's election, the South's most highly respected clergyman, James Henley Thornwell, told his Presbyterian congregation in Columbia, South Carolina, that slavery was the "good and merciful" way to deploy the "labour which Providence has given us." He went on to say: "The relation betwixt the slave and his master is not inconsistent with the word of God, we have long settled... We cherish the institution not from avarice, but from principle." [6]

Thinkers in the South also asserted that theirs was a people deeply attached to the land and an outdoor way of life, in contrast to city-dwelling Northerners, who huddled indoors during the winter. Southerners were, as a consequence of all these features, a distinct and traditional people, even a warrior people. The Southern claim to forming a nationality that merited its own sovereign state exhibited the characteristics of the romantic-ethnic nationalisms that erupted in the mid-nineteenth century. Southern nationalism was a folk ideology, the expression of the Volksgeist of its people. Gone were the touches of Enlightenment nationalism, fused with the rights of man, that were so deeply a part of Lincoln's Northern outlook.

Canada's nation state project was an even more deviant departure from the classic American model. Canadians established their nation state within the confines of the British Empire, and the Parliament at Westminster continued to exercise authority over Canadian defence and foreign policy for many decades after Confederation.

In American thinking, an empire was incompatible, by definition, with a subsidiary state within it that could be an authentic nation state. How could a monarch in London be the head of state of a country in North America that constituted a genuine nation state? All of the American antagonism toward monarchy, aristocracy, and the absence of liberty for the mass of the population boils to the surface when confronted by the launch of the Canadian state in the 1860s. (Fortunately for their psychic well-being, Americans only infrequently consider the implications of the Canadian case when analyzing their own history.) When federal Canada was launched, American sensibilities were taken into account and the inoffensive term *dominion* was used to depict it rather than the emotionally charged epithet *kingdom.*

Over the past century and a half, one persistent line of attack against the authenticity of the Canadian state has been that English-speaking Canada does not possess a national identity sufficiently distinct from that of the United States. On top of that, there are the realities of Quebec and of native peoples within the Canadian state. Canada has often been dismissed as an artificial union between English-speaking Canada and the Quebecois, one in which the whole does not transcend its constituent parts. More recently, Canada has been critiqued as a settler state, built on land stolen from native peoples. According to this analysis, Canada is not, and never has been, a legitimate state.

That the dominion was a white settler state is clear. Ideologists who promoted the virtues of the dominion faced a challenge on the matter of ethnicity. Since one-third of the settler population of Canada spoke French and heralded originally from France, claims that the dominion was a new Anglo-Saxon nation were difficult to sustain. French-Canadian nationalism predated Confederation. In later decades, it evolved into Quebec nationalism and remained a powerful and cohesive political ideology.

The anglophone majority wrapped itself in a British identity, so as to distinguish itself sharply from the neighbouring republic.

As the decades passed, English-Canadian nationalism took on distinctly Canadian claims. Canadians were becoming, as the generations passed, more and more a northern people, it was asserted. Canadian artists created a national style in their portrayal of their immense land. This marked a conscious break from English pastoral painting. Poets and novelists followed suit.

As American power rose while that of Britain declined, Canadians cast off many of the British markers they had used to differentiate themselves from Americans. They did retain British-style parliamentary government and even kept the British monarch as their symbolic head of state. But as Canadians embraced their North American reality and gave up any thought of themselves as transplanted Englishmen, they established new markers intended to affirm their distinctive character. No longer attached to a great European power, Canadians uneasily settled into coexistence with the world's dominant state.

Endnotes

Introduction: Three Nation State Projects and Three Unlikely Leaders

1. Abraham Lincoln, *Selected Speeches and Writings,* pbk. ed. (New York: First Library of America, 2009), 149.
2. *Debates of the House of Commons,* 5th Parliament, 3rd Session (June 6, 1885–July 20, 1885), vol. 2 (Ottawa: Maclean, Roger, 1885), 1589. Accessed online at https://www.collectionscanada.gc.ca/primeministers/h4-4090-e.html.
3. *Jefferson Davis: The Essential Writings,* ed. William J. Cooper Jr. (New York: Modern Library, 2004), 190–94.

Chapter 1: Manifest Destiny

1. Douglas Southall Freeman, *Lee,* abridged by Richard Harwell (1935; repr., New York: Scribner, 1997), 72–73.
2. Ibid., 75–77.
3. James M. McPherson, *Battle Cry of Freedom: The Civil War Era,* pbk. ed. (New York: Oxford University Press, 2003), 48.
4. James K. Polk, Inaugural Address, 1845.
5. James M. McPherson, *Battle Cry of Freedom: The Civil War Era,* pbk. ed. (New York: Oxford University Press, 2003), 51.
6. Ibid.
7. Ibid., 52.
8. Sven Beckert, introduction to *Empire of Cotton: A Global History* (New York: Alfred A. Knopf, 2014), xix–xx.
9. Ibid., 57–58.
10. Ibid., 67.
11. Ibid., 66–67.
12. Ibid., 104–5.
13. Ibid.

14. Ibid., 109–10.

15. James McPherson, *Battle Cry of Freedom: The Civil War Era,* pbk. ed. (New York: Oxford University Press, 2003), 102.

16. Ibid., 100.

17. Sven Beckert, *Empire of Cotton: A Global History* (New York: Alfred A. Knopf, 2014), 109–10.

18. Ibid., 119.

19. Ibid., 244.

20. Ibid., 109.

21. Ibid., 110.

22. Ibid., 120–21.

23. Ibid., 118.

24. James M. McPherson, *Battle Cry of Freedom: The Civil War Era,* pbk. ed. (New York: Oxford University Press, 2003), 100.

25. Paul Quigley, *Shifting Grounds: Nationalism and the American South, 1848–1865* (New York: Oxford University Press, 2012), 89.

26. Walter Stahr, *Seward: Lincoln's Indispensable Man* (New York: Simon & Schuster, 2012), 8.

27. Ibid., 17–19.

28. Bruce Chadwick, *1858: Abraham Lincoln, Jefferson Davis, Robert E. Lee, Ulysses S. Grant and the War They Failed to See* (Naperville, IL: Sourcebooks, 2008), 182–83.

29. Ibid., 185.

30. Ibid.

31. Walter Stahr, *Seward: Lincoln's Indispensable Man* (New York: Simon & Schuster, 2012), 123.

32. Ibid., 123–24.

33. Bruce Chadwick, *1858: Abraham Lincoln, Jefferson Davis, Robert E. Lee, Ulysses S. Grant and the War They Failed to See* (Naperville, IL: Sourcebooks, 2008), 188.

34. Ibid., 189.

CHAPTER 2: IRREPRESSIBLE CONFLICT

1. James M. McPherson, *The Battle Cry of Freedom: The Civil War Era,* pbk. ed. (New York: Oxford University Press, 2003), 122.

2. Ronald C. White Jr., *A. Lincoln: A Biography* (New York: Random House, 2009), 234.

3. Bruce Chadwick, *1858: Abraham Lincoln, Jefferson Davis, Robert E. Lee, Ulysses S. Grant and the War They Failed to See* (Naperville, IL: Sourcebooks, 2008), 47.

4. Ronald C. White Jr., *A. Lincoln: A Biography* (New York: Random House, 2009), 234.
5. Ibid., 235.
6. Ibid., 235–36.
7. Bruce Chadwick, *1858: Abraham Lincoln, Jefferson Davis, Robert E. Lee, Ulysses S. Grant and the War They Failed to See* (Naperville, IL: Sourcebooks, 2008), 49.
8. Ronald C. White Jr., *A. Lincoln: A Biography* (New York: Random House, 2009), 236.
9. Bruce Chadwick, *1858: Abraham Lincoln, Jefferson Davis, Robert E. Lee, Ulysses S. Grant and the War They Failed to See* (Naperville, IL: Sourcebooks, 2008), 48–49.
10. Ibid., 50.
11. Ibid., 141.
12. Steven Lubet, "The Oberlin Fugitive Slave Rescue: A Victory for the Higher Law," (Northwestern University School of Law Scholarly Commons, Faculty Working Papers, 2011).
13. Ibid.
14. Ibid.
15. Ibid.
16. Bruce Chadwick, *1858: Abraham Lincoln, Jefferson Davis, Robert E. Lee, Ulysses S. Grant and the War They Failed to See* (Naperville, IL: Sourcebooks, 2008), 153.
17. Steven Lubet, "The Oberlin Fugitive Slave Rescue: A Victory for the Higher Law" (Northwestern University School of Law Scholarly Commons, Faculty Working Papers, 2011).
18. Ibid.
19. James M. McPherson, *Battle Cry of Freedom: The Civil War Era,* pbk. ed. (New York: Oxford University Press, 2003), 152.
20. Ibid., 48.
21. James Laxer, *The Border: Canada, the U.S. and Dispatches from the 49th Parallel* (Toronto: Doubleday, 2003), 120.
22. John Boyko, *Blood and Daring: How Canada Fought the American Civil War and Forged a Nation* (Toronto: Alfred A. Knopf, 2013), 30.
23. James M. McPherson, *Battle Cry of Freedom: The Civil War Era,* pbk. ed. (New York: Oxford University Press, 2003), 206.
24. Ibid., 208–9.
25. Paul Quigley, *Shifting Grounds: Nationalism and the American South, 1848–1865* (New York: Oxford University Press, 2012), 89.
26. John Boyko, *Blood and Daring: How Canada Fought the American Civil War and Forged a Nation* (Toronto: Alfred A. Knopf, 2013), 23.
27. Ibid., 19.

28. Cheryl MacDonald, "Last Stop on the Underground Railroad," *Beaver*, February/ March 1990, as cited in James Laxer, *The Border: Canada, the U.S. and Dispatches from the 49th Parallel* (Toronto: Doubleday, 2003), 115.

29. James Laxer, *The Border: Canada, the U.S. and Dispatches from the 49th Parallel* (Toronto: Doubleday, 2003), 115–16.

30. Ibid., 116–17.

31. Ibid., 118.

32. Ibid., 115.

33. John Boyko, *Blood and Daring: How Canada Fought the American Civil War and Forged a Nation* (Toronto: Alfred A. Knopf, 2013), 34.

34. "Hon. Otho R. Singleton of Mississippi, on Resistance to Black Republican Domination," delivered in the House of Representatives, December 19, 1859 (Washington: Congressional Globe Office, 1859), 11.

CHAPTER 3: A HOUSE DIVIDED

1.   Doris Kearns Goodwin, *Team of Rivals: The Political Genius of Abraham Lincoln* (New York: Simon & Schuster, 2006), 196.

2.   Walter Stahr, *Seward: Lincoln's Indispensable Man* (New York: Simon & Schuster, 2012), 174.

3.   Abraham Lincoln, *Selected Speeches and Writings*, pbk. ed. (New York: First Library of America, 2009), 149.

4.   Ronald C. White Jr., *A. Lincoln: A Biography* (New York: Random House, 2009), 250.

5.   Ibid., 305.

6.   Ibid., 7.

7.   Ibid., 8.

8.   Ibid., 9.

9.   Ibid., 13.

10. Ibid., 14.

11. Ibid., 16.

12. Ibid., 25.

13. Ibid., 28.

14. Ibid., 30.

15. Ibid.

16. Ibid., 32.

17. Ibid., 36–37.

18. Ibid., 39–40.

19. Ibid., 70, 72.

20. Ibid., 73.

21. Ibid., 74.
22. Ibid., 67.
23. Ibid.
24. Ibid., 67–68.
25. Ibid., 81–86.
26. Ibid., 75.
27. Ibid., 75–76.
28. Abraham Lincoln, *Selected Speeches and Writings,* pbk. ed. (New York: First Library of America, 2009), 9.
29. Ronald C. White Jr., *A. Lincoln: A Biography* (New York: Random House, 2009), 151–52.
30. Abraham Lincoln, *Selected Speeches and Writings*, pbk. ed. (New York: First Library of America, 2009), 117.
31. Ronald C. White Jr., *A. Lincoln: A Biography* (New York: Random House, 2009), 238.
32. Abraham Lincoln, *Selected Speeches and Writings*, pbk. ed. (New York: First Library of America, 2009), 120.
33. Ibid., 120–21.
34. Ibid., 118–20.
35. Armistead C. Gordon, *Jefferson Davis* (New York: Charles Scribner's Sons, 1918), 7.
36. Ibid., 4–6.
37. Ibid., 7.
38. Ibid., 8.
39. Ibid.
40. Bruce Chadwick, *1858: Abraham Lincoln, Jefferson Davis, Robert E. Lee, Ulysses S. Grant and the War They Failed to See* (Naperville, IL: Sourcebooks, 2008), 20.
41. Armistead C. Gordon, *Jefferson Davis* (New York: Charles Scribner's Sons, 1918), 13.
42. Bruce Chadwick, *1858: Abraham Lincoln, Jefferson Davis, Robert E. Lee, Ulysses S. Grant and the War They Failed to See* (Naperville, IL: Sourcebooks, 2008), 20.
43. Ibid.
44. Ibid.
45. Armistead C. Gordon, *Jefferson Davis* (New York: Charles Scribner's Sons, 1918), 32–34.
46. Ibid., 44, 51.
47. Ibid., 53–54.
48. Ibid., 58–63.
49. Ibid., 66.

50. Bruce Chadwick, *1858: Abraham Lincoln, Jefferson Davis, Robert E. Lee, Ulysses S. Grant and the War They Failed to See* (Naperville, IL: Sourcebooks, 2008), 28.

51. Ibid., 29.

52. Ibid., 40.

53. *Jefferson Davis: The Essential Writings*, ed. William J. Cooper Jr. (New York: Modern Library, 2004), 2836–47.

54. Bruce Chadwick, *1858: Abraham Lincoln, Jefferson Davis, Robert E. Lee, Ulysses S. Grant and the War They Failed to See* (Naperville, IL: Sourcebooks, 2008), 41.

55. Ibid., 41–43.

56. Ibid., 43.

57. Ibid., 45.

58. Ibid.

CHAPTER 4: POLITICAL DEADLOCK IN CANADA

1. Adam Shortt and Arthur G. Doughty, eds., *Canada and Its Provinces: A History of the Canadian People and Their Institutions by One Hundred Associates*, vol. 4 (Toronto: Publishers' Association of Canada, 1913), 403.

2. James Laxer, *The Acadians: In Search of a Homeland* (Toronto: Doubleday, 2006), 55–56.

3. Adam Shortt and Arthur G. Doughty, eds., *Canada and Its Provinces: A History of the Canadian People and Their Institutions by One Hundred Associates*, vol. 4 (Toronto: Publishers' Association of Canada, 1913), 403.

4. Ibid., 397.

5. Ibid., 397–98.

6. John Ralston Saul, *Louis-Hippolyte LaFontaine and Robert Baldwin* (Toronto: Penguin, 2010), 173–75.

7. Ibid., 186–87.

8. W. L. Morton, *The Critical Years: The Union of British North America, 1857–1873* (Toronto: McClelland & Stewart, 1964), 1–2.

CHAPTER 5: JOHN A. MACDONALD TAKES THE STAGE

1. Donald Creighton, *John A. Macdonald*, vol. 1, *The Young Politician* (Toronto: Macmillan Canada, 1952), 48.

2. Ibid., 64–68.

3. E. B. Biggar, *Anecdotal Life of Sir John Macdonald* (Montreal: John Lovell & Son, 1891), 17.

4. Donald Creighton, *John A. Macdonald*, vol. 1, *The Young Politician* (Toronto: Macmillan Canada, 1952), 4, 7.

5. E. B. Biggar, *Anecdotal Life of Sir John Macdonald* (Montreal: John Lovell & Son, 1891), 17.

6. Donald Creighton, *John A. Macdonald*, vol. 1, *The Young Politician* (Toronto: Macmillan Canada, 1952), 10.

7. E. B. Biggar, *Anecdotal Life of Sir John Macdonald* (Montreal: John Lovell & Son, 1891), 18–19.

8. Donald Creighton, *John A. Macdonald*, vol. 1, *The Young Politician* (Toronto: Macmillan Canada, 1952), 10.

9. E. B. Biggar, *Anecdotal Life of Sir John Macdonald* (Montreal: John Lovell & Son, 1891), 23–24.

10. Richard J. Gwyn, *John A.: The Man Who Made Us* (Toronto: Random House, 2007), 32.

11. Donald Creighton, *John A. Macdonald*, vol. 1, *The Young Politician* (Toronto: Macmillan Canada, 1952), 19–20.

12. Ibid., 30.

13. *Dictionary of Canadian Biography* Online, s.v. "Mackenzie, George," http://www.biographi.ca/en/bio/mackenzie_george_6E.html.

14. Ibid.

15. Ibid.

16. Donald Creighton, *John A. Macdonald*, vol. 1, *The Young Politician* (Toronto: Macmillan Canada, 1952), 34.

17. Richard J. Gwyn, *John A.: The Man Who Made Us* (Toronto: Random House, 2007), 48.

18. Ibid., 49.

19. Donald Creighton, *John A. Macdonald*, vol. 1, *The Young Politician* (Toronto: Macmillan Canada, 1952), 64–67.

20. E. B. Biggar, *Anecdotal Life of Sir John Macdonald* (Montreal: John Lovell & Son, 1891), 41–42.

21. Richard J. Gwyn, *John A.: The Man Who Made Us* (Toronto: Random House, 2007), 53–54.

22. Ibid., 55–56.

23. Donald Creighton, *John A. Macdonald*, vol. 1, *The Young Politician* (Toronto: Macmillan Canada, 1952), 85.

24. Richard J. Gwyn, *John A.: The Man Who Made Us* (Toronto: Random House, 2007), 59.

25. Ibid., 64.

26. Donald Creighton, *John A. Macdonald*, vol. 1, *The Young Politician* (Toronto: Macmillan Canada, 1956), 198.

Chapter 6: Leaders of Canada's Two Solitudes: George-Étienne Cartier and George Brown

1.   Donald Creighton, *John A. Macdonald,* vol. 1, *The Young Politician* (Toronto: Macmillan Canada, 1952), 216.
2.   Ibid.
3.   Ibid., 256.
4.   Ibid., 268.
5.   Ibid., 272.
6.   Ibid., 275–76.
7.   Ibid., 308.
8.   Ibid.
9.   J. M. S. Careless, *The Union of the Canadas: The Growth of Canadian Institutions, 1841–1857* (Toronto: McClelland & Stewart, 1967), 189.
10. Donald Creighton, *John A. Macdonald,* vol. 1, *The Young Politician* (Toronto: Macmillan Canada, 1952), 308.
11. J. M. S. Careless, *Brown of the Globe,* vol. 1, *The Voice of Upper Canada* (Toronto: Macmillan Canada, 1959), 5.
12. Ibid., 6.
13. Ibid., 6–8.
14. Ibid., 18–24.
15. W. L. Morton, *The Critical Years: The Union of British North America, 1857–1873* (Toronto: McClelland & Stewart, 1964), 33.

Chapter 7: The Election of Abraham Lincoln

1.   James M. McPherson, *Battle Cry of Freedom: The Civil War Era,* pbk. ed. (New York: Oxford University Press, 2003), 214.
2.   Abraham Lincoln, *Selected Speeches and Writings,* pbk. ed. (New York: First Library of America, 2009), 149.
3.   *Jefferson Davis: The Essential Writings,* ed. William J. Cooper Jr. (New York: Modern Library, 2004), 153–56.
4.   Eric H. Walther, *William Lowndes Yancey and the Coming of the Civil War* (Chapel Hill: University of North Carolina Press, 2006), 241.
5.   Ibid., 243.
6.   Ibid., 244.
7.   James M. McPherson, *Battle Cry of Freedom: The Civil War Era,* pbk. ed. (New York: Oxford University Press, 2003), 216.
8.   *Great Speeches: Abraham Lincoln* (New York: Dover, 1991), 35–51.

9. James M. McPherson, *Battle Cry of Freedom: The Civil War Era*, pbk. ed. (New York: Oxford University Press, 2003), 220.

10. Doris Kearns Goodwin, *Team of Rivals: The Political Genius of Abraham Lincoln* (New York: Simon & Schuster, 2006), 257–58.

11. James M. McPherson, *Battle Cry of Freedom: The Civil War Era*, pbk. ed. (New York: Oxford University Press, 2003), 221.

12. Doris Kearns Goodwin, *Team of Rivals: The Political Genius of Abraham Lincoln* (New York: Simon & Schuster, 2006), 259.

13. Ibid., 264.

14. Ibid.

15. Ibid., 265.

16. James M. McPherson, *Battle Cry of Freedom: The Civil War Era*, pbk. ed. (New York: Oxford University Press, 2003), 229.

17. Ibid., 230.

18. Ibid., 232.

CHAPTER 8: THE CONFEDERATE STATES OF AMERICA: JEFFERSON DAVIS'S PROJECT

1. Armistead G. Gordon, *Jefferson Davis* (New York: Charles Scribner's Sons, 1918), 124.

2. James M. McPherson, *Battle Cry of Freedom: The Civil War Era*, pbk. ed. (New York: Oxford University Press, 2003), 257.

3. *Jefferson Davis: The Essential Writings*, ed William J. Cooper Jr. (New York: Modern Library, 2004), 169–70.

4. Alexander H. Stephens, "Cornerstone Address, March 21, 1861," in *The Rebellion Record: A Diary of American Events with Documents, Narratives, Illustrative Incidents, Poetry, Etc.*, ed. Frank Moore, vol. 1, (New York: O. P. Putnam, 1862), 44–46.

5. Thomas E. Schott, *Alexander H. Stephens of Georgia* (Baton Rouge: Louisiana State University Press, 1988), 334–35.

6. Michael T. Bernath, *Confederate Minds: The Struggle for Intellectual Independence in the Civil War South* (Chapel Hill: University of North Carolina Press, 2010), 39.

7. Ibid., 39.

8. Ibid., 40.

9. Ibid., 44.

10. Ibid., 45.

11. Ibid.

12. Ibid., 47.

CHAPTER 9: A VERY POLITICAL WAR

1.   Abraham Lincoln, *Selected Speeches and Writings*, pbk. ed. (New York: First Library of America, 2009), 284–85.
2.   Gary W. Gallagher, *The Confederate War: How Popular Will, Nationalism, and Military Strategy Could Not Stave Off Defeat* (Cambridge, MA: Harvard University Press, 1997), 119.
3.   Alan T. Nolan, *Lee Considered: General Robert E. Lee and Civil War History* (Chapel Hill: University of North Carolina Press, 1991), quoted in Gary W. Gallagher, *The Confederate War: How Popular Will, Nationalism, and Military Strategy Could Not Stave Off Defeat* (Cambridge, MA: Harvard University Press, 1997), 123.
4.   Ibid., 127.
5.   Richard S. Brownlee, *Gray Ghosts of the Confederacy: Guerrilla Warfare in the West, 1861–1865* (Baton Rouge: Louisiana State University Press, 2000), 121–25.
6.   Gary W. Gallagher, *The Confederate War: How Popular Will, Nationalism, and Military Strategy Could Not Stave Off Defeat* (Cambridge, MA: Harvard University Press, 1997), 130.
7.   Ibid.
8.   James M. McPherson, *Battle Cry of Freedom: The Civil War Era*, pbk. ed. (New York: Oxford University Press, 2003), 470.
9.   Ibid., 490.
10. Gary W. Gallagher, *The Confederate War: How Popular Will, Nationalism, and Military Strategy Could Not Stave Off Defeat* (Cambridge, MA: Harvard University Press, 1997), 131–32.
11. John Boyko, *Blood and Daring: How Canada Fought the American Civil War and Forged a Nation* (Toronto: Alfred A. Knopf Canada, 2013), 156–57.
12. Ibid., 157.
13. Ibid.
14. Ibid.
15. Ibid., 157–59.
16. James M. McPherson, *Battle Cry of Freedom: The Civil War Era*, pbk. ed. (New York: Oxford University Press, 2003), 490.
17. Ibid.
18. Ibid.
19. Ibid.

Chapter 10: Lincoln's Project: Total War

1. Gary W. Gallagher, *The Union War* (Cambridge, MA: Harvard University Press, 2011), 90.

2. Abraham Lincoln, *Selected Speeches and Writings*, pbk. ed. (New York: First Library of America, 2009), 336.

3. Ibid., 338–42.

4. Gary W. Gallagher, *The Union War* (Cambridge, MA: Harvard University Press, 2011), 90.

5. James M. McPherson, *Battle Cry of Freedom: The Civil War Era,* pbk. ed. (New York: Oxford University Press, 2003), 503–4.

6. Ibid., 505.

7. Abraham Lincoln, *Selected Speeches and Writings,* pbk. ed. (New York: First Library of America, 2009), 343.

8. Abraham Lincoln, "The Emancipation Proclamation" (1863), accessed online at http://www.abrahamlincolnonline.org/lincoln/speeches/emancipate.htm.

9. Ronald C. White Jr., *A. Lincoln: A Biography* (New York: Random House, 2009), 275–76.

10. Garry Wills, *Lincoln at Gettysburg: The Words That Remade America* (New York: Simon & Schuster, 2006), 38.

11. Ibid., 60–61.

12. Ibid., 38.

13. *Memoirs of General William T. Sherman* (New York: Da Capo Press, 1983), 171.

Chapter 11: The War Threatens Canada

1. P. B. Waite, *The Life and Times of Confederation, 1864–1867: Politics, Newspapers and the Union of British North America* (Toronto: Robin Brass Studio, 2001), 31.

2. Donald Creighton, *The Road to Confederation: The Emergence of Canada, 1863–1867* (Toronto: Macmillan Canada, 1964), 18.

3. Adam Shortt and Arthur G. Doughty, eds., *Canada and Its Provinces: A History of the Canadian People and Their Institutions by One Hundred Associates,* vol. 7 (Toronto: Publishers' Association of Canada, 1914), 400.

4. Mountague Bernard, *A Historical Account of the Neutrality of Great Britain During the American Civil War* (London: Longmans, Green, Reader, & Dyer 1870), 135.

5. Ibid., 152.

6. Walter Stahr, *Seward: Lincoln's Indispensable Man* (New York: Simon & Schuster, 2012), 292.

7.   Mountague Bernard, *A Historical Account of the Neutrality of Great Britain During the American Civil War* (London: Longmans, Green, Reader, & Dyer, 1870), 190.

8.   Alfred H. Guernsey and Henry M. Alden, *Harper's Pictorial History of the Civil War* (New York: Fairfax, 1866), 194–95.

9.   Ibid., 195.

10. Adam Shortt and Arthur G. Doughty, eds., *Canada and Its Provinces: A History of the Canadian People and Their Institutions by One Hundred Associates,* vol. 14 (Toronto: Publishers' Association of Canada, 1914), 409.

11. Mountague Bernard, *A Historical Account of the Neutrality of Great Britain During the American Civil War* (London: Longmans, Green, Reader, & Dyer, 1870), 192–93.

12. Ibid., 193–94.

13. Alfred H. Guernsey and Henry M. Alden, *Harper's Pictorial History of the Civil War* (New York: Fairfax, 1866), 195.

14. Donald Creighton, *John A. Macdonald,* vol. 1, *The Young Politician* (Toronto: Macmillan Canada, 1952), 324.

15. John Boyko, *Blood and Daring: How Canada Fought the American Civil War and Forged a Nation* (Toronto: Alfred A. Knopf Canada, 2013), 98.

16. Donald Creighton, *John A. Macdonald,* vol. 1, *The Young Politician* (Toronto: Macmillan Canada, 1952), 324.

17. John Boyko, *Blood and Daring: How Canada Fought the American Civil War and Forged a Nation* (Toronto: Alfred A. Knopf Canada, 2013), 98–99.

18. Walter Stahr, *Seward: Lincoln's Indispensable Man* (New York: Simon & Schuster, 2012), 315.

19. Ibid., 316.

20. Ibid.

21. Ibid., 317–18.

22. Ibid., 318.

23. Ibid.

24. Ibid.

25. Ibid., 318–19.

26. Ibid.

27. Ibid., 319–20.

28. Ibid., 320.

29. Donald Creighton, *The Road to Confederation: The Emergence of Canada, 1863–1867* (Toronto: Macmillan Canada, 1964), 7–8.

30. Adam Shortt and Arthur G. Doughty, eds., *Canada and Its Provinces: A History of the Canadian People and Their Institutions by One Hundred Associates,* vol. 14 (Toronto: Publishers' Association of Canada, 1914), 409.

31. Adam Shortt and Arthur G. Doughty, eds., *Canada and Its Provinces: A History of the Canadian People and Their Institutions by One Hundred Associates,* vol. 7 (Publishers' Association of Canada, Toronto, 1914), 394.

32. Ibid., 401.

33. Ibid., 403.

34. John Boyko, *Blood and Daring: How Canada Fought the American Civil War and Forged a Nation* (Toronto: Alfred A. Knopf Canada, 2013), 117–18.

35. James Laxer, *Tecumseh & Brock: The War of 1812* (Toronto: Anansi, 2012), 71–72.

36. John Boyko, *Blood and Daring: How Canada Fought the American Civil War and Forged a Nation* (Toronto: Alfred A. Knopf Canada, 2013), 118–19.

37. Danny R. Jenkins, "British North Americans Who Fought in the American Civil War, 1861–1865" (master's thesis, University of Ottawa, 1993), ii.

38. Ibid., iii.

39. Donald Creighton, *The Road to Confederation: The Emergence of Canada, 1863–1867* (Toronto: Macmillan Canada, 1964), 18.

Chapter 12: George Brown Changes Course

1. J. M. S. Careless, *Brown of the Globe,* vol. 2, *Statesman of Confederation 1860–1880* (Toronto: Dundurn, 1989), 86.

2. Ibid., 120.

3. Donald Creighton, *The Road to Confederation: The Emergence of Canada, 1863–1867* (Toronto: Macmillan Canada, 1964), 45–46.

4. J. M. S. Careless, *Brown of the Globe,* vol. 2, *Statesman of Confederation 1860–1880* (Toronto: Dundurn, 1989), 121.

5. Ibid., 121.

6. Ibid., 128.

7. Donald Creighton, *The Road to Confederation: The Emergence of Canada, 1863–1867* (Toronto: Macmillan Canada, 1964), 51–52.

8. Ibid., 52–53.

9. Ibid., 57.

10. Ibid.

11. Ministerial Explanations, Parliament of Canada, Quebec, June 23, 1864. Library and Archives Canada.

12. Ibid.

13. Ibid.

14. Ibid.

15. Ibid.

16. Ibid.

17. Ibid.

18. Ibid.

19. Donald Creighton, *The Road to Confederation: The Emergence of Canada, 1863–1867* (Toronto: Macmillan Canada, 1964), 67–69.

CHAPTER 13: CONFEDERATION: THE HOUSE MACDONALD BUILT

1. Donald Creighton, *The Road to Confederation: The Emergence of Canada, 1863–1867* (Toronto: Macmillan Canada, 1964), 105–9.

2. Ibid., 112–13.

3. Ibid.

4. J. M. S. Careless, *Brown of the Globe*, vol. 2, *Statesman of Confederation 1860–1880* (Toronto: Dundurn, 1989), 155.

5. Ibid.

6. Donald Creighton, *The Road to Confederation: The Emergence of Canada, 1863–1867* (Toronto: Macmillan Canada, 1964), 115–16.

7. Macdonald, Sir John A., *Canada Transformed: The Speeches of Sir John A. Macdonald*, ed. Sarah Katherine Gibson and Arthur Milnes (Toronto: McClelland & Stewart, 2014), 142–43.

8. John A. Macdonald Papers (143) Reel 1503, Tuesday, 11 October, 1864. Library and Archives Canada.

9. Donald Creighton, *The Road to Confederation: The Emergence of Canada, 1863–1867* (Toronto: Macmillan Canada, 1964), 138.

10. John A. Macdonald Papers (143) Reel 1503, Tuesday, 11 October, 1864. Library and Archives Canada.

11. Donald Creighton, *The Road to Confederation: The Emergence of Canada, 1863–1867* (Toronto: Macmillan Canada, 1964), 139.

12. Ibid., 145–46.

13. John A. Macdonald Papers (147) Reel 1503, Monday, 17 October, 1864. Library and Archives Canada.

14. J. M. S. Careless, *Brown of the Globe*, vol. 2, *Statesman of Confederation 1860–1880* (Toronto: Dundurn, 1989), 165.

15. John A. Macdonald Papers (139) Reel 1503, Wednesday, 19 October, 1864. Library and Archives Canada.

16. Donald Creighton, *The Road to Confederation: The Emergence of Canada, 1863–1867* (Toronto: Macmillan Canada, 1964), 154–55.

17. John A. Macdonald Papers (149) Reel 1503, Thursday, October 20, 1864. Library and Archives Canada.

18. John A. Macdonald Papers (159) Reel 1503. Date not legible on original document. Library and Archives Canada.

19. John A. Macdonald Papers (155) Reel 1503, Saturday, 22 October, 1864. Library and Archives Canada.

20. Donald Creighton, *The Road to Confederation: The Emergence of Canada, 1863–1867* (Toronto: Macmillan Canada, 1964), 172–73.

21. Ibid., 173–74.

22. John A. Macdonald Papers (159) Reel 1503. Date not legible on original document. Library and Archives Canada.

23. J. H. Stewart Reid, Kenneth McNaught, and Harry S. Crowe, eds., *A Source-Book of Canadian History: Selected Documents and Personal Papers* (Toronto: Longmans Canada, 1964), 212.

24. Donald Creighton, *The Road to Confederation: The Emergence of Canada, 1863–1867* (Toronto: Macmillan Canada, 1964), 181.

Chapter 14: Debating Confederation

1. J. H. Stewart Reid, Kenneth McNaught, and Harry S. Crowe, eds., *A Source-Book of Canadian History: Selected Documents and Personal Papers* (Toronto: Longmans Canada, 1964), 210.

2. Walter Stahr, *Seward: Lincoln's Indispensable Man* (New York: Simon & Schuster, 2012), 410–11.

3. Ibid., 411–12.

4. Ibid.

5. Donald Creighton, *The Road to Confederation: The Emergence of Canada, 1863–1867* (Toronto: Macmillan Canada, 1964), 212.

6. Walter Stahr, *Seward: Lincoln's Indispensable Man* (New York: Simon & Schuster, 2012), 415.

7. J. M. S. Careless, *Brown of the Globe*, vol. 2, *Statesman of Confederation 1860–1880* (Toronto: Dundurn, 1989), 181.

8. P. B. Waite, ed., *The Confederation Debates in the Province of Canada, 1865* (Toronto: McClelland & Stewart, 1969), 43–44.

9. Ibid., 40.

10. Ibid., 43.

11. Ibid., 50–51.

12. Ibid.

13. Ibid., 58, 71–72.

14. Ibid., 90, 92.

15. Ibid., 95.

CHAPTER 15: SURRENDER AND ASSASSINATION

1. Shelby Foote, *The Civil War: A Narrative,* vol. 3 (New York: Vintage Books, 1986), 627–29.
2. James M. McPherson, *Battle Cry of Freedom: The Civil War Era,* pbk. ed. (New York: Oxford University Press, 2003), 838–39.
3. Ronald C. White Jr., *A. Lincoln: A Biography* (New York: Random House, 2009), 657.
4. Ibid., 659.
5. Abraham Lincoln, Second Inaugural Address, March 4, 1865.
6. Ronald C. White Jr., *A. Lincoln: A Biography* (New York: Random House, 2009), 669.
7. Shelby Foote, *The Civil War: A Narrative,* vol. 3 (New York: Vintage Books, 1986), 945–46.
8. Douglas Southall Freeman, *Lee,* abridged by Richard Harwell (1935; repr., New York: Scribner, 1997), 517.
9. James M. McPherson, *Battle Cry of Freedom: The Civil War Era,* pbk. ed. (New York: Oxford University Press, 2003), 853.
10. Ibid., 851–52.
11. Walter Stahr, *Seward: Lincoln's Indispensable Man* (New York: Simon & Schuster, 2012), 434.
12. Ibid.
13. Ibid.
14. Ibid., 435–36.
15. Shelby Foote, *The Civil War: A Narrative,* vol. 3 (New York: Vintage Books, 1986), 996–97.
16. Howard Zinn, *A People's History of the United States, 1492–Present* (New York: Harper Perennial, 1995), 187–205.
17. Samuel Eliot Morison and Henry Steele Commager, *The Growth of the American Republic* (New York: Oxford University Press, 1962), 19–52.
18. Howard Zinn, *A People's History of the United States, 1492–Present* (New York: Harper Perennial, 1995), 187–205.

CHAPTER 16: KEEPING THE AMERICANS AT BAY: THE *REALPOLITIK* OF CONFEDERATION

1. Reg Whitaker, Gregory S. Kealey, and Andrew Parnaby, *Secret Service: Political Policing in Canada from the Fenians to Fortress America* (Toronto: University of Toronto Press, 2012), 19–20.

2. Ibid., 20–22.
3. Ibid., 21–22.
4. Ibid., 21–24.
5. W. L. Morton, *The Critical Years: The Union of British North America, 1857–1873* (Toronto: McClelland & Stewart, 1964), 19, 130.
6. David A. Wilson, *Thomas D'Arcy McGee: The Extreme Moderate, 1857–1858*, vol. 2 (Montreal: McGill-Queen's University Press, 2011), 100.
7. Reg Whitaker, Gregory S. Kealey, and Andrew Parnaby, *Secret Service: Political Policing in Canada from the Fenians to Fortress America* (Toronto: University of Toronto Press, 2012), 31–32.
8. *Dictionary of Canadian Biography* Online, s.v. "Jervois, Sir William Francis Drummond," http://www.biographi.ca/en/bio/jervois_william_francis_drummond_12E.html.
9. Richard J. Gwyn, *John A.: The Man Who Made Us* (Toronto: Random House, 2007), 285.
10. *Dictionary of Canadian Biography* Online, s.v. "Jervois, Sir William Francis Drummond," http://www.biographi.ca/en/bio/jervois_william_francis_drummond_12E.html.
11. John A. Macdonald Papers, Confidential Report 1865, Reel 1521. Library and Archives Canada.
12. Walter Stahr, *Seward: Lincoln's Indispensable Man* (New York: Simon & Schuster, 2012), 167–68.
13. *Dictionary of Canadian Biography* Online, s.v. "Smith, Sir Albert James," http://www.biographi.ca/en/bio/smith_albert_james_11E.html.
14. Ibid.
15. Ibid.
16. Donald Creighton, *The Road to Confederation: The Emergence of Canada, 1863–1867* (Toronto: Macmillan Canada, 1964), 362.
17. Ibid., 365–66.

Chapter 17: Red River Rebellion

1. W. L. Morton, *The Critical Years: The Union of British North America, 1857–1873* (Toronto: McClelland & Stewart, 1964), 253.
2. Ibid., 267.
3. George F. G. Stanley, *Louis Riel* (Toronto: McGraw-Hill Ryerson, 1963), 39.
4. Ibid.
5. Ibid., 40–41.
6. D. N. Sprague, *Canada and the Metis, 1869–1885* (Waterloo, ON: Wilfrid Laurier University Press, 1988), 26.

7. Ibid., 26.

8. Ibid., 27–28.

9. Ibid., 28–29.

10. Ibid., 30.

11. Ibid., 33–34.

12. George F. G. Stanley, *Louis Riel* (Toronto: McGraw-Hill Ryerson, 1963), 6.

13. Ibid.

14. Ibid., 10.

15. D. N. Sprague, *Canada and the Metis, 1869–1885* (Waterloo, ON: Wilfrid Laurier University Press, 1988), 22.

16. Ibid., 22–23.

17. Ibid., 23.

18. Ibid., 45.

19. Ibid., 34–6.

20. Ibid., 40.

21. George F. G. Stanley, *Louis Riel* (Toronto: McGraw-Hill Ryerson, 1963), 19–34.

22. D. N. Sprague, *Canada and the Metis, 1869–1885* (Waterloo, ON: Wilfrid Laurier University Press, 1988), 38–39.

23. Ibid., 39.

24. Ibid., 40–41.

25. Ibid., 41.

26. Ibid., 42.

27. Ibid., 44–45.

28. Ibid., 44.

29. Ibid., 46.

30. Ibid., 47.

31. Ibid., 47–48.

32. Ibid.

33. Ibid., 50–51.

34. Ibid.

35. *Canada Transformed: The Speeches of Sir John A. Macdonald,* ed. Sarah Katherine Gibson and Arthur Milnes (Toronto: McClelland & Stewart, 2014), 217.

36. *Wilfrid Laurier on the Platform, 1871–1890,* comp. Ulric Barthe (Quebec: Turcotte & Menard's, 1890), 38–40.

37. Joseph Boyden, *Louis Riel and Gabriel Dumont* (Toronto: Penguin Canada, 2010), 1334.

38. Christopher Adams, Ian Peach, and Gregg Dahl. *Metis in Canada: History, Identity, Law and Politics* (Edmonton: University of Alberta Press, 2013), 454.

39. *Debates of the House of Commons*, 5th Parliament, 3rd Session (June 6, 1885–July 20, 1885). Ottawa: Maclean, Roger, 1885. Accessed online at https://www.collectionscanada.gc.ca/primeministers/h4-4090-e.html.

40. George F. G. Stanley, *Louis Riel* (Toronto: McGraw-Hill Ryerson, 1963), 355–60.

41. Joseph Boyden, *Louis Riel and Gabriel Dumont* (Toronto, Penguin Canada, 2010), 159–60.

42. George F. G. Stanley, *Louis Riel* (Toronto: McGraw-Hill Ryerson, 1963), 355–60.

43. Ibid., 367.

EPILOGUE: LEGACIES OF THREE LEADERS

1. *Jefferson Davis: The Essential Writings*, ed. William J. Cooper Jr. (New York: Modern Library, New York, 2004), 428–29.

2. Abraham Lincoln, Second Inaugural Address, March 4, 1865.

3. Richard Gwyn, *Nation Maker: Sir John A. Macdonald: His Life, Our Times*, vol. 2, *1867–1891* (Toronto: Random House Canada, 2011), 566–67.

4. E. A. Pollard, *Southern History of the War* (New York: C. B. Richardson, 1866), quoted in Gary W. Gallagher and Alan T. Nolan, eds., *The Myth of the Lost Cause and Civil War History* (Bloomington: Indiana University Press, 2000), 13.

5. Gary W. Gallagher and Alan T. Nolan, eds., *The Myth of the Lost Cause and Civil War History* (Bloomington: Indiana University Press, 2000), 40.

6. Ibid.

7. Ibid., 42.

8. James M. McPherson, *Battle Cry of Freedom: The Civil War Era*, pbk. ed. (New York: Oxford University Press, 2003), 507.

9. Garry Wills, *Lincoln at Gettysburg: The Words That Remade America* (New York: Simon & Schuster, 2006), 372.

10. John A. Macdonald, speech, May 30, 1881. Accessed online at https://www.collectionscanada.gc.ca/primeministers/h4-4035-e.html.

11. John A. Macdonald, speech before the House of Commons, January 17, 1881. Accessed online at https://www.collectionscanada.gc.ca/primeministers/h4-4013-e.html.

APPENDIX: NATION STATE PROJECTS IN NINETEENTH-CENTURY NORTH AMERICA AND EUROPE

1. Rogers Brubaker, *Citizenship and Nationhood in France and Germany* (Cambridge, MA: Harvard University Press, 1992), 35.

2. Elie Kedourie, *Nationalism* (London: Hutchinson University Library, 1966), 12.

3. Ibid., 59.

4. Stanley Ryerson, *Unequal Union: Confederation and the Roots of Conflict in the Canadas, 1815–1873* (Toronto: Progress Books, 1968), 164–65.

5. *The Writings of Thomas Jefferson*, ed. Andrew Adgate Lipscomb, vol. 10 (Washington, DC: Thomas Jefferson Memorial Association, 1905), 324–25, quoted in Hans Kohn, *The Idea of Nationalism* (Toronto: Macmillan, 1969), 309.

6. Mark A. Noll, *The Civil War as a Theological Crisis* (Chapel Hill: University of North Carolina Press, 2006), 2.

Bibliography

PRIMARY SOURCES

Abraham Lincoln Papers, Library of Congress.

Archives of Ontario.

Ayling, Augustus D. *A Yankee at Arms: The Diary of Lieutenant Augustus D. Ayling, 29th Massachusetts Volunteers*. Edited by Charles F. Herberger. Knoxville: University of Tennessee Press, 1989.

Bernard, Mountague. *A Historical Account of the Neutrality of Great Britain During the American Civil War*. London: Longmans, Green, Reader, & Dyer, 1870.

Berryhill, William Harvey. *The Gentle Rebel: The Civil War Letters of 1st Lieutenant William Harvey Berryhill, Co. D, 43rd Regiment, Mississippi Volunteers*. Edited by Mary Miles Jones and Leslie Jones Martin. Yazoo City, MS: Sassafras Press, 1982.

Confederate Hall, Civil War Museum, New Orleans.

Debates of the House of Commons, 5th Parliament, 3rd Session (June 6, 1885–July 20, 1885). Ottawa: Maclean, Roger, 1885. Accessed online at https://www.collectionscanada.gc.ca/primeministers/h4-4090-e.html.

"Discovering the Civil War," National Archives. Accessed online at http://www.archives.gov/exhibits/civil-war/.

Davis, Jefferson. *Jefferson Davis: The Essential Writings*. Edited by William J. Cooper Jr. New York: Modern Library, 2004.

George Brown Papers, Augustus C. Long Health Sciences Library, Columbia University.

Gould, John Mead. *The Civil War Journals of John Mead Gould, 1861–1866*. Edited by William G. Jordan Jr. Baltimore: Butternut & Blue, 1997.

Greene, William B. *Letters from a Sharpshooter: The Civil War Letters of Private William B. Greene, Co. G, 2nd United States Sharpshooters (Berdan's), Army of the Potomac, 1861–1865*. Edited by William H. Hastings. Belleville, WI: Historic Publications, 1993.

Griscom, George C. *Fighting with Ross' Texas Cavalry Brigade, C.S.A.: The Diary of George C. Griscom, Adjutant, 9th Texas Cavalry Regiment*. Edited by Homer L. Kerr. Hillsboro, TX: Hill Junior College Press, 1976.

Heth, Henry. *The Memoirs of Henry Heth*. Edited by James L. Morrison Jr. Westport, CT: Greenwood Press, 1974.

Historical Debates of the Parliament of Canada, Canadian Parliamentary Historical Resources, http://parl.canadiana.ca/.

Hitchcock, Henry. *Marching with Sherman: Passages from the Letters and Campaign Diaries of Henry Hitchcock, Major and Assistant Adjutant General of Volunteers, November 1864–May 1865*. Edited by Mark De Wolfe Howe. Lincoln: University of Nebraska Press, 1995.

Holmes, Oliver Wendell, Jr. *Touched with Fire: The Civil War Letters and Diary of Oliver Wendell Holmes, Jr., 1861–1865*. Edited by Mark De Wolfe Howe. Cambridge, MA: Harvard University Press, 1947.

Jefferson, Thomas. *The Writings of Thomas Jefferson*. Edited by Andrew Adgate Lipscomb. Vol. 10. Quoted in Hans Kohn, *The Idea of Nationalism*. Toronto: Macmillan, 1969.

John A. Macdonald Papers, Library and Archives Canada.

Kansas Adjutant General. *Report of the Adjutant General of the State of Kansas 1861–65*. Topeka, KS: Hudson, 1896.

Laurier, Wilfrid. *Wilfrid Laurier On the Platform, 1871–1890*. Compiled by Ulric Barthe. Quebec: Turcotte & Menard's, 1890.

Lincoln, Abraham. *Selected Speeches and Writings*. Pbk. ed. New York: First Library of America, 2009

——. *Great Speeches: Abraham Lincoln*. New York: Dover, 1991.

——. "The Emancipation Proclamation." 1863. Accessed online at http://www.abrahamlincolnonline.org/lincoln/speeches/emancipate.htm.

Macdonald, Sir John A. *Canada Transformed: The Speeches of Sir John A. Macdonald*. Edited by Sarah Katherin Gibson and Arthur Milnes. Toronto: McClelland & Stewart, 2014.

Parvin, Daniel J. *An Iowa Soldier Writes Home: The Civil War Letters of Union Private Daniel J. Parvin*. Edited by Phillip A. Hubbart. Durham, NC: Carolina Academic Press, 1991.

Ramseur, Stephen Dodson. *The Bravest of the Brave: The Correspondence of Stephen Dodson Ramseur*. Edited by George C. Kundahl. Chapel Hill: University of North Carolina Press, 2010.

Ray, William R. *Four Years with the Iron Brigade: The Civil War Journals of William R. Ray, Co. F., Seventh Wisconsin Infantry*. Edited by Lance Herdegen and Sherry Murphy. Cambridge, MA: Da Capo Press, 2002.

Remley, George, and Lycurgus Remley. *Southern Sons, Northern Soldiers: The Civil War Letters of the Remley Brothers, 22nd Iowa Infantry.* Edited by Julie Holcomb. DeKalb: Northern Illinois University Press, 2004.

Sherman, William T. *Memoirs of General William T. Sherman.* New York: Da Capo Press, 1983.

Shepherd, William T. *To Rescue My Native Land: The Civil War Letters of William T. Shepherd, First Illinois Light Artillery.* Edited by Kurt H. Hackemer. Knoxville: University of Tennessee Press, 2006.

Stephens, Alexander H. "Cornerstone Address, March 21, 1861." In *The Rebellion Record: A Diary of American Events with Documents, Narratives, Illustrative Incidents, Poetry.* Edited by Frank Moore. Vol. 1. New York: O. P. Putnam, 1862.

Stephenson, Philip Dangerfield. *The Civil War Memoir of Philip Dangerfield Stephenson, D. D.* Edited by Nathaniel Cheairs Hughes Jr. Conway: University of Central Arkansas Press, 1995.

Stewart Reid, J. H., Kenneth McNaught, and Harry S. Crowe, eds., *A Source-Book of Canadian History: Selected Documents and Personal Papers.* Toronto: Longmans Canada, 1964.

Stuckenberg, John H. W. *I'm Surrounded by Methodists: Diary of John H. W. Stuckenberg, Chaplain of the 145th Pennsylvania Volunteer Infantry.* Edited by David T. Hedrick and Gordon Barry Davis Jr. Gettysburg, PA: Thomas, 1995.

Waite, P. B., ed., *The Confederation Debates in the Province of Canada, 1865.* Toronto: McClelland & Stewart, 1969.

Welsh, Peter. *Irish Green and Union Blue: The Civil War Letters of Peter Welsh.* Edited by Lawrence Frederick Kohl and Margaret Cosse Richard. New York: Fordham University Press, 1986.

Secondary Sources

Alford, Kenneth D. *Civil War Museum Treasures: Outstanding Artifacts and the Stories Behind Them.* Jefferson, NC: McFarland, 2008.

Ammen, William. *Personnel of the Civil War.* 2 vols. New York: Thomas Yoseloff, 1961.

Armistead, Gene C. *Horses and Mules in the Civil War: A Complete History with a Roster of More Than 700 War Horses.* Jefferson, NC: McFarland, 2013.

Armistead, G. Gordon. *Jefferson Davis.* New York: Charles Scribner's Sons, 1918.

Armstrong, Richard L. *"God Alone Knows Which Was Right": The Blue and Gray Terrill Family of Virginia in the Civil War.* Jefferson, NC: McFarland, 2010.

Ashworth, John. *Slavery, Capitalism, and Politics in the Antebellum Republic.* Vol. 1, *Commerce and Compromise, 1820–1850.* Cambridge: Cambridge University Press, 1996.

Ayers, Edward L. *What Caused the Civil War?: Reflections on the South and Southern History.* New York: W. W. Norton, 2005.

Barrett, Joseph H. *Life of Abraham Lincoln.* Mechanicsburg, PA: Stackpole Books, 2006. First published 1865 by Wilstach & Baldwin.

Beckert, Sven. *Empire of Cotton: A Global History.* New York: Alfred A. Knopf, 2014.

Bernath, Michael T. *Confederate Minds: The Struggle for Intellectual Independence in the Civil War South.* Chapel Hill: University of North Carolina Press, 2010.

Biggar, E. B. *Anecdotal Life of Sir John Macdonald.* Montreal: John Lovell & Son, 1891.

Bliss, Michael. *Confederation: A New Nationality.* Toronto: Grolier, 1981.

Boatner, Mark Mayo. *Civil War Dictionary.* New York: Vintage Civil War Library, 1991.

Bolotenko, George. *A Future Defined: Canada from 1849 to 1873.* Ottawa: National Archives of Canada, 1992.

Bonenfant, Jean-Charles. *The French-Canadians and the Birth of Confederation.* Ottawa: Canadian Historical Association, 1966.

Boyden, Joseph. *Louis Riel and Gabriel Dumont.* Toronto: Penguin Canada, 2010.

Browne, G. P., ed. *Documents on the Confederation of British North America.* Toronto: McClelland & Stewart, 1969.

Brubaker, Rogers. *Citizenship and Nationhood in France and Germany.* Cambridge, MA: Harvard University Press, 1992.

Bumsted, J. M. *The Peoples of Canada: A Pre-Confederation History.* Toronto: Oxford University Press, 2003.

Burayidi, Michael A. *Multiculturalism in a Cross-National Perspective.* London: University Press of America, 1997.

Calore, Paul. *The Causes of the Civil War: The Political, Cultural, Economic, and Territorial Disputes between North and South.* Jefferson, NC: McFarland, 2008.

Careless, J. M. S. *Brown of the Globe.* 2 vols. Toronto: Dundurn, 1959, 1963.

Catton, Bruce. *The Centennial History of the Civil War.* Garden City, NY: Doubleday, 1961.

Chadwick, Bruce. *1858: Abraham Lincoln, Jefferson Davis, Robert E. Lee, Ulysses S. Grant and the War They Failed to See.* Naperville, IL: Sourcebooks, 2008.

Clavin, Matthew J. *Toussaint Louverture and the American Civil War: The Promise and Peril of a Second Haitian Revolution.* Philadelphia: University of Pennsylvania Press, 2010.

Craven, Paul, ed. *Labouring Lives: Work and Workers in Nineteenth-Century Ontario.* Toronto: University of Toronto Press, 1995.

Creighton, D. G. *John A. Macdonald.* 2 vols. Toronto: Macmillan Canada, 1952, 1955.

———. *The Road to Confederation: The Emergence of Canada, 1863–1867.* Toronto: Macmillan Canada, 1964.

Davis, William C. *Look Away!: A History of the Confederate States of America.* New York: Free Press, 2002.

Dew, Charles B. *Apostles of Disunion: Southern Secession Commissioners and the Causes of the Civil War.* Charlottesville: University Press of Virginia, 2001.

Egerton, Douglas R. *Year of Meteors: Stephen Douglas, Abraham Lincoln, and the Election That Brought on the Civil War.* New York: Bloomsbury Press, 2010.

Egnal, Marc. *Clash of Extremes: The Economic Origins of the Civil War.* New York: Hill & Wang, 2009.

Faust, Drew Gilpin. *The Creation of Confederate Nationalism: Ideology and Identity in the Civil War South.* Baton Rouge: Louisiana State University Press, 1989.

Foote, Shelby. *The Civil War: A Narrative.* 3 vols. New York: Vintage Books, 1986.

Freeman, Douglas Southall. *Lee.* 1935. Abridged by Richard Harwell. New York: Scribner, 1997.

Freehling, William W. *The Road to Disunion: The Secessionists at Bay.* New York: Oxford University Press, 1990.

———. *The South vs. the South: How Anti-Confederate Southerners Shaped the Course of the Civil War.* New York: Oxford University Press, 2001.

Gallagher, Gary W. *The Confederate War: How Popular Will, Nationalism, and Military Strategy Could Not Stave Off Defeat.* Cambridge, MA: Harvard University Press, 1997

———. *The Union War.* Cambridge, MA: Harvard University Press, 2011.

Gallagher, Gary W., and Alan T. Nolan. *The Myth of the Lost Cause and Civil War History.* Bloomington: Indiana University Press, 2000.

Goodheart, Adam. *1861: The Civil War Awakening.* New York: Alfred A. Knopf, 2011.

Granatstein, J. L., and Paul Stevens, eds. *Canada Since 1867: A Bibliographical Guide.* 2nd ed. Toronto: Samuel Stevens, Hakkert, 1977.

Guernsey, Alfred H., and Henry M. Alden. *Harper's Pictorial History of the Civil War.* New York: Fairfax, 1866.

Hamlin, Percy Gatlin. *"Old Bald Head" and the Making of a Soldier: Letters of General R. S. Ewell.* Gaithersburg, MD: Ron R. Van Sickle Military Books, 1988.

Heidler, David Stephen, and Jeanne T. Heidler, eds. *Encyclopedia of the War of 1812.* Annapolis, MD: U.S. Naval Institute Press, 2004.

Hesseltine, William B., ed. *The Tragic Conflict: The Civil War and Reconstruction.* New York: George Braziller, 1962.

Hewitt, Janet B., et al., eds. *Supplement to the Official Records of the Union and Confederate Armies.* 95 vols. Wilmington, NC: Broadfoot, 1994–99.

Holden, Walter, William E. Ross, and Elizabeth Slomba, eds. *Stand Firm and Fire Low: The Civil War Writings of Colonel Edward Cross.* Hanover: University Press of New Hampshire, 2003.

Horwitz, Tony. *Midnight Rising: John Brown and the Raid That Sparked the Civil War.* New York: Henry Holt, 2011.

Huston, James. *Calculating the Value of the Union: Slavery, Property Rights, and the Economic Origins of the Civil War*. Chapel Hill: University of North Carolina Press, 2003.

Irvine, Dallas. *Military Operations of the Civil War: A Guide-Index to the Official Records of the Union and Confederate Armies, 1861–1865*. 2 vols. Washington: Government Printing Office, 1968–80.

Johnson, Pharris Debach, ed. *Under the Southern Cross: Soldier Life with Gordon Bradwell and the Army of Northern Virginia*. Macon, GA: Mercer University Press, 1999.

Johnson, R. U., and C. C. Buel, eds. *Battles and Leaders of the Civil War*. 4 vols. New York: Century, 1887–88.

Jones, Terry L., ed. *Campbell Brown's Civil War: With Ewell and the Army of Northern Virginia*. Baton Rouge: Louisiana State University Press, 2001.

Kearns Goodwin, Doris. *Team of Rivals: The Political Genius of Abraham Lincoln*. New York: Simon & Schuster, 2006.

Kedourie, Elie. *Nationalism*. London: Hutchinson University Library, 1966.

Lankford, Nelson D. *Cry Havoc!: The Crooked Road to Civil War, 1861*. New York: Penguin, 2008.

Laxer, James. *Tecumseh & Brock: The War of 1812*. Toronto: Anansi, 2012.

Long, Everette Beach, comp. *The Civil War Day by Day: An Almanac, 1861–1865*. Garden City, NY: Doubleday, 1971.

Lightner, David L. *Slavery and the Commerce Power: How the Struggle against the Interstate Slave Trade Led to the Civil War*. New Haven, CT: Yale University Press, 2006.

Loo, Tina. *Making Law, Order, and Authority in British Columbia, 1821–1871*. Toronto: University of Toronto Press, 1994.

Lubet, Steven. "The Oberlin Fugitive Slave Rescue: A Victory for the Higher Law." Northwestern University School of Law Scholarly Commons, Faculty Working Papers, 2011.

Madden, David. *Beyond the Battlefield: The Ordinary Life and Extraordinary Times of the Civil War Soldier*. New York: Simon & Schuster, 2000.

Manning, Chandra. *What This Cruel War Was Over: Soldiers, Slavery, and the Civil War*. New York: Alfred A. Knopf, 2007.

Marquis, Greg. *In Armageddon's Shadow: The Civil War and Canada's Maritime Provinces*. Montreal: McGill-Queen's University Press, 1998.

Martin, Ged. *Britain and the Origins of Canadian Confederation, 1837–67*. Vancouver: UBC Press, 1995.

———, ed. *The Causes of Canadian Confederation*. Fredericton: Acadiensis Press, 1990.

Marvel, William. *The Great Task Remaining: The Third Year of Lincoln's War.*
Boston: Houghton Mifflin Harcourt, 2010.

McCurry, Stephanie. *Confederate Reckoning: Power and Politics in the Civil War South.* Cambridge, MA: Harvard University Press, 2010.

McPherson, James M. *Battle Cry of Freedom: The Civil War Era.* Pbk. ed. New York: Oxford University Press, 2003.

Morison, Samuel Eliot, and Henry Steele Commager. *The Growth of the American Republic.* Vol. 1. New York: Oxford University Press, 1962.

Morton, W. L. *The Critical Years: The Union of British North America, 1857–1873.* Toronto: McClelland & Stewart, 1964.

Mosocco, Ronald A. *The Chronological Tracking of the American Civil War per the Official Records of the War of the Rebellion.* Williamsburg, VA: James River Publications, 1994.

Mountcastle, Clay. *Punitive War: Confederate Guerrillas and Union Reprisals.* Lawrence: University Press of Kansas, 2009.

Neeley, Mark E., Jr. *The Abraham Lincoln Encyclopedia.* New York: McGraw-Hill, 1982.

Nicholson, Norman L. *The Boundaries of Canada, Its Provinces and Territories.* Ottawa: Queen's Printer, 1964.

Noe, Kenneth W. *Reluctant Rebels: The Confederates Who Joined the Army after 1861.* Chapel Hill: University of North Carolina Press, 2010.

Nosworthy, Brent. *The Bloody Crucible of Courage: Fighting Methods and Combat Experience of the Civil War.* New York: Carroll & Graf, 2003.

Noll, Mark. *The Civil War as a Theological Crisis.* Chapel Hill: University of North Carolina Press, 2006.

Nudelman, Franny. *John Brown's Body: Slavery, Violence, and the Culture of War.* Chapel Hill: University of North Carolina Press, 2004.

Pickenpaugh, Roger. *Captives in Gray: The Civil War Prisons of the Union.* Tuscaloosa: University of Alabama Press, 2009.

Quigley, Paul. *Shifting Grounds: Nationalism and the American South, 1848–1865.* New York: Oxford University Press, 2012.

Roland, Charles Pierce. *The Confederacy.* Chicago: University of Chicago Press, 1960.

———. *An American Iliad: The Story of the Civil War.* 2nd ed. Boston: McGraw-Hill, 2002.

Rose, Anne C. *Victorian America and the Civil War.* New York: Cambridge University Press, 1992.

Ryerson, Stanley. *Unequal Union: Confederation and the Roots of Conflict in the Canadas, 1815–1873.* Toronto: Progress Books, 1968.

Saul, John Ralston. *Louis-Hippolyte, LaFontaine and Robert Baldwin.* Toronto: Penguin Canada, 2010.

Samuels, Shirley. *Facing America: Iconography and the Civil War*. New York: Oxford University Press, 2003.

Schott, Thomas E. *Alexander H. Stephens of Georgia*. Baton Rouge: Louisiana State University Press, 1988.

Shortt, Adam, and Arthur G. Doughty, eds. *Canada and Its Provinces: A History of the Canadian People and Their Institutions by One Hundred Associates*. 23 vols. Toronto: Publishers' Association of Canada, 1913–17.

Sizer, Lyde Cullen. *The Political Work of Northern Women Writers and the Civil War, 1850–1872*. Chapel Hill: University of North Carolina Press, 2000.

Sprague, D. N. *Canada and the Metis, 1869–1885*. Waterloo, ON: Wilfrid Laurier University Press, 1988.

Stahr, Walter. *Seward: Lincoln's Indispensable Man*. New York: Simon & Schuster, 2012.

Stanley, George F. G. *Louis Riel*. Toronto: McGraw-Hill Ryerson, 1963.

Sweeny, Alastair. *George-Étienne Cartier: A Biography*. Toronto: McClelland & Stewart, 1976.

Symonds, Craig L. *The Naval Institute Historical Atlas of the U.S. Navy*. Annapolis, MD: Naval Institute Press, 2001.

Varhola, Michael J. *Everyday Life During the Civil War*. Cincinnati: Writer's Digest Books, 1999.

Wagner, Margaret E., Gary W. Gallagher, and Paul Finkelman, eds. *The Library of Congress Civil War Desk Reference*. New York: Simon & Schuster, 2002.

Walther, Eric H. *William Lowndes Yancey and The Coming of the Civil War*. Chapel Hill: University of North Carolina Press, 2006.

Waugh, Joan, and Gary W. Gallagher, eds. *Wars Within a War: Controversy and Conflict Over the American Civil War*. Chapel Hill: University of North Carolina Press, 2009.

Werner, Emmy E. *Reluctant Witnesses: Children's Voices from the Civil War*. New York: Westview, 1998.

Whitaker, Reg, Gregory S. Kealey, and Andrew Parnaby. *Secret Service: Political Policing in Canada from the Fenians to Fortress America*. Toronto: University of Toronto Press, 2012.

White, Ronald C., Jr. *A. Lincoln: A Biography*. New York: Random House, 2009.

Wilson, Edmund. *Patriotic Gore: Studies in the Literature of the American Civil War*. New York: W. W. Norton, 1994. First published 1962 by Farrar, Straus & Giroux.

Winks, Robin W. *The Civil War Years: Canada and the United States*. 4th ed. Montreal: McGill-Queen's University Press, 1998. First published 1960 by Johns Hopkins Press.

Woodworth, Steven E. *While God Is Marching On: The Religious World of Civil War Soldiers.* Lawrence: University Press of Kansas, 2001.

Wrong, George M. *Canada and the American Revolution: The Disruption of the First British Empire.* New York: Macmillan, 1935.

Young, Brian. *George-Étienne Cartier: Montreal Bourgeois.* Montreal: McGill-Queen's University Press, 1981.

Young, Elizabeth. *Disarming the Nation: Women's Writing and the American Civil War.* Chicago: University of Chicago Press, 1999.

Acknowledgements

I want to express my gratitude to those who have played important roles in making this book possible.

Working with the support, encouragement, and advice of Anansi publisher Sarah MacLachlan has been of immense value to me over the course of this major project. Knowing that you have the backing of Sarah and of all those who make Anansi so special in Canada makes a great difference.

Janie Yoon, editorial director at Anansi, is unique among editors. As on my previous book, *Tecumseh & Brock*, Janie has been unstinting in her efforts to make this book as effective as possible. Janie Yoon is truly a reader's editor, if I can put it that way. Her constant goal is to work with an author to produce a work that is completely accessible to the reader. And she does that with an energy that is close to superhuman. She is the best editor with whom I have ever worked, and I look forward to the next project with Janie piloting the book to its destination.

Peter Norman copy-edited the book superbly.

Paul-Émile McNab is a highly effective researcher and sleuth. He tracks down what we're looking for with energy and enthusiasm. He's done a wonderful job for me on this project, as he did on *Tecumseh & Brock*. For this book, as for the previous one, he was able to use his skills in his field of specialty, aboriginal history.

Jackie Kaiser has been my literary agent for many years and over the course of a large number of projects. She has always done her best for me. I feel much happier knowing that she is with me as I traverse "the valley of the shadow" of writing and publishing. Thanks again, Jackie.

I'm happy to be working on this project with Emily Mockler, who is in charge of publicity at Anansi. And my best wishes go to others at Anansi — Nan Froman and Michael Solomon — who've been so supportive on previous projects.

Thanks so much to Sandy, who is wonderfully ready to advise me on what I'm writing, while doing her own writing. She offers solace when the going gets tough. No less on this project than on earlier ones.

Index

JAMES LAXER is the award-winning author of more than twenty-five books, including the number one national bestseller *Tecumseh & Brock: The War of 1812*, *Stalking an Elephant: My Discovery of America* (published by the New Press in New York as *Discovering America*), and *The Border: Canada, the U.S., and Dispatches from the 49th Parallel*. He is a professor of political science in the Department of Equity Studies at York University. He lives in Toronto.